Meaty Balls

Vincent Daniels

tiny ★ word books

An Imaginary Friends Division

Detroit – New York – London – France – Underpants

Meaty Balls

Copyright © 2016 by Vincent Daniels   Second Edition

ISBN-10: 148026623X

ISBN-13: 978-1480266230

Author's note: The events described in these stories are real. Deal with it. Any fibby parts are present to protect the innocent or be sort of funny. Other than a few sparse characters and places, most have fictitious names and identifying characteristics, and any similarities to actual persons, either living or dead, are merely coincidental, except everything about your mom is true, sorry.

Library of Congress Cataloging-in-Publication Data

Daniels, Vincent.

  Meaty Balls / by Vincent Daniels – 2nd edition

      p. cm.

  1. Daniels, Vincent – Biography. 2. Humorists, American – 21st century – Memoir

  3. United States – Social life and customs – 21st century – Humor   I. Title

  [Deeter Deeds]   2016   Pankens (2005-2016)

10 9 8 7 6 5 4 3 2 1 0 Blast Off!

Book Design by Vincent Daniels

Limited – eBook version available at Amazon

Printed in the United States of America

Hoo, you are my motivation, purpose, treasure, and butt.

Dedicated to single moms making it work

Contents

Meaty Balls

A Collection of Essays, Expositions, and Insightfully Elegant
Potty Humor (your favorite)

Little voices can say big things – big, dumb things.

The Dirtiest Look *Ever*

I recently went on a family reunion camping trip to the Metamora-Hadley Recreation Area in mid-Michigan. It's the campground my family went to every summer during my childhood. It's the place I learned to ride a bike, swim, and roast marshmallows.

The campground has several perks. It's inexpensive, well maintained by a friendly staff, and only an hour from my hometown. They have a clean beach, groomed nature trails, and a short bike ride takes you to a quaint town where you can get family-friendly stuff like ice cream, fudge, and soda, or, if you prefer, better stuff like booze, rubbers, and porn. Lastly, and key to any campground rating, the bathroom facilities are above average. The population of daddy longlegs and screen-dwelling giant mosquitoes are a fraction of what I've seen at other campgrounds.

One shower room is particularly amazing. (Next sentence best read by Robin Leach, who, if you don't know, has an English accent nicely suited for describing lavish things.) And...*go*. A heavy steel door locks you into a private spa complete with its own toilet, sink, mirror, ample counter space, abundant shelves and hooks, electrical outlets galore, and an expansive bathing area complete with *two* adjustable showerheads – one above your head, and one staring directly into your navel – combining to deliver a fire-hosing of hygiene. It's *very* special. A large, square blue sign on the door denotes the room's grandeur. The sign depicts a stick figure man sitting on a bean bag playing video games, or it could be a man in a wheelchair. That's right – it's the mother flippin' handicap stall! (Cue *Charlie's Angels* theme.)

Do handicapped people camp? *Hmm*, let's see – popping up campers, pounding tent pegs, chopping firewood, shimmying into sleeping bags, and hiking through the forest...for their sake, I sure hope not! Camping requires a substantial amount of physical activity not conducive to wheelchair confinement. I think both sides would agree that they're better off at home in their padded cages. That's not intended to sound mean. Personally, I adore handicapped people of all shapes, sizes, and defects. I even own a wheelchair myself. When I bought my house, the previous owners left one in the garage rafters. Yeah, I've taken it down for a spin, so I think I can relate. So I'm not saying handicapped people *can't* camp, I'm just saying it'd be like a middle-aged white guy hanging out in a jazz club – technically he's allowed, but why bother? Besides, I'm not the one discriminating here, the wilderness is. File a complaint with Earth's HR department.

I'd never seen a disabled camper at Metamora, so when choosing a shower, I always went with first-class over coach. The inclusion of a handicap facility was probably mandated by state law, despite being *completely* unnecessary. I rinsed and repeated in that opulent washroom every time we camped there. However, during this recent trip, my shower choice triggered a series of events that culminated in me being the unlucky recipient of the dirtiest look ever given in the history of mankind.

On Saturday morning at nine o'clock, I entered the shower corridor. Ahead of me was a father holding the hand of his young son. We made small talk about the invasion of the emerald ash borer and the exorbitant price of firewood. An old man in flip-flops and paisley swim trunks exited one of the regular showers. When the father and son disappeared into it, I slipped into the disabled master-bath and locked the deadbolt behind me. When the fluorescent bulbs flickered on, I said, "Good to see you again, you magical, handicapped *whore* of a shower." I meant it in a totally good way.

I took my sweet old time, as the luxuries of life should afford, shampooing my hair into a white, soapy afro while reading the oft-overlooked shampoo packaging. I was glad to see that my shampoo was "Paraben-Free" despite not knowing what a paraben is. (Parasitic forest troll?) A similar thing happened the night before while digging into a bag of Ruffles potato chips that claimed to have "No Trans-Fat." I don't know what trans-fat is, but I sure wished I had a bowl of it to dip the chips in.

I squeezed an extra dollop of body wash onto my loofah and lathered myself until I looked like a snowman. I affixed two lather balls to my ears like Princess Leia buns. It gave the room a hollow and metallic sound reminiscent of when Tom Hanks would zone out during combat in *Saving Private Ryan*. The "Mountain Fresh" scented soap I chose was revitalizing. I wondered what "Mountain Fresh" consisted of, so I took a deep whiff from the spout, detecting traces of Febreze, Dian Fossey's bush, and severed ape heads. I applied a moisturizing facial cleanser, cleaned out my bellybutton pretty well, and let the conditioner set for several minutes before rinsing. I sang *September Morn* by Neil Diamond the whole time (chorus only, I don't know the rest). The dual showerhead torrent was so penetrating that even my distaste for peas washed down the drain. It also temporarily lessened my fear of dogs. I actually thought, "If a dog walked in here right now, I might try petting it instead of screaming."

I stepped to the sink and brushed my teeth for the dentist recommended two full minutes. I recalled the snotty hygienist at my last check-up saying in a mom-knows-best tone, "If you'd floss more this wouldn't hurt so *bad*." She annoyingly sang the word "bad" off key. I had floss in my travel bag, so I pulled off a segment, and sang, "Look at me now, *bitch*," followed by an old-fashioned, mirror-spattering flossing. The point is – I cleansed my soul in that handicap bathroom that morning.

I exited the facility the way an actor in a Pert Plus commercial would – in slow-motion, with a towel around my shoulders, flashing my pearly whites, and running my fingers through the back of my glistening hair. The last thing I expected to see was a double-crutched, Peter Dinklage-looking little person with a rolled towel tucked under his armpit. My first thought was, "Somebody lost their circus!" Then it hit me – this wasn't a standard midget, this was a *handicapped* midget. *Then* I realized something worse. I made him wait to use what was rightfully his. I was in there a long time too. I wondered how long he waited. I never wanted to be in a wheelchair so badly.

The door shut behind me and I froze. He turned to me and made eye contact – scathing, filthy eye contact. The kind that wives who've put on forty pounds give their husband's thin, cleavage-bearing ex-girlfriends at class reunions. The kind Medusa gave Greek treasure hunters. The kind Clint Eastwood gives rapists. It was a showdown. A lone tumbleweed rolled between us. Gunslinger music played – *ooh we ooh we ooh, woh woh woh.*

Have you ever stood at the top of a ski hill on a clear afternoon, overlooking a blanket of fresh snow reflecting the sun's blinding rays, squinting with every muscle in your face as you nurse a murderous hatred for your archenemy while imagining yourself crushing them in a monster truck made of fire ants? Hopefully you have, because that's the introductory offer to the look this handicapped midget had on his face. His thick midget brow amplified the vengeance. Blood vessels were popping in his midget eyes. It looked like he was about to keel over from an aneurysm. I secretly wished for it.

I had preemptively awarded someone else with the Oscar for "Dirtiest Look Ever" about a year earlier. I was backing out of my driveway and nearly hit an old, limping war vet walking his black cocker spaniel. I hurriedly apologized, but the cranky old geezer slapped my SUV and garbled something about it being, "A foreign piece of *shit!*"

A couple months later, I pulled up to the stop sign at the end of my block as he was turning the corner with his dog. I smiled and waved, but in return he gave me a *gigantic* thumbs-down. It wasn't a "Caesar deciding a gladiator's fate" thumbs-down. It was an "I can jam my thumb through steel" thumbs-down. It was so intense that all vegetation within thirty yards instantly withered. For a brief moment, as his thumb descended, my business casual attire morphed into a rainbow-colored, polka-dot clown costume. It was *that* bad.

His accompanying dirty look topped them all. It would've melted a gargoyle. It gave Chuck Norris erectile dysfunction. The old man was carrying a paper bag full of dog shit, and I would've rather had him hurl that into my eyes than see his nasty scowl. His dirty look was amplified by his unkempt, pockmarked, beet red, ugly-as-shit face.

But check this out, that grumpy old vet looked like Mona Lisa compared to this handicapped midget. Handiman's dirty look registered a 9.7 quake in Indonesia. The ripple effect of his dirty look made a herd of Triceratops shit their pants. His dirty look prompted Satan to call his mom just to see how she was feeling.

I stood at a critical crossroad. I had a life-altering choice to make. It was like having your parents dangling from a cliff but only having time to save one of them (assuming you love them equally). It was like being granted the power of invisibility but only having it long enough to either rob a bank, scope out the women's locker room at Planet Fitness, or use it for some form of good, like replenishing the soap dispensers in the women's locker room at Planet Fitness. I had a nanosecond to decide how to handle this malady.

Any other time, I'd quickly apologize, but this time I refrained, reasoning that I had the right to use the fancy bathroom because I got there first. If there were no disabled campers on the premises, it would've gone unused, and I can't take that risk. I wouldn't be upset if he was in a normal person shower and I had to wait. I wouldn't glare at him like Wolverine and say, "Hey Crutches, use your own!" In fact, if he hobbled out of a Homo erectus facility while *I* was waiting, I'd give him a thumbs-up to show my regard for his plight, maybe even add something like, "Nothing like a hot shower, eh?" That's true empathy right there. I wasn't about to apologize for the best freshening-up experience one can have at a fifteen-dollar-a-night campground.

The next logical choice was to break eye contact, focus on a distant tree, and beeline the hell out of there. If I did that, I'd surely get a disgusted headshake along with a loud sigh of pure hatred while his handicapped eyes shot handicapped lasers into the back of my genetically sound head. It was *also* likely that he'd include a sarcastic remark, something like, "*Real* nice," or, "*Yeah*, thanks for making me wait." Sure, I could live with myself after that, but for some reason I wanted to be "off the hook," as nimble people say. I wanted to nullify the confrontation by outwitting my handicapped nemesis. So…I did it. You're thinking, "Oh no, you didn't?" Maybe you're thinking it with ghetto flair, bobbing your head from side to side while shaking a blingy finger with a gaudy fake nail. "*Aw naw you dit-int!?*" Oh yes, *I did*.

I tilted my head loosely to the right and channeled Billy Bob Thornton from *Slingblade*. I smiled the type of easy grin elicited by things like cupcake sprinkles and napping kittens. My toes pigeoned, and I took a step forward with a frothy limp, slightly twinging before pulling the next leg in succession. It was a miracle! I became *handicapped! Hallelujah, praise the Lord!* I wasn't sure what I had, but *damn* was I crippled! You think less of me now? You prejudiced son of a *bitch*. Cut me some slack! I'm quasi-handicapped! If all of this sounds shallow, don't worry, it's cool. I'm allowed to poke fun at handicapped people because some of my best friends are handicapped. Not really…but I wish they were!

The little guy watched intently but kept his handi-eye-daggers on hold. There was no loud sigh, no appalled headshaking. A snide comment was sitting in a turbo-charged wheelchair at the top of a steep porch ramp, but he kept his grip on the brakes. He couldn't let me have it because there was a *very slight chance* I was not acting but was his fellow brethren, his comrade in arms, or in this case, arm braces. Maybe, *just maybe*, instead of being an ignorant bastard who'd sink to the depths of depravity to imitate a disabled person in a pitiful attempt to get away with using their bathroom, I was one of them. If that were the case, our disadvantages would connect us in suffering the way Corvette owners are connected in pretentiousness. Instead of kicking my shin and bashing me in the head with his crutch, he'd owe me a little head nod. Maybe even a fist pound if he could balance himself.

Not to brag, but I'm good at acting crippled. As crude and merciless as it sounds, it's just something American schoolchildren practice a lot. You know you did it. But what if he could tell the difference between a *pretend* handicap and an *authentic* handicap the way I can tell the difference between Hormel chili and store brand? He watched with curiosity, trying to figure me out. I limped another couple steps and added a shaky elbow thing to the mix.

Paranoia crept in during my exceptionally slow escape. It was taking way too long. He had too much time to spot a mistake. I had to seal the deal, so I took it to the next level, a level not for the weak-of-heart, a level requiring tireless training and commitment. I was going for Handicap Impersonator gold at the Nagano Special Olympics. I was going to say something.

I knew saying something would break his trance. Unfortunately, to be viable, it had to be spoken like a complete retard. Again, I'm a pro at this, but what came out of my mouth is indescribable, especially in written form where it can be hard to get the gist. It'd be like trying to diagnose a car problem by reading that the car goes "*squee squee*," or identifying a bird species by reading that its call is "*tweeter twiddle.*" Onomatopoeia can only afford so much. How would you write out the sounds of Beethoven's Fifth Symphony for a deaf person to enjoy? Words simply can't do justice for audible wonders like this.

I turned to him, maintaining deadness behind my eyes, and said, "*Ehh*, it's all yours, *buddy!*" However, you'll have to imagine what that'd sound like coming from a happy-go-lucky cartoon hippopotamus with a learning disability. And he's a baritone. And partially deaf. And German. And gay.

I said, "*Ehh*, it's all yours, *buddy!*" and quite frankly, I nailed the audition. I didn't just deliver the line – I *was* retarded when I said it. My IQ dropped into the low thirties. You could tell from my inflection that I wasn't saying it out of cognitive recognition, but because it was something a down-to-earth caretaker often said to me. I pictured him as a tall, skinny, cool black guy named Levon who had a knack for working with us retards. He said it to me all the time – when I wanted my purple bean bag, the Play-Doh, or a bowl of vanilla pudding. Levon would get them for me and say, "Hey, it's all yours, buddy!" Sometimes he'd put his hand out and say, "All right, now give me some skin!" I'd slap his hand and bellow out a goofy laugh. Man, Levon is the best!

One little line and Handiman's suspicion faltered. His demeanor adjusted and his magma subsided below his tectonic plates. His body language alone proved it worked. He visibly softened and his brow relaxed, thereby granting me safe passage. Now I could go about my day energized and happy, not to mention particularly clean thanks to all those textured handrails that made arranging my bath products a cinch.

"Thanks," he said, as clear as day, with a scholarly accent as if he learned to say *thanks* while attending Yale on a full handicapped scholarship.

Notably, I didn't feel guilty. The old saying is true, what a handicapped guy doesn't know, won't hurt him. What started as the dirtiest look *ever* ended amicably a few moments later. All great confrontations could've been avoided if archenemies would've simply acted like they had gimpy legs and learning disabilities. If Bush and Saddam would've talked things over in their best Corky Thatcher impersonations, we'd be watering our lawns with oil by now.

As the legitimately handicapped man entered the shower, I walked away, healing like Kaiser Soeze. The moment I heard the door latch, I smiled and took off running through the parking lot. I looked back, laughing at my unprecedented victory, and immediately tripped over a parking block, twisted my ankle, threw everything in my arms, and fell face first in the dirt. I stood up covered in pinecone chunks and pebbles. There were evergreen needles in my hair. My travel kit landed in mud. "*Ehh*, it's all yours, *buddy!*" Karma must have a handicapped aunt.

Smashed Puerto Ricans

For the past two years I've been dating a girl whose family is Puerto Rican. I hate to sound cliché, but they're *absolutely fucking nuts*. I don't feel bad saying that, because they'll tell you the same thing. The first time I met her extended family, most of them said something along the lines of, "You're dating in this family? I feel bad for you. We're *absolutely fucking nuts!*"

Her dad looks like Tony Montana. He'll get two inches from your face when talking about things that excite him, like the *Silver Surfer*, *Battlestar Galactica*, and Chi-Chi Rodriguez. If you ask him, "Have you seen *Avatar*?" be prepared for a movie summary that lasts longer than the actual movie. He'll also recite a plethora of quotes from it that'll make you wonder if every character was played by Cheech Marin. I do this great impersonation of him where I get all up in your grill, bug my eyes out, stick out my tongue, and spastically shake my head while screaming, "Aye mang! *Ahhhhhh!*" It's dead nuts.

My girlfriend's wackjob mother tells stories *teeming* with the phrases "They goes" and "I goes." Every sentence starts with one or the other. She'll say, "I goes to the waitress, I goes, I goes, 'These eggs are overcooked!' She goes, she goes, 'You wanted over-medium, right?' So I goes, I goes, 'Hell no I didn't!' I goes, *'Hell* no!'"

While watching sports, she constantly shouts the phrase, "Get 'em guys!" That may not sound that bad, but trust me, it's agonizing when shouted incessantly, like five times every ten seconds, and at inappropriate times like during player interviews and commercials. She also happens to have the dirtiest mouth I've ever heard on an adult woman. She's obsessed with the punishment of shoving her foot up another human being's ass. Apparently the world would be a better place if Barack Obama, Mel Gibson, and whoever finished her bottle of wine were all sodomized by her foot. She refers to other females as "fucking cunts." She describes all aspects of everyday life, whether it's a traffic light, the climate, or a pizza, as "fucking bullshit."

My girlfriend has a brother named Roberto whose phrase tic is "All of the sudden." He begins every sentence with it as if nothing ever happens with a precursor. He'll say, "All of the sudden the phone rang. All of the sudden I answered it and was like 'Hello'. All of the sudden the person was like, 'Who is this?' All of the sudden they hung up. All of the sudden I was like, 'What the *fuck?*'"

Her oldest brother is a dark, skinny Hispanic dude married to a fat, white-trash broad who treats him like utter shit to the point that it's hilarious. It's like *I Love Lucy* on PCP in the Bizarro World. They've been together for five years and have five kids who're all less than a year apart. None of the kids are twins and none have said their first word yet. When his wife is being nice to him, she'll say things like, "Will you get off your lazy, fucking, shitty ass, stop being a little nigger, and get me a piece of fucking cake, please?" That's not an exaggeration. And that's when she's not even mad at him! For the record, she doesn't have Tourette's. I heard a family member referred them to a marriage counselor who in turn referred them to Dr. Kevorkian.

There's an aunt who looks *exactly* like Dustin Hoffman's portrayal of Captain Hook. Another aunt could be Bill Murray's stunt double. There's an aunt with a wandering glass eye who I call *Crazy-Eyed Eva*. Another aunt looks just like Danny Trejo from *Machete* (yes, I said *aunt*). The first thing her sister Luisa ever said to me was, "You have ugly feet."

I replied, "That means a lot coming from you, Frodo."

Then her cousin Tonya says to me, she goes, she goes, "Your face looks like a ninja turtle," so I goes to her, I goes, "Your face looks like it has Down syndrome."

The men in her family put on sunglasses after dark. All of her uncles have mastered the art of dimwitted one-liners. They'll critique my shirt, saying, "Vinny boy don't got no Puerto Rican flavor!" as they stand there draped in orange, harvest-themed wallpaper from the '70s.

I'll say, "It looks like you guys got too much cookie dough flavor," but they don't get it.

Some of them have thick accents making them impossible to understand. They'll ask, or at least I assume it's a question, "*Aye mang da como lee to paws?*"

I'll say, "Yes, or perhaps no, depending on what you said."

The women seem to speak Spanish more often than the men, but to me it just sounds like they're repeating *cootina cootana* over and over.

I've been around these Puerto Ricans for a while now but still can't seem to get their names straight. Miguel, Angelo, Florencio, a bunch of Maria and Tony characters – I don't know who's who. The same thing happens at each family function, I roam around getting sloppy cheek kisses from all sorts of portly women. Early on I thought the traditional kiss greeting would pay off if there were a bunch of cousins who looked like Salma Hayek, but I wasn't so lucky. There are at least two dozen female cousins under the age of twenty-five, but *zero* are hot, unless you consider no neck, a front butt, and a pissy attitude hot.

On my list of "The Top Ten Most Absurd Things I've Ever Seen," number three is the way her cousins dance at family functions. If you've ever seen the 2 Live Crew video for *Pop That Coochie*, which is basically a bunch of sluts bending over shaking their asses, this would look familiar. When the DJ plays Ludacris, a herd of girls ranging from 175 to 300 pounds, dressed in fatty-roll-accentuating whore outfits, start freaking each other as if they're filming a roofie-induced amateur porn titled "Chubby Latina Dyke Orgy 5." The only thing missing are the strap-on dildos. Keep in mind that they're all related, they're the only ones on the dance floor, and their ninety-seven-year-old great-grandparents are watching. It's one of those moments when you're compelled to say out loud, *"Where the hell am I?"*

My girlfriend's youngest brother, Pedro, is a sanity pill in the medicine cabinet. He's pretty normal and has a good sense of humor. We'll stand in the corner at family events doing impersonations of everyone. My buddies who've met Pedro don't prefer him because he's a relentless flirt who'll hit on your wife or girlfriend with no regard for decency. Obviously, I don't have that issue since I'm dating his sister.

Pedro is good at rolling with an absurd joke premise. Topics have included the pros and cons of pissing in toilets vs. urinals, things Sean Connery would say if he were black, and movie roles Dolph Lundgren should've had (his Ace Ventura *"Allll-righty then"* would've been celestial). When my relationship with his sister ends, since there's no way I can keep this up, laughing fits with Pedro may be the only thing I'll truly miss.

Pedro's graduation party took place at his parents' house on a recent Saturday in July. Early that afternoon I threw on some crappy clothes and loaded a party-store Coke cooler, boom-box, and a stack of Latin dance CDs into my truck, and headed to their place. My intention was to drop the stuff off, head to the mall for a new outfit, down a couple shots at home, and return primed and prepped for the extended family barrage. Instead, I got stuck setting up their four-foot-tall disco speakers to their retro amp to my CD player on their back deck. The mess of dusty wires I had to sort through looked like an untamed crop of Puerto Rican pubes. I wanted to scold their Dad, "Why didn't you set up these speakers yesterday?" But instead I said, "Wow, cool speakers!" Then, just when I was about to escape, my parents showed up early to get their appearance out of the way, and I felt guilty leaving them alone with those Spanish nuts.

The stereo and cookers were plugged into a Florida room outlet and every time I turned the music on it tripped the circuit breaker. People started complaining about not having music, so I unplugged the power strip that was heating the food. I'd never seen such a massive pile of black beans and chorizo before and theorized that such a large amount would produce its own heat if required to do so. I wasn't sure if leaving beef enchiladas unheated for hours would pose a health risk, but I figured everyone would get diarrhea regardless of whether or not the food spoiled. Plus, from my point of view, if I'm responsible for giving a hundred Puerto Ricans diarrhea, I just did the world a favor. I could sense Jesus up there giving me a thumbs-up.

People praise the bathroom at Pedro's parents' house because it's the most tastefully decorated room in the place. Admittedly, it's quite nice, almost worthy of a *Better Homes & Gardens* full-page spread. Ironically, it's the only room in the house they didn't remodel when they moved in. They wanted to tear out the white tile and go with a jungle cat theme, but their father's boss talked them out of it. Being the classiest room in the house isn't very difficult, seeing as how the living room is decorated entirely in black velvet, the master bedroom is an Indian reservation gift shop, and the kitchen looks like a Puerto Rican flag puked everywhere and then exploded.

The lukewarm chorizo was disagreeing with me, so I ventured to the bathroom, but there was already a line of people waiting there, all of them slightly keeled over with their hands on their stomachs. My belly was gurgling, and I knew it was go time, but I didn't panic, because I knew about a secret bathroom in the garage. I crept down the hallway, snuck into the garage toilet, and ripped ass in a manner that made me hate my own guts.

Being mid-summer, it was ninety degrees in the garage, and the humidity was god-awful. The bathroom, which is about the size of a coat closet, had no ventilation of any sort. There was no fan or window, just a two-inch diameter peephole where a doorknob should've been. I suffered through my entire shit. Each wipe created the hallucination that my body was being smeared in feces. Each time I moved, my sweaty ass cheeks peeled off the toilet seat like Velcro. I was sitting in the cramped poop oven, dying from my own wretchedness, when I heard the house-to-garage door open. A female voice with a Spanish accent instructed, "It's the door just past the workbench."

The voice of a mature woman replied, "Thank you, Maria."

I had my hand in the doorknob opening when she knocked. "This one's occupied," I said, hoping she'd change her mind and go away. I knew the crud being exorcised from my body was no ordinary dump – it was a mega-shit of spoiled pork parts that scraped every refried bean from my intestinal wall. The atmospheric conditions broiled my shit to maximum stench. It absolutely *reeked*, and I dreaded walking out to face the person about to fill their lungs with my homebrewed methane.

I flushed twice hoping it'd provide some venting, but it didn't. I scanned the shelves for air freshener but came up empty-handed. I grabbed a bottle of sink cleaner and squirted it in the bowl, but it was unscented. I lathered my hands with ten times the normal amount of liquid soap, but it made no impact on air quality. I was left with a tough choice: Upon exiting, do I give this woman some forewarning or pass by without a word? I couldn't deny my responsibility. If the bridge was out, it was my duty to warn an oncoming driver.

I opened the door and saw an older Jewish woman in a paisley top standing there. She was the owner of a mansion in Bloomfield Hills that Pedro's mother cleaned. She was a friend of the family by default. She probably stuffed a hundred bucks in Pedro's card and wrote, "May God bless your life after graduation." She shot me a quick smile and took a step forward. "Whoa!" I said, putting my hands up in the universal gesture to "Hold on a dang second!"

"I'm not promising a rose garden in there," I said.

"Oh, that's okay," she said, smiling casually. But I knew it wasn't. I should've said, "You've heard of those Nazi gas chambers, right?"

When she shut the door, I stepped to the side instead of leaving, and in roughly five seconds, I heard her make this noise, "*Gooooo-aaaaahhhhh.*" I could tell it was combined with a full body shiver and triggered her gag reflex. My pity turned to pride, and I ran out of the garage laughing.

By dusk both kegs were empty. The liquor cabinet was being raided and beer runs were being made. All respectable people had fled the scene, and a slew of kids had filed in. I filled plastic cups with gin and juice and handed them to kids who I pretended were old enough to drink despite that they were wearing their high school class shirts. A couple of my pals rushed over after I sent out a mass text that said there were hammered high school girls freaking each other on the back deck. I did a shot of tequila with a dude I call Nate Dogg. He said, "When should I find you for the next one?"

I said, "Maybe ten minutes or so."

Nine minutes and fifty-nine seconds later he tapped me on the shoulder. Like clockwork, he stuck to the ill-advised shot schedule all night. He'd find me, look at his watch, and say, "Yo, Vincent, what time is it?" When El Toro Tequila is going down easy, you know trouble is coming. I poured him doubles, so I wonder how he fared later.

If the family in *My Big, Fat Greek Wedding* were considered outlandish and eccentric, then the family at *My Big, Fat Puerto Rican*

Grad Party would be labeled smashed and dramatic. Kids were dumping hair gel and kitty litter on cars. Shirtless men were wrestling on the front lawn. Latin dance music was blaring. Daiquiris were flowing. Pedro's brother Roberto was in the street, beating his chest like King Kong, rhetorically challenging anyone to a fight. "Who wants some?" he shouted. "All of the sudden everyone's scared! I will knock you the *fuck out!*"

I was stumbling around, completely shitfaced, and eventually passed out in the backyard shrubbery. Mosquitoes that bit me got hammered and entered karaoke contests. Mosquitoes predisposed to anger flew home and beat their larva. I woke up a little later to the sound of firecrackers, conga drums, and Spanish cursing, or, in other words, the same noise Satan's alarm clock makes. In my drunken stupor, I reasoned that I didn't want my girlfriend's parents to find me in the fetal position in a pool of vomit on their petunias, so I decided to make an attempt to get to the backseat of my vehicle.

When I stood up I instantly fell over and took a couple Tiki torches with me. One landed on a seat cushion and lit it on fire. I immediately vomited on it and put it out. I felt like a superhero. It's probably the coolest thing I've ever done. I did a quick scan of the area to see if there were any other random blazes I could extinguish with my mutant vomit, but, no dice. When I got to the side of the house, I put both hands on the brick and puked my guts out. When I wiped my mouth and looked up, I saw other guests keeled over, puking in the vicinity. At least I wasn't the only wasted idiot. Between heaves I said to myself, "I'm not the only one. I'm not the only one."

I found the spout for the garden hose and stuck my face under it for a while. Could've been ten seconds, could've been ten minutes, I lost track of time. I left it running in case anyone else was thirsty. When I turned the corner to the front yard, I spotted cousin Carlos passed out in the woodchips. "I'm not the only one," I said. Then I saw someone lying face down in the driveway between a couple cars and mumbled the warning, "I'm not the only one. Don't get run over." Eventually, I made it down the block and crawled into the backseat of my ride just as a couple police cars drove by with their lights flashing.

Pedro called the next day to see if I was okay. "Cops shut it down around one," he said. "I couldn't find you and was worried they threw you in a squad car."

"Nah," I said, "I slept in my backseat all night." I was soaking wet when I woke up but didn't relay that info.

"The last time I saw you, I was playing beer pong," he said. "I shouted, 'Yo Vincent! You want to get in on this?' but you just kept walking, saying, 'I'm not the only one, I'm not the only one'."

I'm Hungary

Omnivorous pt. 1

Omnivore: An organism that eats both plants and animals, lots and lots of animals.

"I'll have the spank-uh-no-tina."

I said those words at Hellas Cafe in Greektown and felt like a total jackass. I was trying to order *spanakopita*. They'll either bring out a spinach pie or Tina and a paddle. As much as I love chewing on the world's delicacies, I hate the humiliation of pronouncing them. Asian cuisine got it right by numbering the entire menu A1-N10. I had Thai food for lunch, and instead of trying to pronounce "*Kanah Goong Pad Prik Gang Bang,*" I said, "I'll have C9 with chicken."

"How spicy?" the waitress asked.

"Engulf my esophagus in flames," I said.

There's an Italian restaurant by my house called *Fratello's*. My favorite thing on the menu is called "*Cannelloni ripieni di melanzane.*" I practice saying it ten times in my head before closing the menu, but the moment the waiter arrives, I go blank. I say, "Cannelloni...*uh*, ripe..." Then I reopen the menu and point at the words while he reads it back to me like Don Corleone. Either rename it "Cheesy pasta tubes" or throw a C9 by it. I'd rather order as if it's a game of Battleship than embarrass myself trying to garble through a bunch of *Super Mario Bros.* sound bites.

I've ordered a thousand gyros and still feel like the waitress takes my order to the unibrows in the kitchen and says, "You guys should've heard what this asshole just called a gyro." Then they laugh and spit in it. Guy-Roh. Ji-Roh. Here-Oh. Year-Oh. Jeer-Oh. Screw you. It's spelled like the first part of "gyroscope" so that's how I'm going to say it. I'm not from Athens so don't expect me to know the lingo. I'd rather call it a lamb pita, or better yet, I'll just point at the picture on the menu and say, "That." Most ethnic food ordering is done by pointing and grunting like a chimp trying to tell you the attic is on fire.

Last Saturday I had dinner at a highly recommended Hungarian restaurant called the *Shepherd's Inn*. When the staff learned that our group never dined there before, they treated us like the Hungarian National Wiffleball Team (or whatever sport is popular there). They gave us a kitchen tour and a lesson in Hungarian culture. I've had other waitresses ask, "Have you dined with us before?" but never received such special attention afterward. They usually follow with something like, "Well, we're known for our ribs," and that's it. The Shepherd's Inn took it to the next level.

Our server, Frida, along with her trainee, taught us that Hungary is a landlocked country whose population descended from giant sloths. Their language originated at the Tower of Babel, isn't used anywhere else in Europe, and sounds like sheep talking. She said Hungary's greatest invention is the Rubik's Cube, although no one in the country can solve it. She also mentioned that the owner of the restaurant is a distant relative of Count Dracula.

Frida explained that their menu is quite diverse, or quite limited, based on how irritable you are. Hungarian delights consist of stuffed cabbage, goulash, and kielbasa, or in medical terms, stuff that makes you clench your anus while sprinting to the toilet. Regardless, their introduction made me hungary (sorry, couldn't resist).

My friends and I wanted an authentic experience, so we bypassed domestic beer in order to try a traditional Hungarian aperitif (pre-meal drink). Hungary's most popular liquor is called *Unicum* – the spooge of a mystical unicorn. It sounded gross. I asked Frida to describe it. She said, "It's gross." We ended up with *Zwack*, an Apricot Brandy, and spent the next few minutes trying to swallow our first sip. The repulsed expressions were entertaining. Someone rattled off the obvious joke, "This shit is zwack!" After that it was pancakes stuffed with mincemeat and plates full of dumplings oozing with creamy gravy.

After we finished, Frida said, "Since this is your first visit, I've prepared a complimentary dessert for you." She reached down her pants, pulled out a pastry molded from her vagina, and sprinkled powdered sugar on it. We fingered and licked it and everyone left satisfied. Every restaurant should take a page from how the Shepherd's Inn treats first timers. More places should say, "Never been here before? Well, we're known for our ribs *and* giving customers spycam access into Kate Upton's shower."

Would I go back to the Shepherd's Inn? Definitely...if constipated. On my list of preferred cuisines, Hungarian landed above Cuban and below Indian, same order as the judo medalists in the 1988 Summer Olympics.

Deciphering the authenticity of an ethnic restaurant is a pompous affair. None of us spent a semester in Budapest, nor do we speak Cantonese, therefore we have no basis for judging. Your food critic credentials came from the same place I got mine, Oscar Meyer University. We say things like, "That sushi place is full of Japanese people. It must be authentic," which is a fairly accurate gauge. My favorite Vietnamese restaurant is always chock-full of Vietnamese people. Old Country Buffet is full of portly rednecks, proving its authentic American mish-mash. The Chinese buffet by my house is teeming with Mexicans, which means they run good coupons.

Cultural ignorance often results in arguments over which Mexican restaurants are best and worst.

"El Mariachi is *my* favorite!"

"Really? I *hate* that hole. Tijuana's is the best!"

"What?! Tijuana's *blows!* Too much cilantro in the salsa."

But is there really such a thing as too much cilantro?

We take it personally as if we're co-owners or Food Network consultants, but we really have no idea what we're talking about. Even "authentic" places like *Mi Sabrosa Cocina* on the outskirts of Detroit's Mexicantown are still catering to fat-ass Americans. Only if you resemble Pancho Villa and slip your waiter a hundred pesos will you get the real chorizo and cactus. Otherwise, you're getting the same Johnsonville Brat and stewed celery everyone gets.

I knew a *real* Mexican guy named José Mendoza. Want to know what he ate? Straight up cow head – as in he rearranged his refrigerator shelving so an entire bovine head would fit inside – just a big raw head mooing at you when you opened the door. He'd scrape a chunk off the brain, throw it in a rubbery corn shell with a habanero, and say, "Aye mang, now *that's* an authentic taco!" Authentic hobo taco, maybe. "You want one, amigo?"

"Nah, I'll stick with authentic Taco Bell." I'd say.

Have you ever considered which foods are healthiest based on racial stereotypes? "Chinese people have nice complexion. Chinese food must be good for you." "The French are thin. French food must be good for you." "Black people age well. Drugs must be good for you." If that's the case, Ethiopian food should make you skinny. Bad news though, Ethiopian sponge bread with sautéed lamb and onions will plump you up the same as a cheeseburger and fries. The catch is that Ethiopians take a month to consume what you'd eat in one sitting. Plus they walked twenty miles to get it. And they ate it in sauna-like conditions. Also, being covered in flies ruins your appetite. Actually, now that I think about it, don't Ethiopians have huge beer bellies? Thought I saw that on a TV commercial.

The truth is you can become a tub-of-goo eating *anything*. I work with a guy who eats a few pieces of fruit for lunch but miraculously maintains an enormous gut. I look at him and think, "Are you eating an apple for lunch and a keg of Guinness for dinner?" There's no point in having a salad for dinner if you're going to watch TV all night, hit the

BK drive-thru, down a Double Whopper in three bites, and go to bed. It's a shame that Polynesian ideals which regard fat as an attractive sign of well-being haven't caught on here. Damn western thinking.

What would you rather do on vacation, booze it up or stuff your fucking face? For me the answer is easy, I *love* eating. I'll try any funk when it comes to food. I'll bite the head off a baby horse if it's considered a delicacy somewhere. Deep fried Twinkie, ground buffalo burger with quail eggs, raw eel in seaweed, chocolate-covered ants, durian shake, oysters on the shell, alligator nuggets, stewed octopus, tree bark stew – I loved each and every bite, minus the durian shake. That shit was nasty. Have you ever had jackfruit chips? Squirrel dip? The old 96'er? I have. That's why I can teleport and you can't.

I love food from every culture and era. If confederate soldiers made snuff soup before marching to Vicksburg, I want a bowl. When a frozen Mastodon is excavated in Siberia, I shake my fossilized Open Pit and get on the half-slab waiting list. I'd devour manna off the ground if given the chance. I'd be way more grateful than those runaway Jews. My dining slogan is, "If it's food, I'll eat it."

I consumed mass quantities while roaming Epcot's World Showcase earlier this year. I wanted to taste a specialty dish from each country's pavilion but was stuffed by Morocco. Here's an insider tip: Don't force down a plate of penne and a half-carafe of Sangiovese in Italy and proceed to the ride *Mission: Space*. Gary Sinise's intro video gave fair warning that G-forces can cause motion sickness, but I still wanted to be an astronaut. The result was something like driving your hammered, puking friend home from the bar, except I got smashed on Mars and Tim Robbins drove me home in his spaceship. I slept on a park bench for an hour and puked an estimated nineteen times. The upside was that I made plenty of room for Moroccan lamb meshoui after my tummy settled.

World travelers love bragging about the native cuisine from the places they've visited. How they were in Dusseldorf at The Kraut House with a stein of Füchschen Alt and a pile of sauerbraten. How they were in Nagoya at Shinobi Gardens drinking sake from a volcano spigot and eating dragon rolls made from real dragon. How they found a pizzeria on the outskirts of Rome that makes U.S. pizza taste like albatross shit. It was Nero's secret family recipe. Picasso was born in the cellar. The food was served by Francis Ford Coppola riding a white stallion in the nude. They gloat and sensationalize to make sure you realize that you'll never taste anything remotely close to the clairvoyant, disease-curing pizza they had, because it helps justify the small fortune they spent to get there. Pizza Hut would've sufficed.

Picky eaters can go to hell. If you always order chicken fingers with ranch, you have no idea what you're missing out on. I know two people who started dating based on a mutual distaste for Mexican food. They were among mutual friends who were trying to choose a restaurant where the group could reconvene, and they simultaneously voiced their south-of-the-border abhorrence. Their eyes met, and they said to each other, "Oh my *god*, I hate Mexican *too!*" Their hearts fluttered and music played, *"Why do birds suddenly appear every time you are near? Just like me, they long to be, tortilla free."*

The girl had Del Taco once and got an upset stomach. The guy had enchiladas from a mall food court and got the runs. A relationship based on diarrhea, I'm jealous. I can hear wedding bells over the gurgling. I once dated a girl based on the fact that we both liked the Barenaked Ladies, *Seinfeld*, and preferred toilet paper to dispense over instead of under. It seemed substantial at the time but wasn't enough to keep us together. This couple, however, has stayed together thanks to having only *one* thing in common – pickiness. They've bonded over the fact that they think *everything* is gross. Neither of them are the gracious type who'll keep their mouth shut while you praise food you like either. If you say, "I love crumbled blue cheese on my ribeye."

They'll say, "Oh *gawd*, how can you eat that? It's *so* disgusting! I'd throw up!"

Ever notice the "American Favorites" section on the back of a Chinese menu and wonder who'd order a hamburger at Chopstick Inn? This is the couple. For social purposes, they want to be included when their friends go out to eat, but they prefer Burger King every night of the week. The one and only time I convinced them to try a bite of Lebanese food, the girl nibbled a tiny piece of chicken and acted like she was about to barf. "It tastes like blood," she said.

The guy said, "The rice looks like maggots." You know what really looks like maggots? Your maggoty face. Since then, they've gone a step further and started picking up Burger King and bringing it with them when meeting friends at restaurants. They are, by far, the worst people in the world. Someone should poison them.

Meaty Balls

Omnivorous pt. 2

If I were stranded on a deserted island and could only take one fully-staffed restaurant with me, I'd choose *Masa Al Kabob*, an amazing Lebanese eatery within the Arab-American hub of Dearborn, Michigan. Thinking about their ghallaba sends me into a Pavlovian frenzy. Their mango smoothies cause premature ejaculation. Their kafta smells super good even *after* being squeezed past your sphincter. I'm gaga for their baba. At other places, I pass on the chopped parsley dish *tabouli*, but at Masa, I actually enjoy it, kind of the same way I feel about KFC's coleslaw. Masa will give your mouth a boner, metaphorically speaking.

Masa Al Kabob would be perfect for deserted island life because the only negative with Lebanese food is the high garlic content causes unbearable halitosis, making human contact altogether funky. You could shy away from the garlic dip (toum), but that'd be like ordering sliders without onions or pizza without cheese. After finishing Masa's shawarma platter, you're guaranteed to burp three hours later and wish death upon yourself. Nevertheless, Masa remains the smart choice for island life. The haze of garlic fumes encompassing your body will protect you from the sun's ultraviolet rays. Cannibalistic island natives will think you're a sulfur-bathed demon. Indigenous dinosaurs will run from you.

Back on the mainland, after a garlic overdose at Masa, it's only safe to hang with fellow garlic eaters until sunup. If everyone stinks, you neutralize each other. I learned the hard way that eating there before team sports ruins camaraderie. My only beef with this halal joint is that my girlfriend feels uncomfortable when the Arab guys working there undress her with their eyes. I'm like, "Come on guys, pull it together! You act like you've never seen the hottest woman on earth before!" For Arab-American dudes, ogling a woman is the same as taking her to a fancy restaurant. If the woman glances over while being stared at, it's a clear sign she's inviting sex. Masa's cramped waiting area used to be a problem too, but they finally expanded, so now my ass doesn't hang in the face of diners when I'm waiting for carry-out. Regardless, nothing from this paragraph matters on a deserted island.

If someone asked me to provide a foreigner with an authentic American meal, I'd skip steak and ribs and bring them to *Vic's Coney Island*. VCI is a hole-in-the-wall diner in a south Detroit hood that's open 24 hours a day, 365 days a year. It's a place where seats are repaired with duct tape, waitresses sport tattoos of reptiles wrapped around medieval weapons, and ceiling tiles are stained orange from years of grease and nicotine.

The cook at VCI would be perfect for the lead role in a movie titled *Uncle Buck 2: End of Humanity*, as long as the director can work with the fact that he doesn't speak English – or any language for that matter. I swear I saw Gollum stirring a huge vat of chili in the back. Ron Jeremy's fatter, less-attractive brother is always perched on the first barstool like a gargoyle. The dishwasher resembles the Crypt Keeper wearing a toupee made from a mushroom pizza. If the plot of *Men in Black* were real, half of the patrons at VCI would be extra-terrestrials posing as humans. It's seriously awesome.

A couple years ago, a Vic's Coney cook was shot seven times while putting the finishing touches on a Reuben sandwich. I heard the closest waitress was shot twice and came to work the next morning to mop up her own blood. Recently, a fifty-five-year-old busboy (technically, bus-older-chap) was robbed and killed in the parking lot. I've had to dash out a few times when drunken hoodlums started getting all *Stomp the Yard* inside, but, no worries, it doesn't happen all the time. Thing is, when the surrounding dives and titty bars empty at 2AM, VCI fills up, so get there early unless you're a Shaolin Kung Fu master.

The chili-cheese fries are worth the risk of being mugged, stabbed, and contracting gonorrhea. Here's why:

1. Thick cut, crispy, ridged fries maximize chili-cheese cling.
2. Covered in the tastiest chili known to man or beast.
3. Grated sharp cheddar melted under chili (not lame liquid cheese).
4. No charge for addition of caramelized onions.
5. It's fun to decorate your food with old-school ketchup squirters.
6. They're less than three bucks and ready in three minutes.

If fries aren't your thing, no worries, they also serve chili-cheese covered onion rings, hashbrowns, tater tots, waffle fries, burgers, omelets, fish sticks, and bumpy cake. Their chili-cheese-fries with a coney dog with extra onions would be my death row meal. I dowse mine with Frank's Red Hot. By the time I'm finished, there are thirty balled-up napkins around my plate. To wash it all down, VCI proudly serves crushed ice in your fountain pop, and they recently switched from Pepsi to Coke, a bonus in my opinion.

Is the food at Vic's nutritious? Of course not. Is it fibrous? It would seem so. A health benefit of eating there is that the food is what I call "a tasty enema." I've never proven my theory with a scale, but I'm *pretty sure* the dumps I take after eating there weigh twice as much as the food I consumed. I'm usually at VCI sometime between midnight and 3AM, and, like clockwork, the moment I wake up, a heaping pile of crap that looks like raccoon road kill falls effortlessly out of my butt (into the toilet). As long as VCI is in business, I guarantee I'll never need a laxative.

They also have an original 1986 coin-operated *Arkanoid* arcade game complete with a wood-grain veneer cabinet with built in ash trays. Arkanoid is the best pong-based brick-breaker game ever made. I've cemented myself in the high score spot. Before you get delusions of grandeur and think you can beat me, don't bother, you'll never get to level twenty-three on one quarter, *never*. I'm the master. They also have a jukebox which plays three types of music: Eminem, Toby Keith, and Eminem-Toby Keith duets. Oddly enough, the girls working the rowdy late shift aren't bad looking either. Other coney islands aren't worthy of wiping the anus of Vic's Coney Island, it's that good.

Have you ever eaten a crumb off a counter top and thought, "Man, I hope that was food." I was raised to do that. My parents taught me to eat everything and waste nothing. I'm surprised we aren't a bunch of fatties. Throughout childhood, our dinner table resembled the buffet at an all-inclusive Cancun resort. My mother's famous line before serving meals is, "I didn't know what to make, so I just whipped this together." She plays it down, but the table will be covered with stuffed cabbage, sweet and sour chicken, pigs in a blanket, barbecue ribs, green bean casserole, and Mom's version of a salad, a few sparse pieces of lettuce covered with a pound of diced ham and cheese. My mom is the type who'll douse your spaghetti with another gallon of meat sauce after you say, "No, thanks."

As a kid, I thought daily seven-course meals were the norm. Not until my mid-teens, when I started spending more time at the homes of my friends, did I realize that good food isn't easy to come by. My pals were eating Corn Flakes for dinner. At Connor's house we'd share a can of refried beans. At Hank's house it was PB&Js. His mom also served potato chips with her homemade onion dip, a gelatinous coagulation with the consistency of watered down cottage cheese. It was disgusting. One time, at Dustin's house, I choked down an entire square of chicken bouillon left in his mom's casserole. I was bloated for a week. My mom would never do that to me!

Even their groceries were suspicious. Dustin's cupboards were stocked with white cans labeled in large black plain font, "KIDNEY BEANS," "PEAS," and "TUNA." They were devoid of barcodes and nutritional data. It looked like cartoon food. For reasons unknown, when his mom made hot dogs, biting into one released a vapor that stung my eyes. We once found metal shards in his grape juice. I'm not kidding either! Forget about suing the company, there was a warning on the jug that read, "May contain foreign objects." That was followed by "May contain peanuts." *Peanuts?* In *grape juice?* It was as if they were cutting and pasting from a general warning database to cover their asses. "Wear safety goggles when pouring." "May cause nausea and vomiting." "Do not look directly at juice." "Stop drinking if suicidal thoughts occur."

My mom and dad's obsession with meat was passed down to their sons. As a force of habit, I still order pizzas topped with ham, sausage, double pepperoni, bacon, hamburger, and extra sausage. I make no apologies for the fact that I *love* balls of meat. Remember that giddy feeling you'd get as a kid when you knew you were going to a waterpark the next day? I felt that every time my mom made meatballs. Nothing is better than her Hawaiian meatballs, Swedish meatballs, Italian meatballs, and barbecue meatballs, as well as her meatloaf, burgers, and stuffed cabbage, which use the same meaty concoction. I'd pile them onto my plate and she'd say, "Save some for everyone else!"

I'd think about it for a sec and say, "Nah."

So, in conclusion, if I could have sex with one food for the rest of my life, it'd be my mom's meatballs. I don't know her secret recipe, but I assure you that every other meatball I've ever tasted doesn't even come close. I'd sing this catchy jingle on meatball nights:

> *Meaty balls, meaty balls, I want meaty balls!*
> *Meaty balls, meaty balls, let's eat meaty balls!*
> *Meaty balls, meaty balls, tay-stee meaty balls!*
> *Meaty balls, meaty balls, I love MEATY BALLS!*

When I was thirteen, my parents invited some families from church over for dinner. The adults sat in the dining room and the kids sat in the kitchen. A kid name Matt Cobblestone stabbed his fork into one of my mom's meatballs, took a bite, said, "These meatballs are gross!" and slung it into the garbage can. I got up, walked around the table, kicked the legs of his chair out, rubbed his face in the rug, and said, "Don't put them on your plate if you're going to waste them, *ya freakin' retard!*" Harsh words for a young Christian boy. After that, while he cried, I recovered the meatball from the trash, rinsed it under the faucet, and added it to my pasta. I'll kill any motherfucker who disses my mom's meatballs.

Thanks to my meat fascination, my midsection started getting pudgy in my late-twenties. First, I paid a tailor to let out the waist in every pair of pants I owned. When those got too tight, I bought bigger pants. When I got to the point where I was relying on my belt buckle to hide the fact that I couldn't button any of *those* pants, I knew it was time to cut back. A friend of mine who successfully dropped a few pounds suggested I cut back on bacon, fried chicken, and burgers, and try eating a salad or veggie dish once in a while. I had a hard time grasping that concept because I was deeply ingrained with the notion that meat was the central part of each meal. To make a long story short, I made the transition and it paid off – I lost thirty pounds.

When my parents noticed that I slimmed down, I told them I felt like a million bucks. I was sleeping better, my clothes fit comfortably, I was faster when playing hockey, and I had more energy throughout the day. I proposed that they try to cut back on their meat intake, but they reacted as if I was asking them to pack up and move to an offshore oil rig. However, when my dad started having digestive issues in his mid-fifties, my parents bit the bullet and incorporated Meatless Mondays. Their meatless menu consists of seafood dishes like bacon-wrapped shrimp and cheese-stuffed tilapia, usually with a side salad covered in diced salami.

Last winter, after my mom was released from the hospital following a major heart procedure, one of my parents' friends from church, a woman with a reputation for being a good cook, dropped off a tray of vegetable lasagna for them. I was visiting the day they were eating it. They each took a bite followed by a slow, apprehensive second bite. Each of them inquisitively inspected the lasagna, making faces as if someone was trying to sell them an incomplete set of encyclopedias from 1975. Finally, they simultaneously put their forks down and shook their heads at one another. "What's wrong?" I asked.

"This lasagna isn't good," Dad said.

"Not at all," Mom said.

"Here," I said, "let me try it."

I reached over and scooped up a hefty bite. The pasta was tender, the sauce was tangy, the cheese was plentiful, and it was filled with a tasty medley of grilled zucchini, eggplant, and bell peppers. "*Hmm*, it's actually pretty good!" I said.

"But there's no meat," Mom said plainly, as if she was being asked to drive a car with no wheels.

"It's *vegetable* lasagna," I said, "that's kind of the point."

"But I put *a lot* of meat in my lasagna," she said.

"Right, and yours is the best," I said, "but for a healthy, non-meat option, since you're supposed to be cutting back on meat, this is pretty good veggie lasagna!"

"This is nowhere near as good as your mother's lasagna," Dad said. "There isn't any meat in this!"

"But it's *vegetable* lasagna," I said.

"It needs meat though," he said.

"Then it wouldn't be vegetable lasagna anymore," I said.

"Yeah, it'd be better," he said. "Either way, this has cheddar on top. Your mother only uses mozzarella and ricotta."

"Instead of comparing it to mom's meat lasagna, you've got to try to appreciate it as its own unique dish," I said.

"Your mom's is better," he said.

"I don't think we're looking at this from the same perspective," I said.

He replied, "Well, what's the old saying? We'll have to agree to disagree."

They said I could take the rest of the lasagna home if I wanted to, because they weren't going to eat it, so I did, but over the next few days, each time I microwaved a piece, I felt like a total sellout.

Not long ago, a girl I'd been dating for several months invited me to a homemade dinner at her parents' house. I met them for the first time and enjoyed a few of her mother's specialty dishes. The next time I saw my mom, I told her about it, and her first question was, "What did they make for you?"

"Bean and cheese enchiladas," I said.

"What, no meat?" she said.

"No, but they were pretty good!" I said.

"Why wouldn't they add meat?" Mom asked. "You can drain the fat from ground beef so it's not bad for you. At least use chicken!"

Then she said, "Are they *vegetarians?*" Implying that being a vegetarian is equivalent to being a devil-worshipping nudist listening to Nickelback.

"No, I don't think so," I said. "They also made pasties."

"What kind?" Mom asked.

"Potato and rhubarb," I said.

"*No meat!?*" she said in a complete state of shock. "What's *wrong* with them? You must've been so hungry afterward. I *always* add meat!"

"I know, mom."

For my parents, quantity reigns supreme over quality. Their restaurant critiques are based solely on portion size. They love a local joint called *China Star* because one $4.95 lunch special provides enough sweet & sour chicken for four meals. I should know better than to buy them gift certificates to fancy restaurants on their wedding anniversary, because the same thing happens every time. "So did you like that place?" I'll ask.

They'll give a sheepish, "It was...*good*," followed by the truth, "but they *barely* gave us any *meat!*"

Atmosphere, presentation, freshness, service – who gives a shit – only weight matters! If my parents visit your restaurant and you don't stuff them and fill a couple to-go boxes, they'll rate your establishment as subpar. If they nod toward their plate while saying, "*Hmm*, lots of meat," that's code for, "We like this place."

I've heard such remarks countless times. My mom will take two bites of a taco, turn the inside view toward you, and happily say, "Look at all that meat!" Conversely, her saddest face accompanies viewing a taco section while pouting, "*Hmph, not much meat.*"

A gourmet restaurant that serves a thirty dollar, five-ounce braised lamb shank garnished with a dab of mango chutney in the center of an oversized plate would be an absolute laughing stock to my parents. If presented with it, they'd literally keel over in sarcastic laughter. My dad would say something like, "Why don't I just give you a hundred bucks for a bologna sandwich?"

If there was a restaurant called *Meat City* that would pile five pounds of beef on a plate for two bucks, my parents would never go anywhere else. I was raised by ravenous carnivores and bred to devour heaping stacks of animal muscle. I'm particularly proud of this. Thanks ma and pa.

Dickfacia

If they don't end up in prison, movie bad guys typically get one of two fates. Emperor Commodus in *Gladiator* – dead. Belloq in *Raiders of the Lost Ark* – dead. Clarence Boddicker in *Robocop* – dead. Hopper from *A Bug's Life* – dead. But, once in a while, they'll pull a one-eighty, learn their lesson, and become an expatriate villain. Vader did it in *Return of the Jedi*. Sato from *Karate Kid 2* realized that "Hate is wrong!" In his final moments, Doc Ock decided that doomsday was a bad idea in *Spider-Man 2*. And thanks to Chunk and a Baby Ruth, Sloth joined the Goonies.

Real life is no different. Some of your enemies need to die, while others just need rehabilitation. Maybe you got off on the wrong foot and simply need to start from scratch. At one point you wanted to crane kick them in the face, but look at you now – you're clanking bottles of

Rolling Rock and singing *Piano Man* together. Miscommunication causes rife. Benefit of the doubt causes unity.

Before I started high school, an older kid in my neighborhood named Justin gave me a warning. He said, "The drafting teacher, Mr. Mason, is a total dickface." I looked up to Justin because he wore the newest Air Jordans and was always picked first in basketball. I believed what he said about Mr. Mason and didn't need further evidence to formulate my opinion. From then on, despite never meeting him, I also claimed Mason was a dickface.

Justin graduated and faded away from the neighborhood scene. Then, during my sophomore year, after years of signing Mason off as the biggest dickface the world's ever known, I landed in his dick drafting class. I'm not saying we drew dicks to scale with T-squares or anything; I'm just saying it was a dick *run* drafting class. My dad encouraged me to take the course, but I wanted the other teacher, Mr. Crawford, so I was bummed to say the least. I disliked dickfaces of Mason's magnitude because, really, who likes mega dickfaces? Certainly not me.

I didn't know what was so dickfacey about him yet, but I was sure it would surface. Yet, a few weeks into his class, Mason's dickfacedness remained hidden. I looked for telltale D-face signs but couldn't find any. I thought he'd eventually fail everyone because he was having a bad day, or keep the class after the bell for no reason, but it never happened. Justin couldn't have been wrong, *could he?* Sooner or later Mason's dickfacia would show.

In the meantime, Mason sent us to Caprara Bakery for pepperoni rolls. He played the Smashing Pumpkins and Pearl Jam while we worked. He held *Tetris* competitions on Friday. He joked to the class about my tardiness but never marked me tardy. He made a concerted effort to help me learn the new CAD software. Then, midway through the year, he hooked me up with my first drafting job – co-op work modifying blueprints for a local tool and die shop. The referral spawned a worthwhile career for me. Not *once* was Mason a dickface. Justin was dead wrong, and I had to come to grips with the fact that I wasted time harboring ill will against someone for no fucking reason at all. Based on what I heard, I wanted to avoid him forever, but he turned out to be the best teacher I ever had.

Maybe he tried to set Justin straight on something and he took it too harshly. I'm not sure. Either way, Justin obviously had a run in with him and wanted to make him sound like a dickface to anyone who'd listen. So whether it's your drafting teacher, the new girl, or a familiar face you never got to know, it's best to form your opinion of them based on unbiased observation. Going off hearsay can lead to pegging someone completely wrong, and that makes *you* the dickface.

Complimenting someone behind their back is rare because bad-mouthing comes naturally. If you were cool, generous, and thoughtful all year but made *one* half-assed mistake, a lot of people are going to hear about your offense and nothing else. It's easy to relay saucy stuff like, "Vincent was so wasted that he mooned a bachelorette party bus and puked on the dance floor. What an *idiot!*" That's seldom followed by, "But…he also bought everyone Taco Bell, let us crash at his place, and helped me move my dad's billiard table the next day. The guy's practically a saint." I love when people freely discuss my benevolence when I'm not around. *Psshh, yeah right!* I won't hold my breath.

I was at an end-of-summer bash at a friend's place, chatting with the host about the cash he was raking in from buying and selling superhero statues. The two of us attended the previous Comic Con together where a limited edition Doctor Doom statue caught his eye. The vendor was selling it for $500. I knew it went for way more than that online and told him it was an awesome deal, so he splurged and bought it. His wife was freaking furious when she found out he spent $500 on what she called "a doll." He tried explaining that it was an investment – that such statues are produced in limited quantities and highly collectible, but she didn't believe him. However, a few months later, after he flipped it on eBay for $1,500, she halfheartedly forgave him after blowing the profits on stuff for herself.

He'd been on a roll with the side business ever since. "That's awesome!" I said. "I give you props, man, because I could never do that. When I buy a cool statue, I get too attached. Plus, I'm too lazy to take pictures, post ads, and ship stuff."

He pulled me aside at the party to offer me a celebratory sip of something special he treated himself to – a bottle of twenty-one-year-old Glenfiddich single malt scotch whiskey. "I don't want everyone drinking it," he said, "so I've got it stashed in the hallway closet. Let's go to the kitchen to get some glasses and ice."

We made our way through the crowded kitchen, pulled a couple fancy glasses from the cupboard, and waited to get to the dispenser on the front of his fridge. As can happen with unfamiliar ice dispensers at fast food drink stations, in hotels, and on other people's refrigerators, I misjudged the mechanism and a handful of cubes shot over my glass and onto the floor. "*Aww* sorry, man!" I said.

"No worries, it's just ice," he said. "Just kick them under the fridge." He laughed and kicked a couple cubes out of view.

Now, to properly understand this story, you need to grasp that the following events happened within a three second window:

1. I said, "Okay," laughed, and reared my foot back.
2. The host turned to greet another guest.
3. The host's wife approached the fridge with a plastic cup.
4. I pulled a David Beckham on the remaining ice chunks.

His wife stopped, her jaw agape, and she looked at me with an "I can't believe you just did that" look. "Not cool, Vincent," she said. "Not cool." She kept repeating it as she grabbed a towel and began wiping the floor, refusing to let me take over as I stammered through an explanation. After several attempts of getting through to her failed, I gave up, walked away, and enjoyed the scotch. Before long, the incident faded from my conscious memory. That was over five years ago.

The host and I are still friends who hang out, but his wife, a traveling trade show model, is scarce. Over the past five years, I can only recall a handful of times that I've seen her, let alone interacted with her. One time was a few years ago on a vacation with a group of friends in Palm Springs, California. She had quite a scare on the trip. We were hiking in Mount San Jacinto State Park, attempting to cross a log over a rushing, icy creek, when she slipped and nearly fell in. Fortunately, I was close enough to grab the straps of her backpack and pull her to safety, and the only thing she suffered was a soaked leg and mild embarrassment.

Another moment we shared was when they hosted a graduation party for the guy's little sister in their backyard a couple years ago. Late that night, after two kegs were emptied, a bonfire fit for Pagan sacrifice was constructed. It got out of control when drunken partygoers, along with the host, poured gas on a stack of wooden pallets and surrounded them with a teepee of old doors retrieved from their garage rafters. When I approached the blaze, everyone was standing around wondering why the doors weren't catching fire. The host's wife was sitting in a nearby lawn chair. I said to her, "I've seen the movie *Backdraft*. I think we should move back." Seconds after walking her to the patio, there was an enormous explosion that sent wood shards flying across the yard, fireballs onto the rented party tent, and a mushroom cloud into the power lines. Her lawn chair was toppled and covered in ash.

Besides those significant instances, our interactions whittle down pretty quickly. I remember buying her and her husband a couple drinks at a concert while supporting a mutual friend's rock band. Then there's the time she and I were teammates for a few minutes during a beer pong tournament at a house party. We high-fived a couple times and shared a couple laughs despite losing. Most recently, though, I saw her after her husband invited me to a new tapas restaurant in downtown Detroit.

It was a Saturday night, they reserved a table for ten, the place was packed, and the service was *horrible*. According to our waiter, two servers called in sick at the last minute, leaving them severely understaffed. Honestly, though, it didn't matter much to us. The bar was fully staffed, so as long as we didn't mind getting our own drinks, it allowed plenty of time to sample the entire specialty drink menu – a side effect of which was inevitable inebriation.

It goes without saying that I've never felt a particularly friendly vibe from this guy's wife, but I assumed it was because we barely knew each other. However, that evening, the more she drank, the more she glared at me. Finally, while her husband was at the bar catching up with friends, I addressed it. "What?" I said.

"*What?*" she said, as if I should already know. She held her martini beside her cheek and stared at me with a furrowed brow. "I'm still mad at you," she continued.

"Mad at me?" I said. "Why are you mad at *me?*"

"You don't go to someone's house and kick ice cubes under their appliances," she said. "It's *rude.*"

The memory flooded back, and I tried to explain, assigning blame to her husband, but she replied, "Well, that's *not* what I saw. I've been mad at you for *years*, and I still can't forgive you."

"Wow," I said. "Sorry, but I'm completely blown away! You don't even live in that house anymore, and you're *still* upset about *that?* You'd think the times I saved your *life* would supersede kicking a couple measly ice cubes!"

She burst into mocking laughter. "Saved my *life?* You've never saved my life!"

When I reminded her about Palm Springs, she said, "If you didn't force us to go on that stupid hike, my foot would've never gotten soaked in the first place!" When I reminded her about the bonfire explosion, she said, "That only happened because you were running around with a pitcher all night, forcing everyone to drink beer until they were too drunk to know better!" I was afraid to bring up the seemingly good time we had playing beer pong, because something I did that night might've given her grandma cancer or caused the death of some baby seals.

I was completely taken aback. She wasn't expressing herself to get an apology – she simply wanted me know that she hated my guts. It's funny how a tinge of attitude can completely alter someone's point of view. I might've been her hero if not for those damn ice cubes. Then I thought, "Maybe I never had a chance. Maybe she hated me *before* the ice cube incident."

"Well, I'm really sorry," I said. "I wish there was something I could do to fix the ice cube thing, but, unfortunately, my time machine is broken, and if saving your life *twice* didn't help, I don't think anything will."

"Probably not," she said smugly, "and since we're having *this* discussion, I also want to tell you to stop pressuring my husband into buying stupid superhero dolls."

"They're statues," I said.

"Whatever," she replied.

I never had a chance.

Later that night I pulled her husband aside and said, "What the *fuck*, man? Your wife's been holding a grudge against me for *years* because of some stupid fucking *ice cubes*? I told her you were the one who told me to kick them under the fridge to begin with, and she didn't believe me. How come you've never explained to her what really happened?"

He laughed and said, "Dude, better for her to be mad at you than me."

"Oh, *real nice*," I said sarcastically. "And can you explain why she thinks *I'm* the only reason you buy superhero statues?"

"Same thing," he said, "self-preservation."

I thought for a moment and realized I couldn't blame him – she was scary. "Okay," I said, "but you owe me a shot."

"Done!" he said and immediately flagged down the bartender.

Instead of being the cool guy who bought her drinks, was an awesome beer pong partner, gave wise investment advice, and rescued her from drowning and fire – I was simply the asshole who kicked ice under her fridge and forced her husband to waste money on dolls. To her, I was a total dickface, and she probably led every one of her female friends to think the same thing, which makes sense since none of them ever flirt with me. I'd like to think that over time, and based on personal observation, some of them have realized I'm not a dickface, but, then again, passed-down judgments can *really* stick.

In an expanded circle of friends, your rep is like the price of gas – up and down based on discernibly nothing. All you can do is hope that when your friends hear crap about you, they'll blow it off. A good friend might even refute the gossiper. A *really* good friend will tell the gossiper to fuck off. A *super-duper* good friend will punch them in the face. A *best friend in the whole wide world* will murder them. If that's you, call me and we'll dispose of the body together, because that's what best friends do.

Parched Elbows

My elbows are sore; like *really* fucking sore. Like I was in a karate exhibition at the mall and my job was smashing cinderblocks with them for hours. I don't do karate though. I mean, I'm *sweet* at karate, I've just never had formal training – but I could easily open my own dojo if I wanted to. I'm sure that someday my elbows *will* be sore from clobbering the skulls of students from rival dojos, but that's not why they're sore today.

I play hockey, and I've had sore elbows after being tripped and falling on them during games. I wear elbow pads, but I bought the cheapest used pair I could find at Play It Again Sports, so they pretty much suck. A couple paper towels with rubber bands would probably provide more protection. It couldn't be hockey though. I've been doling out the trips lately, not collecting them.

My elbows used to get sore after doing a few reps on a tricep machine, but the last time I did that was during a semester of weight training in tenth grade. I didn't really want to take the class, because in my opinion weights are too heavy, but a Phys Ed course was required. It was the obvious choice because the teacher, Coach Frampton, who had the same build as Mr. Incredible, gave everyone an "A" as long as they brought gym clothes. Whether or not you exercised didn't matter. I did, however, *love* staring at Cher Zewicky doing reverse leg curls. The one thing I learned in weight training is that it's hard to hide a boner in basketball shorts.

I suppose you could carry stress in your elbows as opposed to other common stress-bearing zones like the neck and shoulders. If that were the case, looming layoffs could result in sore elbows, but I don't give a shit about my shitty desk job. I paid off my car loan and credit cards last summer, and since then I've been praying for layoffs. I think I have what it takes to collect unemployment and sleep until noon every day.

So why are my elbows sore? My guess: *Dehydration*. A lack of fluid in my body is representing itself in my elbows of all places. It's true, dehydration causes muscle soreness, ask any doctor, AA rep, or Egyptologist. Some get it in their quads, some in their delts, others their lats. If you drink too much alcohol, or, to be precise, drink over a long span without pausing to guzzle a bucket of aqua, *bam*, you get all sore. In this case it's centralized in and around my elbow area. It's weird but scientifically indisputable. Bill Nye that shit, his drunk ass will back it up.

Supposedly, you can survive up to forty days without eating, less if you see a fast food commercial with a close-up of a juicy, steaming cheeseburger. I find those zoom-ins pointless because nobody peers into their burger with a magnifying glass, it's unappetizing. It's like staring at clouds, you start seeing things. Last time I was at my older brother's place for a barbecue, I looked too closely into a burger he grilled and thought I saw a canary beak, baby caterpillars, and Jesus winking at me. Regardless, I'm in a White Castle drive-thru an hour after seeing their commercial, so it obviously works. Anyhow, forty days before starving to death seems generous. If you can't find something to eat within that time frame, you deserve to die, because almost everything is edible. Look around, you can eat half of the stuff within arm's reach, at least babies and dogs can. You're more of a survivor than a baby or dog, aren't you?

But get this – humans can only live *eight days* without water. Eight lousy days and that's it, you're toast! I picture a lost explorer exiting the desert on his seventh waterless day thinking, "Good *lord*, I am thirsty!" Then he walks into 7-Eleven, spots a bag of Honey BBQ Fritos, and says, "*Yes! My favorite!*" The next morning he's fucking dead, all pasty and shriveled, with a half-eaten bag of chips in his mummified hand. It'd be even more ironic if he made it out of the desert, fainted while crossing a bridge, fell over the edge, and drowned. That aside, here's the point – dehydration is real, and it's nipping at my elbows.

I attended good ol' churchy-church on Sunday. Well, Jehovah's Witnesses don't call it "church" they call it "a meeting," and it doesn't take place in a "church" because the building is called a "kingdom hall," but it's the same gist – sit and listen to a sermon (except it's called "a talk") given by a minister (except he's called an "elder"). But for clarity's sake, I'll just call it church. After church, the plan was to get lunch at a local bar with my pals Kate and Shoomer.

Kate is a short blonde who I've known since I was thirteen. I hung around her older brother when our family moved to their kingdom hall, but he wanted to move up the congregation ranks and went all "holier-than-thou" on me in his late teens. For example, one time I wore a teal dress-shirt to the meeting and he told me it displeased God because it wasn't white. Shit like that. What a wiener, right? It was around that time when Kate and I realized we shared a mutual love for biting sarcasm and ruthlessly impersonating weirdoes at the hall. Needless to say, Kate and her brother aren't very close.

Kate's the Elaine Benes type, a little more practical and raunchy then her prissy peers. I think of her as "the little sister I never had," which is usually a line of BS that guys use until they bone their so-called "lil' sis," but I'm going to stick to that claim because we've partied together, bitched at each other, laughed our asses off, survived rough patches, and I'd rather see her fall down a flight of stairs while carrying a tray of hot coffee than see her boobs. I don't have a real sister, but I'm assuming that's how it feels to have one.

Shoomer is one of my hockey teammates. His nickname is derived from his last name. He's a distant relative of the nineteenth century composer Robert Schumann. As far as I know, Shoomer doesn't have any symphony writing skills, although he does play the trumpet. I'm glad he's on my hockey team because he dangles a puck as if he's the spawn of Patrick Kane and Pavel Datsyuk. Sometimes I call him Shumanov in tribute to Russian hockey legends. Sometimes I call him Shoomily Shooms in tribute to the show *Zoobilee Zoo*. Sometimes I call him Pablo Shumanovich because, well, it's just fun to say.

Some guys on the team call him *Shooms*. One of them got married last year and asked me and Shooms to be in his wedding. The groomsmen gifts were beer steins engraved with our nicknames. Mine said "Deeter Deeds," since that's the name of my fantasy hockey team. Shooms' was engraved "Schums," because that's how the groom thought it was spelled. To me, Schums is pronounced *Scums*, which sounds like a member of Bobcat Goldthwait's gang from *Police Academy 2*. Anyhow, that's enough background on Scums. Now that you've met my post-church drinking buddies, let's learn about sore elbows together. *Follow me, kids!*

Kate and I had a tradition of going to the aptly named *Mugs Saloon* after Sunday services for half-pound burgers, pitchers of Bud, and a steady mix of engaging and off-color conversation consisting mostly of humorous lies. For example, Kate asked, "Have you ever seen that *Alien vs. Predator* movie?"

"No," I answered, "I *lived* it. *Alien vs. Predator* is my biopic."

The motto being, it's not a lie if you're joking. It's only a lie if it hurts someone's feelings, and even then you can still say absurdly offensive stuff as long as you follow it with, "I'm kidding." I test this theory on my tablemates. "Shoomer, man, your mom looked *hot* today! My penis got all throbby just staring at her legs...I'm kidding. But seriously, Kate, Krissy's butthole (Kate's mom) is so tight I could barely get my thumb in it last night...*ha ha ha*, again, I jest."

Since I qualified my statements, no permanent offense was taken. I may as well throw in the footnote that the term "Krissy's butthole" is an expression that's been used within my crew for a long time. Most of the time it's interchangeable with "Damn it." For example, a few days earlier, while helping my friend Hank change his brake pads, he broke a lug nut, sighed loudly, and groaned, *"Krissy's butthole!"*

It can also be used to convey drastic conditions, such as, "This locker room smells worse than Krissy's butthole!" or, "This lid is tighter than Krissy's butthole!" Or if your golf ball is buried in a sand trap, you might say to your partner, "You've got a nice lie, but my ball is in Krissy's butthole!" When I watch the show *Hoarders*, I expect them to walk into people's cluttered homes and say, "It looks like Krissy's butthole in here." Conversely, it can also denote something especially nice, e.g., "Your new rims are sweeter than Krissy's butthole!" Either way, Kate isn't really a big fan.

We arrived at Mugs Saloon around three o'clock in the afternoon. Shoomer and I were wearing suits. Kate was in a dress. It'd been a while since we consumed dive bar delicacies, so we eagerly awaited our pickle-filled condiment tray, onion ring pile, and first swig of beer. On Sundays, Mugs sells a sixty ounce pitcher of domestic beer for five bucks. We killed the first one before the food arrived, so the decision to order a second was easy. The next pitcher washed down delicious grilled meat. After a couple bites I peered into my burger and thought I saw a foam packing peanut but quickly reminded myself to look away.

The next moment was crucial to the day's outcome, whether or not to order a third pitcher despite being satiated. Normally, we'd pat our bellies, throw an "I'm stuffed" look at each other, and ask for the bill in unison. "I should go home and do laundry," I thought. I was wearing my last clean pair of socks *and* underwear. We'd been there for an hour and collectively downed two pitchers, a pound and a half of ground beef (weight before cooking), a basket of onion rings, a basket of fries, and a medley of gherkins. Still, something was missing. We guessed it was another pitcher. We were right.

The minister's sermon that morning debated whether or not God uses natural disasters to punish people. I say *yes*. Hurricane Ivan lambasting Florida wasn't random. Pensacola is full of dirty old men yanking it to kiddy porn. Some God-fearing people say the same thing about Katrina hitting New Orleans. Actually, there are grubby people doing vile stuff everywhere. Send more hurricanes. Maybe throw some locusts in there too. Maybe give the locusts little swords for the hell of it. Maybe dip the swords in Tabasco sauce. I don't know, just trying to be creative, God.

I was bored during the sermon, so I zoned out and read Bible rape stories in *Judges* while Shoomer made a pop-up book out of his *Watchtower* (a Jehovah's Witness magazine). I got a text from Kate that read, "Mugs Saloon after?" so I shot her a thumbs-up from across the auditorium. About halfway through the meeting, the hall lost power for thirty seconds. The lights and PA system went out. Nobody knew what to do. It was exciting. Ten more seconds and everyone would've started fondling each other.

Don't get the wrong impression, just because I went to church doesn't mean I consider myself exemplary. I know my attitude and lifestyle are lax from a religious standpoint, but I was raised to attend church, I've got longstanding friends there, and nothing makes my parents happier, so I go when I can. I don't do it hypocritically; I do it out of dutiful respect. I appreciate that my parents birthed me, put spaghetti on my plate, braces on my teeth, and Pumas on my feet (copycat Pumas from Payless Shoe Source, but still). So, if staying on the member roster pleases them, doctrine aside, I've got no problem with it. If they were Aztecs who wanted me to wear a feather headdress and worship the sun once in a while, I'd do that too, even if I thought it was a useless, bullshit tradition.

I don't claim to have any insight as to what's really going on in the soupy spirit realm of the universe, but if history is any indicator, it seems to me that families used to worship Gaia, Baal, Marduk, Zeus, Osiris, Jupiter, and a ton of other defunct deities. When successive generations doubted their validity, it upset the parents. After a while, though, it didn't matter, because those gods we're replaced, over-thrown, voted out, or fizzled out. Billions of people worshipped, warred, and abided by gods that are now considered myths. Egyptian gods win the prize for sticking around the longest, lasting several millenniums, but they eventually tanked too.

So what I'm about to say might make staunch churchgoers want to gouge my eyes out, but, odds are, the gods and saints we believe in today will someday fade into obscurity too. Their stories will become peculiar old myths, and their icons and paraphernalia will be found only in museums. People in the 31st Century will look at it and say, "Wow, people used to believe in some screwy bunk!" Current religions will be replaced by new beliefs, maybe science, aliens, or whatever fits the needs of the populous, and as upsetting as that may be, it's pretty much already happening. Regardless, officially revoking the belief system of my parents would decimate them, so why bother.

I think spirituality is great, and I see the structural, moral, and social value of organized religion, but I also think there's some evil to dodge in there, like the risk of becoming a haughty, judgmental prick. Who knows, maybe someday I'll have a Lieutenant Dan moment and hash it out with the Almighty. Hopefully I'll get the shrimp and titanium legs too. Anyhow, I bring up church for a reason. If that morning's sermon was about the sin of drunkenness, perhaps citing the time Lot got hammered and had kinky cave sex with his daughters, or when Noah got wasted and passed out buck-ass naked in front of his kids, resulting in the beginning of slavery, we'd have been less apt to order pitcher number four. If you're rusty on your Bible stories, yes, those things happened.

Green lighting pitcher four was almost as difficult as pitcher three because we knew it'd be similar to the point of no return that Doc Brown explained to Marty regarding the train tracks in *Back to the Future III*. Pitcher four is a tender little guy with hopes, dreams, and feelings. Treat him kindly. Encourage him to keep on keeping on. Show him you love him by ordering an accompanying round of shots. At five o'clock, pitcher four was thriving among us, surrounded by a fan club of whiskey.

Let's fast-forward. Pitcher four and the shots tasted extra tasty so we asked for another round. After ganging up on pitcher five, a blissful yet eerie feeling set in. I looked around the bar. It was too dark to see the back wall. The place felt like an infinite tunnel. To our backs was an empty stage surrounded by out-of-date wood paneling. I could only imagine the flawless mullets and gleaming leather pants that must've rocked that stage in years past. The walls were covered with dust-caked mirrors advertising Busch, Fosters, Stroh's, and other beers that no one orders. Our waitress scurried around behind the bar like a rat in a maze. I looked at her and thought, "You were a young waitress thirty years ago."

A cowardly tingle shivered up my spine. *What am I doing here?* Last Sunday I took underprivileged church kids to a roller hockey rink where I proceeded to whip their asses. Don't worry, they still had fun. The previous Sunday I took my parents to dinner at a Lebanese restaurant. The Sunday before that, well, I can't remember that far back, but I probably did something more productive than this. Then it popped in my head again – I had laundry to do at home.

By seven o'clock we had five pitchers under our belt, and the laughs were flowing like booze into a hobo's esophagus. Our waitress Wanda walked up and said, "Another large pitcher and three *frosty* mugs?" If she hadn't used the word *frosty* we might've called it quits. *Frosty* conjured up fantasies of being served golden ale by glee-filled snowmen. She obviously went to Beer Selling School. For the previous one, she said, "Another *ice cold* pitcher?" Wanda was a pro. She'd consult a thesaurus before returning. "How about another *glacial* pour of *sweet, sweet* lager?" she'd say. If she came out in a Chilly Willy costume and said, "More beer?" that'd work too. However, in a moment of weakness, we panicked and ordered a *small* pitcher in lieu of the regular one.

When the small pitcher came, we felt like chumps, like total sell-outs, like we won the World Series and immediately licensed our name to a vegetable chopper and online dating service. The small pitcher was half the size of the previous ones. A toddler would order this pitcher. Paranoia kicked in, and I sensed other customers snickering at us. To retain dignity, I suggested we order two more baby pitchers to use as mugs. Instead, we did three double shots of beer and requested it be swiftly ushered from our table and replaced with a full-size daddy version. In order to get back on track after the mishap, we manned up and ordered another round of whiskey shots along with it.

By eight o'clock we were buzzing as if someone punted the hive. Admittedly, I'm not a huge fan of the term "buzzed." I don't care for proclamations of inebriation in general. One of my pet peeves is when people insist on running a ticker on their blood-alcohol content. I don't call anyone out or get angry or anything; it's only a *mild* peeve. On my list of pet peeves it falls somewhere between using the word "Chillaxin'" and flooring that makes my shoes squeak. It's not up there with stuff like food going down the wrong pipe or being jumped on by a dog when walking in someone's front door. Fuck that shit!

"I'm *freaking* buzzed right now!" "I'm *so* tipsy!" "I'm *totally* drunk, dude!" It gets obnoxious. Hey, we all make descriptive claims of drunkenness at some point, and that's cool, all I'm saying is, "Let's drink together, friend. We'll assist each other in maintaining equal consumption and telepathically know how the other feels because *we've drank the same amount!* When I fill my mug, I will fill yours. When you drink, I will drink. We will be beer brethren!" Then we'll cheers our glasses and say, "Wonder Twin powers...*Activate!*" It'll be the best! Although it kind of sucked that the Wonder Twin guy could only turn into water-related stuff, while the chick could become any creature. She'd say, "Form of a silverback gorilla!" And he'd say, "Form of a mop bucket." I felt bad for him.

By nine o'clock we'd pulled a Houdini on seven pitchers (technically, six-and-a-half). We'd been sitting in our Sunday best for six hours. Shoomer wondered why his girlfriend hadn't called. "I wonder if it's because I'm a loser wasting my day in a seedy bar," he said. Kate stood up a friend she was supposed to meet for a matinee. An hour earlier, a guy I knew sent me a text message requesting a jump because his car stalled somewhere in my neighborhood. I kept thinking, "I've *got* to get home and do laundry if I want clean undees for work tomorrow."

Since beer makes you smarter, we discussed relationship ideology, hypothesizing on fault-finding behavior, subconscious jealousies, and shepherding a dramatic circle of friends. After that we ripped on girls who wear pajamas in public. I bemoaned the addition of print on the butts of girls' pants. It's already hard enough to not stare at young female asses like a total perv, let alone if they have words like "Pink" and "Juicy" written across them. I then listed my top three *least* favorite current female fashion trends:

1. Capri Pants – Don't say they're practical for summer, they're just nappy floods. You wear them because you're self-conscious about your knees, but I like your knees. Way better alternative: Daisy Dukes. (PS – Nice knees.)
2. Baby doll tops – They may show the shape of your boobs, but they also make it look like your crotch starts directly below them. Only acceptable after your first trimester.
3. Shawls – Shoomer calls them "Frocks." Kate refers to them as "Ponchos." Either way, you cut a hole in a blanket and wear it. They cover everything on a woman worth looking at. They make fat chicks look like tents, and skinny chicks look like fat chicks. Should be reserved solely for gunslingers.

Wanda's shift was over so we cashed out with her and met her replacement. The new waitress was younger but looked like she'd been smashed in the forehead with a hot iron. When she walked up, I said, "Whoa! That's quite a contusion!"

"What happened?" Kate asked.

"Oh this?" she said, gesturing toward her gaping wound and giggling as if having half of your brain hanging out is no biggie. "I tripped over my cat and hit my head on the stove." In other words, your redneck boyfriend got pissed about your skanky work outfit and clocked you. Can you blame the guy? Anyone would be insanely jealous of those pale, veiny tits in that training bra. Despite being nearly brain dead, she swapped our sweaty mugs with icy ones and brought us pitcher ocho. Nice job, zombie waitress!

While hanging with a fresh, bubbly pour, we came to grips with the fact that it was after ten o'clock. That alone made us laugh. Mugs Saloon was devoid of clocks and windows like a casino. It was a black hole time vortex. Time flew by. I was worried that we'd walk outside and there'd be flying cars and androids everywhere.

We spent the next hour swapping stories about crazy exes while spinning dime novel versions of our sex conquests. We talked about sneaking in bedroom windows, hiding naked in closets, and getting caught by the cops in steamed up backseats. Shoomer took the cake with a dry-humping story involving skin-tight anti-erection jeans, an itchy straw blanket, and an intrusive ping pong playing robot. We argued over who dealt with more crap and who got the best retribution for said crap. By 11PM, pitcher eight was three-quarters gone, or one-quarter full, depending on your take on life. All the sitting left us famished, so we entertained the thought of ordering food again.

We told the bludgeoned waitress we were hungry. She said we could order a pizza. "A large cheese and pepperoni sounds *super* good!" I said. "Better bring us another pitcher and a round of shots while we're waiting!"

While drooling over the thought of a piping hot pizza, we passed the time discussing our pizza preferences. Kate dips every bite in ranch and picks off mushrooms. Shooms loves 'shrooms and stacks his slices into a poor man's calzone. I like small pepperonis that curl up into little grease hot tubs. I like dipping my crust in marinara, otherwise I skip it. I crave deep dish about once a year but hunt down Italian style pie with sweet sauce and thick cheese nearly once a month. I eat more Hawaiian pizza than they do in Honolulu. My favorite mom n' pop joint is Riopelle's. My favorite chain is Jet's. Pizza was going to be perfect for sponging up the gallons of beer sloshing around in our tummies.

At midnight we were huddled closely, laughing at everything. Saying *vagina* or making a fart noise (via butt or mouth) was hilarious. We took turns saluting pitcher nine with heartfelt yet incoherent tributes. Kate started hers with, "I feel like this pitcher is my dad." Shoomer started with something about appreciating cheap beer, but by the time he was done he was rambling about his car payment. I was wearing my nicest suit and had the sleeves rolled up like a sweatshirt. Shoomer was wearing his tie as a headband. Kate misaligned her mug to her lips, pouring beer on her lap for the fourth time.

Around twelve-thirty we asked about our pizza and learned that the waitress wasn't telling us we could "order a pizza" but that we could "*order* a pizza" – as in use the payphone to call Domino's and have it delivered. *Krissy's butthole!*

We were finishing pitcher ten when Kate's friends walked in, two girls wearing foam trucker hats printed with "Spoiled Kitty" and "Mrs. Timberlake." Her friend Trish called us "freaking morons" and took the keys. I call Trish "Beedeebee" in reference to what Martin Lawrence called Gina's meddling friend Pam on the sitcom *Martin*. Some say

Beedeebee was a reference to her nappy black hair, others claim it was an acronym for B̲ig D̲umb B̲itch. B̲ig D̲umb B̲londe is fitting for Trish. The girls drove us to Taco Bell and then to my house where Kate washed down a chalupa with the half-mug of beer she walked out of the bar with. Five minutes later, Kate was out cold on the couch with a steady stream of drool dripping from her chin. Shoomer was next to her spitting out crunchy taco debris while cracking up at a TV commercial for the Bernstein Law Firm because one of the lawyers was blind.

If my math is correct, we collectively drank the equivalent of forty-seven-and-a-half beers, roughly sixteen each, in addition to the whiskey. It was 2AM. I ate my burritos and bemoaned the fact that I had to work the next day. I couldn't walk straight but had the where-withal to wipe Kate's drool with her shawl or frock or whatever those lesbo things are called, and seconds later I was asleep in bed, which in this case is technically referred to as "passed out." An hour later I woke to the sound of Shoomer puking his guts out in the bathroom.

Three hours after that I woke up with sore, throbbing elbows. Each one felt like it had the palpitating heart of a meth addict in it. I stumbled to the kitchen, guzzled two glasses of water, and crashed back in bed. However, it must've been too little, too late, because Monday evening, a good sixteen hours later, my elbows were still aching like bitches. In case you were wondering, I got to work two hours late and went commando. The moral of the story is that if you're ever lost in the Sahara, on the verge of dehydration, and come across an oasis with two glistening pools, one full of water and one full of beer – don't be greedy, take water breaks.

Comb-Over for the Deceased

I recently attended the funeral of a twenty-six-year-old guy who went to my church. His name was Harris. Last Friday they found him face down in a bathroom stall at the Westgate Theater, dead from a heroin overdose. We weren't best buds or anything, he only came to the kingdom hall once in a while, but he seemed like a cool guy. During our brief encounters, he was always friendly and quick to smile. All I knew about Harris was that he played electric guitar, had a bonkers mom, and a smoking hot stripper sister.

When his mom got the unfortunate news, she understandably lost it, repeatedly calling him a "motherfucking son of a bitch" in front of the congregation elders. A few days earlier, she argued with him about substance abuse, and he told her not to worry. He told her you can't OD on heroin, and she believed him. They had obviously reached a bizarre stage in their relationship, because it's hard to imagine when you'd stop arguing about whether or not to *do* drugs and *start* arguing about whether or not your particular drug addiction could have ill effects. I mean, come on, its goddamn heroin, it's not exactly packed with nutrients. Last I checked, Dr. Oz wasn't endorsing banana-kale-heroin smoothies.

I saw Harris at church a week before he died. I shook his hand and said, "What sub?" When he started to answer, "Not much…" I interrupted and said, "Did you have for lunch at Subway?" because I think retarded stuff like that is funny. He kind of laughed, but we both knew it was stupid. I do similar stuff to my cousin Laura whenever I see her. I'll walk up to her, look down, and say, "*Oooh*, I like those shoes!"

She'll say, "Really? Thanks, I just got them!"

Then I'll say, "Oh, no, I was talking about mine. But yours aren't bad."

Anyhow, I asked Harris, "You still jamming on that guitar?"

"It's been a while," he said.

I pantomimed playing a heavy metal riff and said, "All right, man!" Then we parted ways with an imitation gang-member hand-shake, the kind that usually goes wrong, but we nailed it. Had I known it would be the last time I'd see him, I probably would've done some-thing more sentimental, maybe pantomimed *Stairway to Heaven* followed by a bro-hug.

The funeral home was packed. I sat there wondering if anyone in the place thought Harris was a jackass who deserved his untimely demise. I considered leaving afterward and forgiving every annoyance I've ever had with anyone, because I don't want anyone attending my funeral secretly thinking I'm a jackass. On the other hand, if you gather a couple hundred people together, odds are at least one of them thinks you're a jackass. I'm not a jackass though! Why would someone attend my funeral if they had such a low opinion of me? To save face? Out of spite? They're the *real* jackass. I can't wait until they bite it so I can be spiteful at *their* funeral. I'll say, "I'm sorry for your loss. Kevin will be missed. Well, except for the times he was a total jackass, which, honestly, was all the time."

I zoned out during the eulogy. The death of someone so young made me ponder my life. I envisioned my funeral, hoping everyone was super bummed, crying, and struggling to console one another. Then I imagined myself sitting up in the casket and saying, "Guess what? I'm still alive, everyone!" After that I hoped they'd be really happy and cheer and no one would be like, "Dang it." I'll probably leave my extensive hockey jersey collection to my younger brother, so I understand if he gets upset that he has to give them back. Out of principle, I guess I'll have to let him keep them after I fake my death.

I nominated the two men sitting in front of me for the "Worst Comb-Over Award." I'm not sure what those twenty greasy strands over your bald scalp are contributing. Whatever boosts your confidence I guess. The guy on the right combed his comb-over with a comb three times during the service. Regardless, the guy on the left won because his comb-over was drenched in pomade, and if allowed to fall naturally, would hang to his nipples.

If I start losing my hair, I'll go with either the Bruce Willis buzz cut or the Jason Statham shaved head. I know it's probably easier said than done, and I'll end up desperately hanging on to every last strand like a two-year-old with a baby blanket. Still, no comb-overs, toupees, or Ron Howard's ballcap-for-life thing for me. No worries though, my hair currently looks like a heaping plate of dark brown Pad Thai (minus the bean sprouts and crushed peanuts). Seriously, last time I had lunch at Thai Palace with a workmate, he said, "Dude, I just realized something funny, this plate of Pad Thai looks *exactly* like your hair!" I pretended it was a compliment.

I sat there pondering the ridiculous nature of comb-overs and didn't zone back in until my row was dismissed to pay final respects. Walking past a dead body is uncomfy. I'm glad morticians exist, because for common folk, prepping a cadaver would be as unnerving as disarming a bomb without a manual while it's teeming with centipedes. "Red wire or blue wire? *Ahhh!!!* I don't know! *There's fucking centipedes everywhere!*" No thanks. Harris was lying peacefully, immune to alarm clocks, pale and swollen, and wearing a nice suit. I noted that his facial expression was the same one you'd have after taking a sizeable bite of a cheeseburger. Admittedly, while beside the casket, my only thought was, "I hope my face looks somber enough."

Thankfully, the deceased aren't laid out in the manner of death. Car accidents would be tricky. Tub suicides would be visually invasive. Gardening heart attacks would be okay depending on the garden. Harris would be face down on crusty tiles beside a puddle of foamy drool. His face would look strangled, instruments of drug addiction would be dangling from his arm, and he'd be surrounded by graffiti laden stall partitions. What a way to go. Plus, he'll never know what happened at the end of *Wedding Crashers*. Death doesn't care about Owen Wilson. Death doesn't care about finishing a tub of popcorn. Harris' guitar was on a stand by the casket. I wanted to pick it up, strum an E-minor, and sing, "*Fuck you, Death.*"

Ideally, I'd like to die painlessly in my sleep of old age. You too? What a coincidence! My next choice would be during sex with two or more supermodels, although that puts them in a precarious situation. Third place would be while saving people's lives, preferably the entire planet, or at the very least, two or more supermodels who'd thereafter diddle themselves in memory of me. If none of those, I hope to die from multiple things. "Vincent died of prostate cancer," sounds boring and cliché. "Vincent died from multiple sword wounds, a fifty-story fall, poison frog darts, a tragic equestrian accident, and a broken heart," sounds bad ass. Maybe add, "The autopsy revealed that he was also allergic to the bees that stung him during the fall. Thank God he saved that bus full of supermodels though. They'll be rolling their beans in memory of him for an eternity!"

I went to the post-funeral get-together at Harris' mom's house. I arrived the same time as my parents. My mom was carrying a container filled with pinwheel cookies and honeyballs. I had empty Tupperware in my car from dinner leftovers that she packed for me the previous week. I tried to get her to lend me some cookies to make it look like I brought something, but she didn't go for it. She said, "I'll say these are from all of us."

I said, "Yeah right, like anyone will believe that."

When everyone was lining up for refreshments, I tried to hug Harris' mom, but it was awkward because she was holding a freshly poured cup of coffee in one hand and a collapsing paper plate full of bean dip and meatballs in the other. When I said, "Sorry," I felt like I was apologizing for the inconvenient hug instead of her loss. When I tried to give Harris' hot sister a hug, it turned into an awkward, one-armed "Buddy ol' pal" sort of thing. She had a new boyfriend in tow anyway, some cage-fighting meathead who looked like he wanted to choke-out every guy that hugged her. I felt bad for him though. It would totally suck to face a huge crisis in your girlfriend's family after dating for only two weeks when all you really wanted was a beejer.

Harris' sister is what a lot of girls would call a skank. She steals the spotlight by bearing more cleavage and showing more leg than any normal girl comfortably would. She's the girl that makes girlfriends slap their boyfriends when she struts by. She makes her money dancing at a topless joint called *King Louie's Go-Go Lounge*. Ever wonder what a stripper dresses like for a funeral? Like a stripper. She was in a tight, low-cut top and a clingy, black miniskirt that barely covered her ass. I appreciated it.

I once saw her in pre-strip gear at a coin car wash during my lunch break. She was in painted on jeans and black stilettos. I was watching her vacuum her mats from my bay and accidentally hosed my shoe. I went back to the office with a drenched sock. My office building only had one bathroom with an air dryer, so I went in, took off my shoe, and held my foot under it. My boss walked in and shot me an odd look. "What's up, Vincent?" he said.

"A stripper got my sock wet," I replied. There was an awkward pause. "It's not as bad as it sounds," I said.

I walked into Harris' basement and had a series of clumsy chats with his relatives. His uncle spewed raunchy details about his recent wild visit to Cabo San Lucas, in particular, the crazy nights he spent at Sammy Hagar's *Cabo Wabo*. "The girls down there *really* know how to party," he said, "I mean *oooh weee* can they party!"

I reminded Harris' teenage cousin about the time she sat next to me at church and complained that I breathe too loud. I told her I had it checked out and the diagnosis was that, unfortunately, yes, I *do* breathe too loud. I assured her that I'd hold my breath when she's nearby. She said, "Good, because I just got my hair done," which I thought was pretty funny.

One of Harris' aunts flew in from Texas and didn't hide the fact that she was grumpy. She complained about how difficult it was to fly in for the funeral. "I'm an accountant," she said, "and tax time is my busy season." I asked her if it's true that there's no *actual* law forcing people to pay income taxes, and she got overly defensive. She gave me the sleazy feeling you'd get if you offered someone a bribe and they tucked it back in your shirt pocket while preaching some Boy Scout honor code bullshit. Give me a break, it's just a question. I'm not asking you to help me sneak anthrax and an oscillating fan into the Pentagon, geez. I heard someone at work ranting about taxes being unconstitutional and I just wanted to get confirmation from an accountant before I stopped paying them.

The whole post-funeral scene was awkward. Some people were flipping through photo albums, some were eating, some were laughing, some were crying. All of it seemed like an act of futility. People have been dying since the dawn of humanity, and there's still no satisfying way to go about consoling the bereaved. You'd think it'd be easy by now. You'd think there'd be a step-by-step procedure in place or a How-To manual, but no, it's still all awkward hugs over collapsing meatball pyramids and annoying small talk to avoid the topic at hand.

I went back to the food table, made a pita roll-up, and exited the premises. I took a bite as I drove away but realized I wasn't even remotely hungry. I only made it to avoid talking to anyone else, so I threw it out the window. Don't worry, it's not littering. I'm sure a raccoon will find it and say, "*Oooh weee* those mourners *really* know how to party!"

Then I had an epiphany and stopped at Blockbuster. I thought, "I'll bet attending a funeral amplifies the scare factor of horror movies." Guess what – it did. The pale, meowing Japanese zombie kid hiding under the bed in *The Grudge* was *extra* freaky. The heightened effect was like watching slapstick comedy with a wine buzz, or watching kung fu after eating Chinese take-out. If you like scary movies, take advantage of this life hack next time someone you vaguely know kicks the proverbial bucket.

Thirteen-Incher

An old friend of mine named Dustin was visiting from Colorado recently. As teens we built a half-pipe in his backyard, had pellet gun wars, poured salt on slugs, played tons of Sega Genesis, watched scrambled porn, snuck into R-rated movies, and had Taco Bell eating contests. We were good pals until he got married and moved out west to be near his wife's family.

Last Saturday we sat around a bonfire in his mom's backyard reminiscing old times. I said to Dustin, "Hey, remember the time we were skateboarding by the high school and you had to crap super bad, so you took a squat behind a dumpster and wiped with weeds and couldn't stop itching your butthole the rest of the day?"

"Yeah," Dustin said with a chuckle, "I think I've taken more emergency craps in my life than normal ones. I even crapped my pants at Sears once." He paused for a moment and then said, "Last week."

The ensuing story was classic, a relay of the entire spectrum of human emotion. Dustin had to take a fiendish dump while waiting in line to buy a circular saw. He snapped at the girl working the register as she spelled out the benefits of applying for a Sears credit card. He watched the aisle to the restrooms stretch out like a hallway in *The Shining* because his bowels were about to burst. I laughed through the entire story, especially the crescendo when he entered the men's room, kicked open the stall door, and blew a load in his pants while trying to undo his belt buckle. "*Wait!?*" I said. "You made it all the way into the stall and *then* crapped yourself?"

Inconceivable but true. That's what happens when you love greasy junk food but suffer from IBS. That poop is exiting your bunghole, and God with all his angels can't stop it. It's also a sign that you need a belt with a simpler latch. Anyhow, hats off to Dustin, the guy I know who's most likely to Hershey squirt his drawers in public.

Before I go any further, I should throw a little disclaimer out there. First, the facts: Humans have bowel movements, and this chapter discreetly touches on that subject, minus the discreetly part. Sometimes the need to take a wicked dump outweighs your dignity and all considerate options. Afterward, though, such instances can often be amusing. Anyhow, if you're about to eat lunch at an Indian buffet, or, I suppose, any buffet for that matter, or you're not someone who "poops," go ahead and sit this one out.

It only takes a couple nights of binge drinking to learn the drunken tendencies of your pals. There's usually a guy who barks at women, a guy who pukes early, a guy who gets touchy-feely, a guy who dances by himself, and one who'll pick a fight with a crew of towering black guys because he thinks he's Mr. Miyagi's chosen one. R.I.P. Colin Bruckner, even though you're not dead, *you should be.*

The guys I hung around with during my hardy partying phase were associated with a gaggle of familiar party gals. They weren't our girlfriends, just random chicks who'd text us every Saturday to find out where we were. They had drunken tendencies too. Some mistakenly thought they'd win hot body contests, some threw their drink at anyone who bumped into them, some got ravenously hungry, some wanted to make out, and some puked out the car window while shouting, "I need *ano-la-ther* drink!"

My crew had a typical version of the latter. She had a pretty face, big tits, and followed Meg Ryan's hair trends. Unfortunately, she also had a *thunderously* huge ass and shapeless sausage-like stumps for legs. Her merciless girlfriends often gave her elephant-themed shit as a gag gift. Genetics screwed her, because her proportions weren't even attractive to black guys. At least this is a female we're talking about, because I went to school with a guy nicknamed Kenny the Butt who had the same shape and never spoke a word through four years of high school. Anyhow, this girl was the type who'd look really good if she pulled up beside you in her car. In fact, if she could go through life holding a car door beside her, she'd be a knockout. With a permanent car door shield, she could easily score a rich, handsome guy. She can roll the window down at their wedding to say *I do.*

My friend Connor was at the bar one night when she was up to her usual drunken antics. Her friends disowned her, so she asked him for a ride home. They got in his Dodge Dakota, and within a couple minutes, she passed out. He shook his head in a "Poor thing, look what you've done to yourself" manner and continued driving. A couple minutes later he heard a faint gurgle and raised a suspicious eyebrow. Next, she uttered a mumbled moan. Seconds later, the cabin filled with a sulfuric smell. "She shit herself!" he said.

I interrupted, "Come on, dude. Are you sure she didn't just rip a nasty fart?"

He explained, "There's a *distinct* difference between the smell of a horrid fart and the smell of fresh shit." He had a point. The thought of it made me gag a little. I can only imagine how disgusted he was. This girl just shit her pants, or more accurately, her skirt, in the passenger seat of his truck. I guarantee it was diarrhea, and I *guarantee* she was wearing a thong. "It gets worse," he said.

When Connor pulled up to her house, she rolled out, face first, onto the lawn. He considered helping her inside, but when the cabin light revealed a puddle of poop soup on his passenger seat, he blurted out, "Oh, that's just *fucking sick!*" and peeled rubber out of there. He drove straight to Meijer and bought a dozen shop rags and the strongest upholstery cleaner he could find. She spent the night passed out in the grass in her shit-filled skirt. Time to lay off the Smirnoff, eh?

The first place I ever played organized hockey in full equipment was an arena in Flat Rock, Michigan called the *Ice Box*. One of the church dads rented the ice and organized games for young guys in our church circuit. When it became a weekly event, a bunch of girls started showing up to watch. One of the girls lived in a nearby trailer park, and my older brother liked her. A few of us started hanging out with her and her friends in her Mom's mobile home after games.

One night, on our way to the rink, my brother and I went through the Taco Bell drive-thru. Without weighing the consequences, I ordered my usual – two soft tacos, two crunchy tacos, and two bean burritos with sixty-thousand packets of hot sauce. After the game, my innards were a gurgling cesspool. On our way to the trailer park, I did everything I could, physically and mentally, to hold back the barrage of low-grade meat pounding on my colon door. I rubbed my belly, unfastened my belt, unbuttoned my pants, tried Lamaze breathing techniques, visualized calm waters, and moaned like a bitch. Nothing helped. Nature was calling something fierce.

It was dark and there was a foot of snow on the ground when we pulled into the trailer complex. I said to my bro, "I can't make it!"

"Hold on, dude!" he said. "We'll be there in like thirty seconds!"

He wasn't grasping the urgency, I didn't have thirty seconds. I was about to blow. Besides, I'd been in this girl's trailer before. The front door opened directly into the living room where there'd be a dozen kids, half of them cute girls. Aside from the humiliation of running past them while clutching my anus, the bathroom was connected to the living room. The walls were paper thin. It was a *fucking mobile home* for Pete's sake! Do the math. They'd hear every ker-plop, sploosh, and sputter as I destroyed her toilet.

I demanded he stop the car. He rolled his eyes and conceded. I grabbed a handful of Taco Bell napkins and dashed out the door, hurdling over snow piles, trying to get to the nearest mobile home. It was the only time I've ever thought, "I'd give my left nut for a pair of snowshoes right now!" I ran behind a random trailer, dropped my drawers, and exploded in the most relieving crap known to man or beast. It was a shapeless mass, nothing like the usual kielbasa logs.

My butthole was like a demon-possessed soft-serve machine hosing a Dairy Queen kitchen in a hellish rage. Yes, it felt good. Yes, it splattered on the vinyl siding. I breathed a deep sigh of relief and watched the steam rise from my hot feces into the frigid night air. My first thoughts were clairvoyant. I understood why Native Americans believed that the steam rising from the wounds of a slain animal was its soul rising to the afterlife. My turd's soul was rising to its afterlife. Perhaps it'd be reborn as the Lincoln log of a king, wizard, or noteworthy mobile home innovator.

I waved goodbye to my shit mound and stated a rhetorical apology to the homeowners. Tomorrow they'd find the frozen brown splatter, footprints, and crap-smeared napkins, and realize this wasn't the doing of a wild animal but a disgusting human being. I entered the girl's mobile home five pounds lighter and more charming than Johnny Depp.

To ease my nerves during public speaking, I picture the audience on toilets with their pants around their ankles. I do the same thing when talking to a girl at a bar. If she's particularly sexy, I imagine her constipated, trying to shit a brick. It calms my nerves. Don't judge me. The fact is – the hottest of hot chicks poop. The wealthiest of the wealthy poop (colostomy bags count). Homeless people poop (just not in toilets). Terrorists poop. The Pope poops. Germaphobes poop. Gourmet chefs poop. Your parents poop. You poop. I poop, a lot. What do you think Jesus and his 4,000 disciples did after he miraculously provided an all-you-can-eat buffet of fish sticks and biscuits in Bethsaida? Let's just say Jewish plumbers have never seen so much action. See, even Jesus pooped. There, I said it – even Jesus took huge, smelly, sometimes-urgent dumps. You can almost picture him writhing back and forth on a clay toilet seat saying his own name.

Messiah or not, we've all had a desperate need to empty our bowels no matter how cool we are. Hell, even the best of us have sharted in a pair of clean underwear, stuffed them in an Outback Steakhouse trash can, and gone commando unbeknownst to our family. No? Just me? Dang it. Generally, it starts with bad food – an undercooked burger, spoiled egg salad, questionable fish fillet, or suspicious kumquat. Intestinal pressure builds, you try to fart, and *Plbbb* too late, you just junked your drawers, clown! Welcome to humanity!

Going number two in your pants is the ultimate slippage. Don't feel bad though, it happens to everyone. I guarantee you that even our nation's founding fathers sharted in their knickers. Benjamin Franklin has stuffed several pairs of soiled undees in Outback trash cans. Ulysses S. Grant is banned from Outback. Everyone you look up to does it. Ralph Fiennes shits himself. Martha Stewart does it *all the time*. It's part of Randy Moss' touchdown celebration. Bill Gates started a charitable foundation for sharters because he identifies with the plight. If you read any of Ian Fleming's *James Bond* novels, you'll find that *007* shits his pants at least *five times* per book, often to thwart enemies. I heard marathon runners are champion pant crappers. It's a blur of confusion and lesson in humility. Add it to your bucket list. Already checked off? *Good for you!*

While on a rustic camping trip, I made it my goal to shit in the same spot in the woods for an entire week. By Friday it looked like that pile of Triceratops shit from *Jurassic Park*. On the last day, after a meaty breakfast and one last giant dump, I tricked my cousin into looking at it. "You've got to see this cool thing I found in the woods," I said, "it's seriously *awesome!*"

"A mushroom?" he said.

"Better!" I said.

"A dead animal?" he said.

"Close…but *even better!*"

I led him into the forest and stopped him just before he stepped in it. "Look" I said, pointing down. "I made that."

He made direct eye-contact with my heaping pile of dung, shook his head, and said, "Dude, you're sick." It was *totally* worth it. As he walked away, I kept saying, "Not bad, huh?" because I sincerely wanted some recognition for my poop mountain, but he refused to humor me.

That's why I hate auto flushers in public restrooms. They purge your achievement every time you lean forward. It's a guilty pleasure to elevate a dark continent out of the sea or relax your sphincter enough to squeeze out a thirteen-incher. It's the same satisfaction you get from hocking up a huge phlegm wad or splattering a mirror when popping a pimple. You want to show someone but rightfully doubt that your girlfriend will be equally impressed.

We usually get a short window of opportunity to poop in a civilized manner. I was at a breakfast buffet joint called *Reggie's Family Restaurant* with a slew of churchgoers on a Sunday morning. Reggie's serves up all-you-can-eat sausage, bacon, eggs, ham, corned beef hash, and pancakes. Gossiping over fatty treats is heaven for churchgoers. Covering that stuff with sausage gravy and hot sauce is heaven for me. I was at a table of ten, already on my second helping, when urgency struck.

I usually think of my anus as being on a first-come, first-served basis, picturing my intestines stacked sequentially with previous meals. I can't explain the science of it but sometimes a disagreeable food pushes the other customers out of the way and gets to the front of the line. I have difficulty grasping exactly how a bad sausage takes cuts, but this phenomenon was happening to me at Reggie's. One moment I was laughing with everyone about Brother Moore's comb-over, the next I was grinding my teeth in a cringe of nuclear gut pressure.

The initial pangs of priority diarrhea are as evident as getting blasted in the stomach by a cannonball. I sat through the first phase of discomfort to make sure it wasn't a false alarm. When the feeling that Mike Tyson was raping ten alligators in my colon returned, I knew it was go time. No sweat though, the cure is simple – I'd excuse myself, gingerly walk to the restroom, and shit it out. "I'll be right back," I said nonchalantly as I finished a chuckle while patting a napkin to my lips. My external demeanor was no reflection of my internal suffering as I headed toward the men's room.

Upon entering I came across an old man combing his hair at the sink mirror. He nodded and smiled as I pranced by. That's when the relative calm was broken. There was only one stall and it had a hand-written sign taped to it that read, "Do Not Use – Out of Order!" At that point, the toxic waste in my bowels was stinging particularly bad. I feigned using the urinal and waited for Old Man Smooth to finish grooming his gray. As soon as he left, I barged into the stall. The toilet was filled to the brim with toilet paper soup. There was a plunger in the corner, so I grabbed it and plunged like a madman. Beads of sweat were forming on my brow from the hell fury boiling inside of me. I flushed the toilet, hoping to god it would empty. I jumped back as it overflowed and rushed to the center floor drain.

I left the men's room with a bright idea. I turned the corner in the hallway and knocked on the door to the women's restroom. Yeah, I was that desperate. Just as I was about to peek inside, a mother with two little girls entered the hallway. "Damn it!" I said loudly. The mother shot me a dirty look and corralled her girls as I leaned against the wall and tried to act normal. After they went in, I dove back into the men's room, which was empty at the moment. I was seconds away from tearing a hole in my dress slacks.

What could I do? I looked at the sink. No way. The urinal? I would've if there was a lock on the door, but there wasn't. The trash can? The floor drain? I didn't want to get caught doing that. Could I make it to the Dunkin Donuts down the street? How about the dumpster in the alley? Shit into a handful of paper towels? I was out of time.

"I hate you Reggie's!" I said. "You serve old ass eggs from a trough under a heating lamp, install a *goddamn second toilet!*"

I sighed and came to grips with my predicament. I wasn't proud of what I was about to do, but quite frankly, Reggie's brought this upon itself.

I tore the *Out of Order* sign off, latched the stall door, stepped out of my shoes, stripped off of my pants, and hung them on the coat hook. Then I took hold of the handicap rails, hovered over the seat, and violently sprayed shit into the overflowing bowl. It was the splashiest shit I've ever taken. I lifted my feet as brown chunks spilled over the porcelain edge and floated downstream on the tile floor. My piss poured onto the ground like Niagara. I took my first wipe, flung it against the wall, and said, "You did this to yourself, Reggie's!" I threw the rest of my wipes on the floor because, what was the point? When I was done, I reapplied the sign, now more fitting than ever.

During the episode, the rest of my party had finished their meals and paid. When I came out, the family I drove with was waiting by the cash register. "I was about to come in and check on you," the father said.

"Be glad you didn't," I said.

"Are you okay?" he asked.

"Never been better!" I answered.

I paid, left a generous tip, donated to the children's hospital charity jar at the check-out counter for the first time in my life, and told the lady at the register, "The men's room could use a little attention."

On the ride back, I relayed a PG version of what happened, not that they wanted to hear the gory details, but poop pangs are universally funny. The mother pretended to be grossed out, but I think it was a guise. Everybody loves poop stories, right?

I was sitting in the backseat of their car beside their toddler who was strapped into a car seat. The little boy followed suit and laughed along with everyone despite not really comprehending the whole story. Then he shouted a keyword he picked up on. "Poop!" he said.

I looked at him, gave a thumbs-up, and said, "You couldn't have said it better, buddy. *Poop!*"

Thelma's Organs

I was invited to a going-away party for an elderly woman named Thelma Organ who goes to my church. Her youngest son, exiting puberty at the ripe age of seventy-three, is moving her out to his condo near Phoenix. Adding to the festivities, Thelma's going away party coincided with her one-hundredth birthday.

Despite being older than dirt, Thelma doesn't really need a caretaker. She lives by herself in my neighborhood. I see her sweeping leaves off her lawn a couple times a week. I used to beep my horn, shout her name, and wave, but the fearful gaze she gave in return made me worry that I was giving her Battle of Gettysburg flashbacks.

A few years ago I attended a weekly Bible study group that met in Thelma's basement. Back then she was only ninety-seven and much hotter. I heard she quit working at Hooters since then. Anyhow, I was always amazed at the way Thelma defied physics. She had no trouble getting up and down stairs, she baked a lot, and she pedaled a mean sewing machine. The only thing lacking was her hearing. Thelma requested that you literally yell in her face during conversation. It was awkward at first but fun when you got used to it. The louder you'd yell, the happier she was. Putting a megaphone to her ear would've been pure bliss for Thelma. Too bad it's not that way with everyone.

It was raining the day of Thelma's party. I arrived late and immediately noticed that there were hardly any cars parked on the street and little to no activity at her house. "Can't believe everyone dissed Thelma," I thought. "What a bunch of twat-faces!" I didn't really want to go inside without buffers present but figured I may as well stop in to say goodbye. To avoid getting stuck there, I premeditated an excuse that I couldn't stay long because I had plans to take my niece and nephew to Chuck E. Cheese's. (Remind me to actually do that someday.)

I entered Thelma's living room, took off my shoes, and sat on her sofa, the material of which felt like coarse grit sandpaper. A few moving boxes were stacked against the wall. There was a formaldehyde-scented candle burning on her coffee table. Besides Thelma and her son, I seemed to be the only one there.

Her son, baby Richard, introduced himself and told me about his oasis town in Arizona with all the arrogance of an overcompensated Ford retiree who drives a brand new Navigator with, and I quote, "every option and upgrade available." "It's got backup cameras," he said. I can see how that'd be useful when your neck stops working, but I didn't think people his age cared about backing into things.

As expected, the conversation was dull. Richard said he lives in a senior community with perfect weather where nobody works and everyone golfs. I'm sure it's awesome if you don't mind living on the set of a George A. Romero movie. While sitting beside him, Thelma asked me three times if I'd met her son Richard. I guess her mind is starting to slip too. One can only take so much yelling. He said she can remember 1918 but not what happened five minutes ago. "So, Thelma," I shouted, "Spanish Flu really sucked, didn't it?"

I asked her if she had any old baseball cards or comic books lying around. Unfortunately, she said she didn't, but I had to try. It's my dream to find a grandma with a shoebox containing a Honus Wagner baseball card, the holy grail of card collecting, or a copy of *Action Comics* #1, which is the first appearance of Superman. Either would fetch a million bucks at a Sotheby's auction.

Back when I was attending the study group at Thelma's, I'd peer around her basement thinking, "There must be *something* down here worth some serious collector's cash! A plunger or turkey baster from 1904 has got to be worth money." But Thelma didn't have anything valuable, just a bunch of knit doilies and a mantle lined with river rocks, the only super old things that are totally worthless.

Most people go tits up in their eighties, so I wondered what the key to her longevity was. She drank beer and ate beef jerky. She enjoyed Charlie Chaplin and listened to Fats Waller. She baked a carrot cake good enough to cure (or cause) crack addiction. She wore a night gown all day and did her own yard work, if sweeping your lawn counts. She loved to chill in her rocking chair. Her lifestyle was ordinary. I couldn't pinpoint a key factor. I assumed she had a self-portrait in her attic that aged for her, or a laboratory beneath her toolshed where she constructed steam-powered organ replacements, making her name, Thelma Organ, more of a moniker.

I can't fathom being a centenarian. I'll be one hundred years old in 2077. Maybe, as a birthday present to myself, I'll fulfill my lifelong desire to be in a high-speed car chase with the cops. I'm not talking about a down-the-freeway, O.J. Simpson joyride with helicopters tracking me from the sky. No, I want an inner city chase through alleys and abandoned warehouses as if I just botched a bank robbery and everything's gone to shit. I'll be driving a 900-horsepower Buggati Veyron with Gatling guns mounted to the doors. It'll also have the oil slick and smoke screen mechanisms from *Spy Hunter*. It'll be like *Gone in 60 Seconds* meets *Mad Max* mixed with the Death Star trench scene, and maybe somehow I'll work in that scene from *Titanic* when Kate Winslet shows her boobs.

Who am I kidding? By 2077 they'll have the technology to drop a nuke in my lap from outer space. That sucks. They're always ruining my fun. Actually, there probably won't even be cars in 2077. By then we'll be piloting dinosaur-shaped Power Ranger hovercrafts. Either way, insane, topless dinocraft chase *will* happen.

I know everyone gets stopped by red lights, but I've had more than my fair share lately. They reprogrammed the lights on a stretch of road I take to work, and now I catch six reds in a row *every day*. It totally pisses me off. Five of six are *screechers*, you know, the kind that turn yellow when you're ten yards away, requiring you to either slam on the brakes or punch the gas knowing it'll turn red while you're under it. It drives me nuts. I want to run them, but it's a busy area near a police station.

By the time I exited my teens, I had so many points on my driving record from speeding tickets that it was equivalent to two-and-a-half vehicle manslaughters. My insurance gave me the boot, and I had to pay an ungodly fee for special coverage underwritten for a driver who steamrolled two adults and a midget at a crosswalk. Therefore, I stop at screechers.

Speeding tickets are unquestionably a painful waste of money. Paying a ticket is like having your driveway replaced or buying new tires – you fork out a wad of cash to keep things exactly the same as before. Last summer, when my homeowner's insurance forced me to replace my warped driveway, the lowest estimate I got was a whopping *six grand!* I told the guy, "For a few slabs of cement? Your crew better be Victoria's Secret models working in thongs!"

Tire shopping sucks just as much. Getting a new set of tires doesn't quite convey the same level of enthusiasm as, say, getting a new pair of sneakers when you were a kid. Back then, new rubber made you feel "super-fast." New tires cost hundreds of dollars, and if they make you feel "super-fast," you'll end up getting a ticket super-fast.

I enjoy driving. I like my gas-guzzler. I love jamming my favorite tunes with the windows down. But the traffic lights ruin it. That's why I want to blow through them. But if I blow them, I'll get pulled over. I can't afford any more points, so I'd have to run for it. Fleeing would initiate a car chase. A car chase would be *awesome*, but the *only* way I'd get away with it would be if I were a hundred years old.

They'll pardon any offense at that age. You could shoot the President and say, "Sorry, sonny. I was aiming at them pigeons," and they'll just ask you to be more careful. If they convict you, you'll die during the trial and waste everyone's time. If you survive long enough to start your life sentence, it'll be two months max. If they put you on death row, you'll get the last laugh by dying in the electric chair of natural causes. Generally though, one-hundred-year-old assassins are let go with a warning and a small fine. I'm basing that on the fact that I've seen a number of crazy old geezers get away with some crackpot antics because nobody felt right about chiming in to correct them. I'm assuming it applies to crime too.

There was an old guy at my church named Ben Whitman who got away with some really tweaked stuff simply because he was older than shit. Ben was a congregation elder in his late seventies when he asked a group of young girls if they knew how to suck cock. Here was a minister of God offering BJ lessons to teens, and everyone just shrugged it off. He once used a seatbelt as a prop to explain to a family how a penis enters a vagina. One time he played his harmonica into the microphone during the opening song. It sounded like ten thousand squirrels committing suicide. Try singing along with that. Everyone would smile and say, "Well, that's old Ben for ya!"

Ben was clearly going senile, but they still gave him church duties. He introduced a ministry demonstration by saying, "Pay attention to this demonstration by two sisters with nice *breasts.*" While announcing a new member of the congregation, he once said, "We'd like to welcome Sarah Freeman to our hall...that's *Freeman*, not *semen.*" Nobody stopped him, reprimanded him, or removed him from his responsibilities – they just giggled at his perviness and turned a blind eye.

Another old minister named Henry Kohler once paused on stage during a rambling sermon and blurted out, "*I love guns!*" He then made the gesture of two guns with his outstretched hands and slowly waved them around, aiming at people in the audience, freaking everyone out. He did it for almost a whole minute, which felt like an awkward eternity, before finally snapping out of it.

There's an interactive segment during midweek church services where members can voluntarily speak about the blessings they've received after finding God. There's an old Armenian vet who gives the same diatribe every time about how he gutted a Korean soldier with a bayonet, smoked a bunch of weed, and banged a bunch of diseased prostitutes. He says Jesus changed him, but when he's talking about the immoral stuff he did, it totally sounds like he's bragging. If I tried to pull off any of the stunts those old loons pull, I'd be ostracized. Being old is liberating, and that's why I'm planning my big car chase on my one-hundredth birthday!

Confused as to why nobody showed up for Thelma's party, I asked Richard, "Where is everybody?" and found out the hard way that, due to the weather, her going-away party had been rescheduled to take place in the church foyer after Sunday's meeting. Thanks for telling me, everyone. Seriously, you guys are the best. I hate you.

When I approached Thelma on Sunday, she didn't remember me. Just to be sure, I asked again if she had any old baseball cards or comic books, but she claimed ignorance. I wanted to interrogate her further but felt like a creep shaking down an old woman. I wondered if there was any value in having the going-away party to begin with, since she wouldn't remember it. It felt like we were putting on a big show to appease ourselves.

Somebody was retarded enough to tie a helium balloon around Thelma's neck. Seriously, *what's wrong with people?* I considered untying it but was afraid I'd tear her fragile throat skin and she'd bleed to death right there in the lobby. Gossipy churchgoers would have a field day with that. "Did you hear about Vincent murdering Thelma at her going away party?"

"Yeah, I heard she wouldn't hand over her baseball cards so he tore her throat out."

That's not a stretch for those gossip-crazed zealots.

I leaned over and gently hugged Thelma. "Have you met my son Richard?" she asked.

"Arizona Navigator guy?" I said.

"Come again, honey," she said, cupping her hand to her ear.

"YES!" I shouted, "I MET RICHARD!"

I got in line for a piece of cake when something peculiar happened. While Thelma was hugging some other people, she looked at me, made eye contact, and gave a knowing smile. It struck me as odd, especially since I didn't think she could see beyond a foot or two. I wondered if that wry grin was her way of letting me in on her secret. She wasn't losing her wits or moving away to wither and die – she was moving away to continue her ancient ritual of sucking the souls out of thirteen virgins, regaining youth, and living another century in a new town. She'd been doing it for millenniums.

Farfetched? Maybe. Maybe she's just plain-old old. Either way, I'm sure she's somewhere in Kansas right now, trekking along in the backseat of a cushy SUV, reading her copy of *Action Comics* #1 and using her Honus Wagner card as a bookmark.

Pirate Snatchy

Everyone wanted to make a good impression on the first day of junior high. A year earlier, we were in the safe confines of elementary school, where, for better or worse, we'd long known our social status. Someone had to fill the slot of funny kid, poor kid, hot girl, smart guy, fat chick, cooties kid, and trouble-maker. If you liked your old typecast, you'd have to re-earn it. If you didn't like it, you better steal some new clothes or lay off the Happy Meals. No matter what though, everyone got labeled. I'd like to think I was the artistic, smart kid, but I was just a foreign-looking geek.

The first opportunity to screw up in junior high was the initial homeroom roll call. When the teacher said my name, I answered in a non-cracking voice, "Here," and sighed relief. Fortunately, my name is easy to pronounce, and, unlike Steven Butkis, Nick Knipple, and Kristine Hairy, isn't associated with anything weird, although one kid called me Farmer Daniels. The teacher continued down the list. "Brian Davidson?" she said.

A naïve looking boy with dark-rimmed glasses and a mop cut answered, "Here, but you can call me *BJ.*" A third of the class giggled. Some kid shouted, "Hi BJ!" and the laughing escalated. In seventh grade, a handful of kids knew the colorful meaning of the term "BJ." I sort of knew what a BJ was. I knew it had something to do with a boner, so I cracked a little bonerific grin. BJ, on the other hand, had no idea what a BJ was, and I felt bad for him.

His middle name was probably James or Jonathan, and he'd been responding to BJ his entire life, just hopefully not from his priest, pee-wee coach, mustached uncle, or chubby, bald neighbor. I wondered what would go through his mind when he learned that a BJ had something to do with a boner. Shit, what went through BJ's mind when he finally realized he was calling himself a sucker of dicks? Life is cruel, man.

It could've been worse though, his name could've been Dylan Donaldson and he could've said, "Here, but you can call me Dildo." Or Ronald Imjoba. "Here, but you can call me Rimjob." Actually, Rimjob wouldn't have been giggled at until eleventh grade, at least that's when I learned the dirty meaning of the term thanks to Larry Ferguson. Larry didn't show me, he just explained what it was. Anyhow, the point is, for some reason Brian didn't want to go by his actual name and made it public ASAP that he liked the nickname BJ. In his particular case, it simply didn't work out.

Pop culture teaches us to embrace nicknames. A guy named Gordon Sumner tells people, "Here, but you can call me *Sting.*" A guy named Paul Hewson says, "Here, but you can call me *Bono.*" Trevor

Smith disregards his birth certificate and goes by Busta Rhymes, and you can't really blame him. What would you rather be called, Calvin Broadus or Snoop Dogg? Exactly. Even their nicknames have nicknames. Sean Combs' nickname is Puff Daddy. Puff Daddy's nickname is Diddy. Rogers Nelson, known around the world as Prince, chose a squiggly mark as his nickname's nickname.

Hollywood does it all the time. John Wayne's actual given name is Marion. Chevy Chase's is Cornelius. Chuck Norris is badass, Carlos Norris, not so much. Do you remember Demetria Guynes and Thomas Mapother's roles in *A Few Good Men*? You do. They go by Demi Moore and Tom Cruise.

The WWE is another proponent of name enhancement. Hulk Hogan is far more intimidating than Terry Bollea. Bob Remus chose Sgt. Slaughter. Can you *smell* what *the Rock* is *cooking?* No, but Dwayne Johnson is making a bologna sandwich.

It's nothing new. Nicknaming has gone on for centuries. After the Indian girl Matoaka saved Captain John Smith's life, she was nicknamed *Pocahontas*, which loosely translates to, "The slut who banged a white dude." In the Bible, the Apostle Paul said, "Here, but you can call me *Saul of Tarsus*." His name wasn't Saul and he wasn't from Tarsus, he was just telling people his rapper name. Abraham Lincoln's rapper name was Honest Abe. Edward Teach's was Blackbeard. The thing is, rappers and the like usually choose their nicknames, and we buy into them. In ordinary life, though, it's not that easy.

All of my pals have nicknames. Some are based on their actual name, some not. Hank's last name is Preiser so we call him Prize. Nash's last name is Fischer so we call him Fish. My friend Connor has a French last name that resembles the word "Suave," so that's what we call him. In the early nineties we called him *Rico Suave* thanks to an overplayed single by an Ecuadorian rapper named Gerardo, but it reverted back to just *Suave* in the new millennium. Based on Connor's notoriety for drinking himself into alternate personas, we sometimes call him Mr. Hyde. I've got a pal named Arroll who we call Eggroll. Based on his pale, gaunt look, we sometimes call him AIDS. Most of the time, the funnier the nickname, the more it sticks.

I'm currently working for a big company that supplies parts to major auto manufacturers. I'm in the Audio-Climate-Telematics Department where a bunch of cutting edge electronic shit is developed. I'm not sure if I'm the only one who's in way over their head and totally fakes it every day by spewing off oodles of bullshit in meetings, but it seems to be working. Anyhow, I work with a woman named Mary Travis. She's a Mechanical Engineer who sits on the second floor of my building. She was introduced to me by a Program Manager. "This is Mary Travis," he said. "She's the new engineer on the Honda climate control project."

When I shook her hand and said, "Nice to meet you, Mary," she interjected with, "You can call me *Emmy*."

"As in *Emmy* Award winning actor Kelsey Grammer?" I asked.

"Sure," she said.

The first thing I wondered was if Mary had gone by Emmy since childhood or if it was something new she was endorsing. Then it hit me, Mary was pulling off the perfect scam! Life doesn't afford many opportunities to nickname yourself and force others to use it. Friends, family, and peers usually supply nicknames, some flattering, others demoralizing, and you have little say. Emmy, however, figured it out and beat the system. Her nickname growing up was probably "Peanut Crotch" or "Chubbers," but she realized that in a professional setting, if she asked her workmates to call her something else from day one, they'd have no choice but to do it. It feels cheap calling her Emmy, but everyone's done it for years now. If she'd have said, "You can call me *Pirate Snatchy*," I'd have no choice but to introduce her in meetings as such.

Everyone should be informed of this naming loophole when starting a job. It should be in the company handbook and the first they cover during orientation. If I could revisit my first day, everyone in the department would be calling me "Pimp Master Fresh" or "Samurai 3000." I'd love to hear my supervisor start my performance review with, "You've been a real asset to the team, *Samurai 3000*." Then I'd make robotic sounds while doing kung fu poses. Instead of the department directory listing Kevin Robertson, April Bowden, and Richard Glickson – it'd be Special K, Strawberry Shortcake, and Assman. I suppose there are reasons why we're not in charge of nicknaming ourselves.

My company's overseas partners discovered the naming loophole. I've been working with the China Tech Center on a project that re- quires me to stay at work until 7PM on Thursdays so the Shanghai office can conference call with us at 7AM their time. The problem with these meetings is that Xianghou Wulaoqishang is too hard for Pete Sims to pronounce. Since subtitles aren't available, the Chinese were tasked with providing their own Americanized name to ease confusion. The result was a Chinese syndicate of engineers named Elton, Ocean, Indiana, Dash, Storm, and Lebron. I wish we had to give ourselves

Chinese aliases. I'd be Ryu from Street Fighter. Too bad "Vince" is easy to say.

In my late teens, I dated a girl from Toledo named Misty. She was a hot blonde with big blue Sailor Moon eyes. The only time I ever heard my father use the term "foxy" was in reference to her. When we first met, she said, "I'm Misty, but everyone calls me *Butterfly.*"

We dated for six months, and not once did any of her workmates, friends, or family ever refer to her as Butterfly. She obviously made it up hoping I'd use it. Nice try, but I'm no sucker. Even if you had wings and tasted food with your feet, I'm not going to be the only one calling you Butterfly. It was evident that she liked butterflies – as they were featured on her wallpaper, bedding, jewelry, and panties – but, come on, I like dinosaurs but don't ask to be called Triceratops. Plus, Butterfly has too many syllables for a nickname. I should've called her "Butt" for short. If she was really attached to the idea, I would've compromised and called her "Moth" – similar genus, quicker delivery.

Real names are tricky enough as it is. At work and church, I call people by the wrong name all the time. I'll be like, "How's it going, Sharon?"

"It's Colleen."

"That's weird, I thought you were Sharon."

"Nope, Colleen."

The more people you meet, the more names you forget. When I'm at a grocery store and run into someone I graduated with, our exchange sounds like this, "Hey...*dude!* How've you been...*man?* Good to see you...*bud!*"

What's funnier is when you've known someone for a long time and *only* know their nickname. For years I played hockey with a guy that everyone called *Fingers*. It wasn't until his wedding ceremony that I found out his real name was Frank. Similarly, for over a year I partied with a club-hopping guy in our crew who we called Dave Diggler, but I didn't know his real last name until I got an invitation to his engagement party. When I read that it was Leggo, as in "Leggo My Eggo," and pronounced like the plastic toy blocks, I was rolling on the floor laughing. I've only recently learned that some of the girls I've seen at parties for years have last names that sound like intestinal disorders (Gasteritis) and sausage manufacturers (Frankenhoffer).

No matter who's in your circle of friends, nickname usage is undeniably popular. In my expanded world, here are some of the names my friends and acquaintances are known by: Ghostface, Buddha, Worm, Waffle House, Goat, Bits, Deeds, Shooms, Jarhead, Jerky, Pest, Rinky Dink, Jibs, Beezer, Papp Smear, Rufio, Rosshole, Ugnaught, Chatchie, Poo Bob, Ghetto Booty, Pa Deeter, Hamel Toe, Melonbees, Senor Strugs, Fruity Top, Big Bird, Burger, McNuts, the Führer, and Bitch …all real people. They don't all make perfect sense, and a few aren't necessarily said to the face of who they represent. As a side note, Bitch isn't a girl.

Calling a friend by a nickname is a bonding element. If you have a friend you still refer to as Nathan, Edward, Jennifer, or Rachel, do them a favor and give them a nickname. Here are some pointers to get you started. Think of something they're insecure about and formulate a moniker around that. Maybe "Shnoz" for a girl with a big nose, "Slash" for someone who's taking guitar lessons, or "Professor X" for a balding buddy. Otherwise, go with one of their immoral vices. Call your alcoholic pal *Dewey*, the literal pronunciation of DUI. Call your smoker pal *Little Nicky*, because he likes a little nicotine. Call someone with a temper problem *Ruprecht* – a reference to the movie *Dirty Rotten Scoundrels*.

Be careful though, Bitch is taken, and we can't have two Bitches running around, it'll be confusing. Also, never use nicknames that sound inherently cool, like Cobra or Steel, because they come across as douchey. And, to keep it in good taste, show a measure of compassion. You wouldn't want to call a guy whose mom has cancer "Tumor Boy." Same goes for "Widowmaker" if there was an unfortunate car accident. Don't try naming yourself either, it'll sound lame. Nobody cool has ever said, "I'm Brian, but you can call me BJ."

Jim Bacon the Jamaican

FYI, an oncologist studies tumors, not birds. An ornithologist studies shitfaced birds. I hate being flagrantly wrong, but it's bound to happen from time to time.

I was having lunch at Lafayette Coney Island with three female friends – a hairdresser, a receptionist, and an orthodontic assistant. The girls are sweet but ditzy. The topic of conversation inexplicably turned to areas of scientific study, and I began quizzing them for self-amusement. Little did I know that I was about to be humbled.

"Do you know what a geologist studies?" I asked.

"Maps?" the receptionist said.

"Not quite, Magellan. A geographer studies maps, although *cartographer* would suffice. A geologist, on the other hand, studies the earth's crust."

"The earth's crust?" she said, puzzled.

"Yeah," I said, "the earth has a crust, and since nobody eats the crust, they give it to geologists. How about a zoologist, what do they study?"

"Zoo animals," the orthodontic assistant answered.

"Close enough," I said. "How about a seismologist?"

"Size?" the hairdresser said.

"*Size?*" I said. "No. A seismologist studies the movement of the earth plates."

"The earth's plates?" she repeated, baffled.

"See," I said, "the earth sits on plates, and at dinner time they move around."

It didn't matter what I said, the information was being instantly rejected by their brain's defenses since it wasn't related to anything covered in *People, Cosmo,* or *Us Weekly.*

"Do you know what an astrologist studies?" I asked.

"Planets?" the receptionist said.

"Close, Galileo. An *astronomer* studies planets. An astrologist studies constellations."

"Constellations?" she said. "What's that?"

"Constellation, you know, when you can't poop."

"Oh!" she said.

"Do you know what an assologist studies?" I said.

"No, what?" she asked.

"You," I said, but she didn't get it.

The quizzing then flipped to *Jeopardy* style. "Do you know what the study of birds is called?" I said.

"I don't know," they answered unanimously.

"Oncology," I said.

"No, it's not," the receptionist said.

"Yes, it is," I said.

"No," she said, "oncology has something to do with cancer."

"Yeah," I said, "if you consider barn swallows a cancer."

"I'm pretty sure though," she said.

I fluffed it off, and then the quizzing degraded to questions like, "Do you know what a bonerologist studies?" "What is the study of taints called?" etc.

As soon as I got home, I busted out the Webster's dictionary that I won in my fifth-grade spelling bee, and there it was:

on-col-o-gy: *noun* \ has something to do with cancer – the end.

I got owned. Oh well, it's not the first time I've been dead wrong.

An abandoned gas station near my parents' place was recently renovated. I was happy about it because it was an eyesore in their neighborhood, and the renovation added a full-fledged snack wing to the previously cramped building. Having a new destination for pump cheese, microwave burritos, and flaming hot chips excites me. I crave that shit. Gas station food deserves a spot on the USDA food pyramid right between fruits and veggies.

Anyhow, before the grand opening, the owners lined the windows with neon signs advertising their wares: HOT DOGS, CHIPS, FOUNTAIN POP, NACHOS, CANDY, PIZZA, SUSHI. "Wait...*sushi!?*" I thought. "What the *butt?*" I re-read the sign. "*Sushi? That's so weird.*"

The next time I was over my parents' house, I said, "They did a nice job on that gas station, but what a strange place to serve sushi!"

"Sushi?" my dad said. "What do you mean by that?"

"Yeah," I said, "one of the neon signs they put up says they serve sushi. Hot dogs, I understand, but sushi, that's odd. Not sure if I'd trust gas station sushi. A Subway would've been more fitting."

"Sure you don't mean *Slushi?*" he said.

"Oh wanker," I thought.

Staring at a computer all day is ruining my eyes.

Last winter I spotted a billboard in Detroit that read, "Radiation for Winter Survival." It was beside a picture of a young, wide-eyed black boy with the plea, "Help keep a child warm – Radiation." I was slightly troubled. Exposing children to radiation was a warming innovation I hadn't heard of. I sped by the billboard every day and couldn't help but envision a guy in a Hazmat suit waving a glowing uranium rod around kids in the projects while their hair fell out. I thought, "Well, at least they're warm I guess. That can't be safe though. Whatever happened to donating coats and mittens?"

Fortunately, I kept my confusion to myself until a traffic jam allowed my brain enough time to distinguish that the "Radiation" was, in fact, a "Radiothon."

In my early teens I delivered newspapers on my skateboard while listening to Bad Religion on my Walkman with the volume on full blast. Thanks to that, my hearing isn't much better than my eyesight. When the Usher song *You Don't Have to Call* was getting radio play, I thought the line, "Listening to friends, now it's the end," was, "Listen *ninja* friends, now it's the end." It never crossed my mind as absurd. I assumed Usher's posse was called "The Ninja Clan" or something. I innocently sang about Usher's ninja friends until the time I sang it in front of a date and she interrupted with, "What did you just say?" I instantly knew I was a world-class dum-dum. Whatever. She thought Kanye West's *Jesus Walks* was *Jesus Rocks*, and when we ended the night at Taco Bell, she ordered a "Maximelt." It's MEXI-melt you, you...super cute girl.

I actually met Usher once at Disneyworld on a spring break trip. I was at Pleasure Island one afternoon while he was rehearsing on an empty stage. The girls I was with started screaming, "Oh my *god!* It's *Usher!* Usher can we take a picture with you!"

It was early in his career, so I was like, "Who the hell is *Usher?*" When they handed me a camera, I sarcastically said, "Everyone say, 'Usher me to my seat'," before snapping a photo. I didn't have a clue. In retrospect, I wish I would've said, "Yo Usher, check out these dance moves," and hoola-hooped a necklace around my neck while doing a sideways moonwalk. We'd probably be best friends now.

On another side note, a notable occurrence of vomiting happened after that. My group of friends was strolling around Pleasure Island because we were too hung over to handle anything else that day, but we made the mistake of taking a bumpy speedboat ride to get there. That, coupled with the unbearable humidity, made everyone nauseous. After the Usher sighting, we were waiting in a bus stop for a shuttle when one of my buddies leaned over and puked. When the splatter hit the girls' feet, they gagged and started yacking too.

One of them ran behind the bus stop while another took off down a grassy incline toward a pond. She had her hand over her mouth, trying to hold it in, but started projectile vomiting. And that shit sprayed *everywhere*. A flock of ducks mistook it as a feeding frenzy and rushed her. She was keeled over, trying to escape two dozen mallards and gulls while raining vomit on them as they devoured her chunks out of the air. It was so disgusting and hilarious at the same time that the rest of us started laughing, gagging, and blowing chunks too. By the time the shuttle arrived, the bus stop was dripping with vomit. As our pale-faced group sluggishly boarded, the driver looked out and said, "Oh my gosh! What in the world happened here?"

I said, "Uh, it was like that when we got here." However, I digress, as that has little to do with misunderstandings.

There's a guy in my circle of friends named Jim Bacon. I know he sounds like a burly pig mascot for a Jazz and Rib Festival, but he's just a regular guy with a delicious name. Several years ago, I was at someone's apartment watching the *MTV Video Music Awards*. Everyone but Jim was there. During the show, when Fat Joe performed his song *Lean Back*, I said, "Wow, Fat Joe looks like an obese, bald Jim Bacon."

A girl named Trish chuckled and said, "He totally does! That's hilarious!"

Everyone in the room knew Jim, but nobody else reacted. I said to Trish, "Thanks for the support."

A few minutes later, they showed Fat Joe backstage, and Trish restated, "He really *does* look like Jim Bacon!"

"An *obese, bald* Jim Bacon," I repeated.

The rest of group laughed and acknowledged the resemblance, and I thought, "Why laugh this time?"

"Is that what you said?" someone asked. "I thought you said he looks like an obese, bald *Jamaican.*" They all did. Obese, bald Jim Bacon. Obese, bald Jamaican. One is chuckle worthy while the other is an inane comment destined to fizzle into obscurity. When communication breaks down, crucial information is lost.

At times though, a mishearing can work in your favor, like the time I went to Bed Bath & Beyond to buy a wedding gift. I approached the customer service desk and the girl there said, "Can I help you?"

"Yeah," I said, "I'm wondering how to buy a gift for someone with a registry?"

The girl started laughing hysterically. "*Ha ha ha!* 'For whoever started a registry!'" she said, misquoting me. "That is *so* funny!"

She thought I said, "I'm wondering how to buy a gift for whoever started a registry," and, oddly enough, it struck her funny bone. No, I don't really get it either, but I took credit for it and played along as if I say funny shit like that all the time. For the rest of our conversation, she laughed at everything I said. "I wonder who'll get this Keurig in the divorce."

"I know, right!" she said while slapping the counter and cracking up. It was *fantastic*.

After that I went next door to a store called *The Half-Off Card Shop* to carry on my tradition of buying an entirely unfitting card for the occasion. I usually buy a card that reads, "Hooray, You're 4!" or, "Sorry You Have AIDS." This time I found a perfect card on the clearance rack. It read, "To a Strong, Beautiful, Black Woman." It had pastel-colored African-style artwork of a black woman who looked like Morgan Freeman being cradled by the big, black inmate from *The Green Mile*. I was giving it to a skinny, white couple. It was marked down to thirty-three cents.

I had a hard time suppressing my laughter when I presented it to the checkout girl, but she didn't crack a smile. When she said, "With tax your total is thirty-five cents," I thought we'd both lose it, but I got nothing. Hey, at the last store they thought I was super funny, what gives?

What's worse than being misheard is being heard correctly after saying something moronic. I was in a car full of churchgoers on our way back from Sunday brunch. The guy driving was a thirty-seven-year-old know-it-all named Mark. Mark's the type of guy who's quick to correct your grammar, hates domestic beer because he brews mead, and enjoys defending the accuracy of the science portrayed on *Star Trek: The Next Generation*. His favorite topic in the whole wide world is debunking the Apollo 11 moon landing. I get that it's mildly interesting, but really, who gives a shit?

The Knights of Columbus guys were collecting donations at road intersections that afternoon. Their yellow vests read, "Help Retarded Children." Each donation was rewarded with a Tootsie Roll. That's all fine and dandy, except that they're at *every* intersection in town. So if you donate to one, you still feel bad at the next light because those K of C guys think you're a retard-hating cheapskate for not pitching into their pail, or at least that's the paranoia I feel. I'll hold up my Tootsie Roll wrapper when they walk by, as if to say, "See, both of us are saving retarded children!" But I still feel like a jerk for some reason.

To break the monotony, I started ranting in Mark's car about how annoying and intrusive those pain-in-the-ass beggars are, and how I wish they'd all fall face-first into a pit full of spikes and get covered with pythons, scorpions, and lava. Generally, I was kidding, but when I finished, Mark said, "Actually, my father is a proud Knights of Columbus member who does this."

"Aw crap," I thought.

He spent the rest of the drive pontificating on the selfless good they do for the community, and how "ignorant people," AKA *moi*, consider them nothing more than a nuisance. I thought, "Well, yeah." All I could do though was make a long "*Ehhhh*" sound and call it quits on speaking for the rest of the day. Putting your foot in your mouth sucks.

One time I was driving with an Australian couple from church, sitting in the backseat of their Chevy Malibu, on our way to visit a senior citizen in the hospital. The couple was exploring different methods of discipline for their rambunctious five-year-old. They knew the Biblical advice, "Do not spare the rod," but were reading about alternatives such as privilege removal, point systems, and time-outs. "Screw that," I said, "I got my butt spanked as a kid and it did me good. My opinions lean toward the corporal aspect." I told them, "I say beat 'em, Beat 'Em, BEAT 'EM!"

Suddenly, the woman's eyes rolled back into her head and she started foaming at the mouth. She was kicking the glove box so hard that her seat back broke and slammed against my knees. Her husband and I were freaking out as she thrashed around in the front seat. He sped to the hospital and we helped her inside. In the waiting room, he shared the fashionably late news that his wife had an abusive father, and recollections of his beatings can trigger epileptic seizures. My bad. But from now on, if you know it's a sensitive topic, try steering the conversation away from discipline and toward something easy like, "What's your favorite candy bar?"

Here's an important foot-in-mouth rule: *Never* ask a woman if she's pregnant. Even if she's got a big belly and you see her shopping for a stroller and baby food, don't assume there's a bun in the oven.

She might've gained forty pounds, is suffering from a toothache, and needs a way to transport her cat. The reason to keep your trap shut is obvious – telling a non-pregnant woman she looks preggers is the same as saying, "Wow, you got fat!" While this faux pas is usually a hopeless foot-in-mouth scenario, I cleverly dodged it once.

The human resources lady at a past employer had plumped over the winter, most noticeably in her gut region. I was so confident that she was with child that I mentioned it while signing insurance paperwork in her office. "So when's your baby due?" I asked.

She gave me a strange look and said, "What? I'm not pregnant."

My heart did a cannonball into the pool of uh-oh.

"Oh," I said, "*uh*...I thought someone said you were. They must've been talking about someone else." Phew. A solid deke. Or maybe not. Yeah, she probably hates me.

Still, my long list of flubs is ever increasing. One time I called a friend of a friend a pussy for ordering an O'Doul's, not realizing he was a recovering alcoholic. On a different occasion, I learned that you shouldn't publicize your contempt for capri pants when you can't see what the women in your group are wearing underneath the table. Another time, while at a house party chatting with a friend in a spare bedroom, I called the host's wife "a fucking bitch" unaware that she was standing in the doorway. The air turned to ice. "I meant that in a totally *good* way," I said, "like when Sam Jackson calls himself a *bad ass motherfucker*. You know what I'm saying?"

I have a friend who moved to Dallas years ago. After getting engaged there, he brought his fiancée to Michigan to meet his family and friends for the first time. We made plans to see *The Lord of the Rings: The Two Towers* and have dinner at an Italian restaurant afterward. At dinner we started discussing the odd customs of other cultures. His fiancée said she thought it was repulsive that Burmese women elongate their necks and expand their earlobes to attract males. I countered with the absurdity that American women have giant silicone globs surgically implanted in their chest to garner male attention. My buddy shot me a look of alarm. Then I panned down to his fiancée's fake double-Ds. We awkwardly slurped fettuccine in silence until I said, "So…that Gimli fella was pretty cool, eh?"

Then there's this one from way back in the day: My older brother and I used to listen to the old-school rap group *3rd Bass*. During the intro to the song *Kick 'Em in the Grill*, MC Search says to Chubb Rock, "What up, Chubbs?" Chubb replies, "What's up, G?" We adopted it as our greeting. I always said, "What up, Chubbs?" He always said, "What's up, G?"

We did it all the time until the day I was at a local street fair and ran into an old girlfriend who I hadn't seen in years. She bounced up, smiling, and said, "Long time no see! What's up?"

My instant reply was, "What up, Chubbs?"

I instantly cringed. Her demeanor hit the pavement, and she flatly stated, "I know, I've gained weight."

What made it ten times worse was that she *had* gained weight, substantial weight, like she'd been living under a Ponderosa buffet. My explanation failed to heal the wound. It was proof that I'm retarded. Please donate to help me. I'll give you a Tootsie Roll.

Lime-Green Dickeys

On my drive to work, I get stopped by three traffic lights while doing a loop-dee-loo to get from Dix Avenue onto the Southfield Freeway. All three lights put me in view of a place called *Retirement House of America*. It's a dreary, prison-like, bare-bones nursing home suspiciously attached to a pharmacy, carpet cleaning business, and secondhand clothing store. That's one shady operation right there.

You know those adorable little grandmas with silvery-blue up-dos wrapped in plastic head dressings that you see having breakfast at Bob Evans? Well, none of them live in this place. This old folks' home isn't the sort that houses senior citizens with loving sons, daughters, and grandchildren. It isn't the sort that houses elderly folks with a decent nest egg or pension. Retirement House of America is chock full of grandmas who don't bake or crochet. This place houses limbless vets who spent their youth shooting at Krauts and Japs, came home with a permanent snarl on their face, and felt as if society turned its back on them. They can barely move. They can barely breathe. They're barely hanging on.

It'd be pointless for them to advertise with a color brochure, because the entire place is gray. This is a facility with a rec room that has a ping pong table with no net, puzzles with missing pieces, and cribbage boards that look like ash trays. It's a place where a retiree finishes a lonely existence and dies in their room while watching an episode of *The Price is Right* they've seen seventeen times.

The city installed handicap-crossing signs at the busy intersection. Waiting at those lights, watching the seniors hobble across the street or hunch by the curb, is a lesson in humility. They're taking a break from their nicotine stained wallpaper to get some exercise in their motorized wheelchairs, or a breath of fresh air strewn with copious amounts of exhaust. There are frail old men with white comb-overs walking wheeled oxygen tanks. There are old ladies whose heads slump perpendicular to their spines as if they forgot to take off their Hunchback of Notre Dame costumes. There are fogeys in wheelchairs moving at a snail's pace, rearing back and forth to get over the weeds in the cracks of the sidewalk ramp. There are women in bulky diapers crossing the street with walkers, holding up rush hour traffic at the "No Turn On Red" sign. It's a sobering sight. Retirement House of *America?* More like Retirement House of *Zombies.*

I sit there idling in my fancy-schmancy SUV, bumping bass-filled MP3s with the AC kicking full blast, feeling an abundance of vitality, wondering how the transition occurs. These people once contributed to society the same way I do. Not that I *really* think I contribute that much, but I do pay a shit load of taxes, including social security and

Medicare, which in essence means I hooked some of these guys up with their heart meds. Either way, at their advanced age, they appear to be nothing more than traffic obstacles. Their existence is meaningless to passersby.

Most of these handi-*crappers*, as my girlfriend calls them (isn't she sweet?) are attempting a trip to one of two mainstays on the opposite side of the road, Rite Aid or Dunkin Donuts. If they're feeling especially vigorous and trek an extra half-block, they'll be rewarded with a Chicken Shack or Radio Shack. The neighborhood is a little dicey, which makes Rite Aid the safest bet, since they have a 400-pound security guard on duty. I can't help but laugh every time I see that uniformed elephant by the door. Shoplift at will; he's not going to chase you. If he does, don't worry, you can count on him having a coronary in your escape plan. Plus, his fingers are bigger than Ball Park Franks, if he tries to dial 911, he'll end up calling a 1-800 number instead.

I've been getting stuck at those lights every day for a while now, long enough to recognize a lot of the old loiterers. I've nicknamed my favorites. There's Old Man Jenkins, Mummy Time, Dolores Diapers, Gandalf, Wobbles McGilicutty, DJ Moses, and Uncle Owen. There's a woman I call McNugs because she constantly charades as if she's gobbling invisible chicken nuggets. She's hovers her hands in front of her chest, kind of like a T-Rex, one holding the invisible box, and the other in a pinch shape which she repeatedly touches to her bottom lip. She doesn't seem to prefer dipping sauce. She's missing out. Invisible honey mustard is *so* good.

I recently observed Gandalf chatting with McNugs. They were sitting on the landscaping blocks in front of Dunkin Donuts. I saw him smile and pat her arm, and it dawned on me – the old farts were flirting! An eighty-year-old man who looks like Colonel Sanders' granddad, the founder of Kentucky Fried Mastodon, was putting the moves on a woman who could easily be his daughter. Don't get me wrong, she was pretty old too, but I'd guess that she was only in her sixties. What a cradle robber, or in this case, grave robber. Can a thirty-year-old date a ten-year-old? Why not? It won't matter when they're eighty and sixty.

If you fill an apartment complex with a bunch of young to middle-aged people, there will undoubtedly be lots of sex happening before long. Hell, put eight strangers in an apartment on national television and they're screwing in the shower in less than a week. What about a re-tirement home full of geriatric singles? Were these wrinkled denizens going to head back to his room for some hot sex with the aid of Viagra and a gallon of lube? Okay, that's gross. But is it really? Don't you want them to bump uglies? Imagine their wrinkled, furry, fossilized genitalia penetrating each other. Okay, I'm sorry, that *is* gross. But what other forms of excitement do they have? Pork chop night? Pressing a pair of lime-green dickeys? I say we root for them to *GET IT ON!*

McNugs stood up, turned around, and brushed some debris off the seat of her pants. I couldn't hear their conversation but dubbed Gandalf's mouth movements with, "What up, sexy? Turn around and smack that ass. Damn, bitch, *you fine!*" It seemed fitting. I found it fascinating that her pants were a color I'd never seen before, like poop-brown mixed with rust-red mixed with iridescence. You can't find that color fabric anymore because the dye was made from lichens that went extinct due to Glyptodont overfeeding.

I, for one, hope they hook up. Maybe they'll fall in love, get married, and have a family. Their first kid will be fifty when exiting the womb. Instead of the usual, "It's a boy!" the doctor will say, "It's a *grown-ass man?* And he has a beer gut and is wearing sweatpants." Since McNugs hit menopause at least twenty years ago, maybe they'll get lucky and find a red-headed, orphaned senior to adopt.

Chances are, in their younger years, the residents of the Retirement House of America were just like me and my friends. That liver-spotted guy had a knack for barroom games. That gangly fellow wore trendy clothes. That pruney woman was a tramp who pissed herself when laughing. That elderly chap was unbeatable at *Halo*, except his version of *Halo* involved running around Germany looking for a real rocket launcher to blow people up. They had house parties, played drinking games, ate sliders, and loyally followed their favorite TV shows (or radio shows). They tried to make their friends laugh by doing impressions of Abbott and Costello and Harry S. Truman.

Driving past the place provides me with a daily glimpse of an outcome that I hope to avoid. It makes me reflect. I wonder why these people ended up in such a dismal place. Did they have a falling out with their kids? Did they gamble their savings away? Did they struggle with alcoholism? Did they bomb in the stock market? Did they fail to rebound after a divorce? Did they push away those who cared about them by being too picky, grouchy, or pessimistic? Will I be alone in a shitty retirement home in fifty years?

Such pondering is beneficial because it motivates me to call my mom to remind her that I love her and her meatloaf. It compels me to buy my friends a round of drinks the next time we're out. I tell myself that it's okay to play a great song a few times before moving on to the next track. It helps me make light of stressful situations, like when my boss says my project is due on Friday and I know it won't be done for months, or maybe never. It's a reminder to not only watch out for pitfalls, but to stop and enjoy the simple things, like a cold beer, a vibrant sunset, or a well-played peek down a girl's shirt. I think about how important it is to just pause, take a deep breath, and enjoy the hilarity of an old fogey in a motorized wheelchair that can't get up a sidewalk ramp because it's stuck on dandelions while a forty car backup of impatient drivers are waiting to turn at the intersection. Love life, kids, because guess who else is going to be super old someday – yep, *you.*

The Queen of Assumptions

There used to be a kid at my church named Andy who everyone called "AC" in reference to Andy Capp's fry snacks. He was a grade behind me in school, but we attended Driver's Ed together. We weren't super close, but we got along, and I considered him a nice kid.

AC had a younger brother and two older, ruffian brothers named Gavin and Zack. Gavin once chopped Zack's nose in half with a snow shovel while playing a game they called *Battle Axe*. Gavin was a senior in high school when I was a freshman. I'll never forget watching him pummel a kid wearing braces and then throw the dude's bloody face through a glass door outside of Mrs. Butz's math class. Noteworthy side point – During my era, the school's math faculty consisted of the following teachers: Mrs. Finn, Grabs, Butz, and Cox. *You're so naughty, Mrs. Finn!* Anyways, when guys from church got together to play wallyball, it inevitably ended in a Gavin versus Zack cage fight.

AC's brothers were also responsible for my first waistband tearing wedgie.

AC didn't follow suit and was a renowned mama's boy. Comparing him to his brothers was a common topic of idle chat amongst churchgoers. Gavin and Zack were outgoing, whereas AC was attached to his mother's hip. The other boys were into firecrackers and moto-cross, whereas AC liked watercolors and baking. His brothers listened to Guns N' Roses. AC preferred Air Supply. Their father built an awesome tree fort in their backyard but AC wouldn't go in it because he was afraid of heights.

Our church had a thing on Tuesdays called the *Ministry School* that put all young men on a scheduled rotation to read short Bible passages from the stage. Whenever AC got up there, he'd read a few sentences, start quivering, and burst into tears. His father would coddle him offstage and someone would have to finish for him. So, all things considered, AC was sort of a girly kid. Then, after he graduated from high school, him and his family moved a few hours north.

Ten years later, AC and his family visited our church again. It was a reunion for them. Gavin, drastically matured since the old days, was the guest speaker giving a sermon about resisting the devil's temptations. His parents reportedly hadn't been to church in a while but attended to see their sons. Zack put on fifty pounds of muscle. His neck looked wider than his head, which was shaved and tattooed. He was fresh out of prison, doing time for being hopped up on crystal meth and beating a cop into critical condition. AC's younger brother, a recovering heroin addict, attended with his pregnant sixteen-year-old girlfriend. AC sat in the front row with his wife and two children. His baby fat was gone. He looked gaunt in his suit. His hair was thinning, he had dark circles under his eyes, but he seemed content and refined.

I approached him after the meeting and noticed that his demeanor was completely different. When I called him AC, he replied like Obi Wan Kenobi, *"AC? That's a name I've not heard in a long time...a long time."* He goes by Andrew now, serves as a minister in a Traverse City congregation, and runs his own construction company. We reminisced about driver's training for a few minutes – how our instructor made us drive between his Subway franchises and taught us that fast food profits come primarily from fountain drinks. Then, with a handshake, we exchanged well wishes and parted ways.

After the meeting, I went to lunch with other churchgoers, and the main topic of conversation was the dirt on AC's family. I sat and listened, observing how gossipers deduce the current state of some-one's existence while presuming the path that led there. They turn thinking, feeling people who're trying to overcome difficulties, into brash, one-sentence judgments. "Zack turned into a real monster!" they said. "Their parents hate the religion now," they said. "I heard Gavin foreclosed on his house," they said.

What I found particularly disturbing was that everyone accepted the family's downward spiral, but no one would acknowledge that AC left as a prissy mama's boy and returned as a responsible, mature man. Why was his success hard for them to accept? Perhaps they sub-consciously wish failure on others because their lives are cemented in the doldrums of complacency.

A woman at the table said, "I'm surprised AC got through the meeting without crying!" I shook my head in disgust. What a cunt bag. Her list of failures is a mile long, but she has no trouble proclaiming the failures of others. Human nature is envious of progression. Plus, people are assholes. AC may have been a wuss a decade ago, but now he's fine – let it go.

Years ago, when I was a teenager, I was at a place called *Louie's Diner* with friends. The daily special was beef pot roast. It sounded good so I ordered it. "You want anything to drink with that?" the waitress asked.

I didn't feel like drinking only water, but I wasn't in the mood for soda, tea, or chocolate milk either, so I spun the dial of randomness and asked for a glass of orange juice. A girl sitting across from me said, "Orange juice? With *dinner?* That's *so* weird!" I figured an explanation was pointless, so I shrugged and ignored her.

Years later, when I was in my twenties, I was at Hella's Cafe in Greektown with a group of friends. We were all perusing the wine list, making suggestions that exposed our wine-choosing incompetence. When I suggested a Greek Nemea to go with grape leaves, a girl sitting across from me said, "You *always* order the *weirdest* drinks with your dinner!"

It was more than a cutesy comment. It came across as a snide judgment evoking that my taste is, and always has been, substantially skewed. "What makes you say that?" I asked.

"Well," she said, "like you *always* order *orange juice* with your dinner and stuff like that."

I always order orange juice with dinner? My mind indexed, and I realized what she was referring to – the one and only time I ever did that was years ago at Louie's Diner, and she was present. Again, an explanation was pointless, so I said, "Well, ordering weird drinks helps suppress my craving for human blood." Nevertheless, I was irritated that someone could be presumptuous enough to sum me up based on a solitary instance. As it turned out, the offender was the same woman bashing AC at lunch.

I've since crowned her "The Queen of Assumptions." Her presumptuous nature is only the tip of the iceberg. Extreme gossiping is her hobby. She works at *Macy's*, and just for the hell of it, she told everyone at the table about a woman from church whose application for credit was denied. Why tell us? Nobody asked. Nobody cares. She did it simply because it's frivolous gossip to spread. After spilling the beans on her credit score, she made assumptions regarding her lifestyle. "I don't see how she can afford to drive that Lexus," she said, "and didn't she just come back from a cruise?"

If anyone at the table relayed information, personal or otherwise, the Queen's expression would deform into an absurd O-face of delight. It didn't matter if she knew the people or not. Her eyes bugged out. Her mouth went agape to one side. It was all juicy to her. She'd light up the same way whether she heard you ate McDonalds's while dieting or 69'ed your sister.

Next, she flexed her exaggeration skills. After hearing that an engaged guy at church thinks Adriana Lima is attractive, she spun it into, "So he thinks he could do better than his fiancée? He probably complains all the time that she doesn't look like a Victoria's Secret model! I don't know how she puts up with him! I bet she wants to kill him!"

"Damn, that escalated quickly!" I thought.

Then she said, "Oh, and get this, I saw Dave Lindberg at Meijer last week and he wasn't wearing his wedding ring. Isn't that weird?"

"Was he by himself?" someone asked.

"No," she said, "his wife was there, but I noticed she didn't have her ring on either! I wonder if they're having problems."

I had to chime in. "Wait, what? No. That's ridiculous. Seeing a guy grocery shopping with his wife is way more proof that they're fine than whether or not they're wearing rings. Buying broccoli and toilet paper isn't exactly something separated couples do together. It's perfectly normal for married people to run errands without their rings on."

"Yeah, but they had hardly anything in their cart," she said.

"Maybe they just started," I said.

"They were in, like, aisle *ten*," she replied, as if it was DNA evidence at the crime scene.

"Well, they must be getting divorced for sure," I said.

I know why she does it. It's simple – her life got shittier as the lives of her peers improved. Human nature is at the root of most exhibitions. For example, I play hockey with a guy named Nash who perpetually trash talks my teammate Shoomer. At first it was behind his back but gradually became a head-to-head power struggle. Shoomer didn't understand. "Why's he so angry with me all the time?" he said. "I've always respected him as a good player. I just don't get it."

"Let me ask you this," I said, "did Nash's girlfriend ever have the hots for you?"

"Chelsea? *Um*...yeah," he answered, "but that was like *three* years ago."

Bingo. It had nothing to do with hockey. Nash's girlfriend used to like Shoomer, so Nash hates him, end of story. Ironically, three years ago, after Chelsea chased Shoomer and he didn't reciprocate, she went around telling people he has a small penis. Talk about sour grapes! For the record, I've seen Shoomer's penis in the locker room, and while it's small compared to mine, it's otherwise average. The point is – if you consider human nature, you'll pop the lid right off of people's actions. Also, penises are dangly.

By most standards, the Queen of Assumptions leads a miserable life. She's in a dysfunctional marriage to a philandering, alcoholic husband. Her child is the spawn of Satan, literally exhibiting all the signs of a future serial killer at age six. She packed on a hundred pounds over the past five years and declared bankruptcy this spring after the bank repo'ed her car. It's easy to see why she craves smut on everyone else. It's a double-negative uplift. It makes her feel as if she's not alone. If the rumors aren't nasty enough, she muddies them until they qualify. Misery doesn't just love company – misery *needs* company.

My brother Vito is three-and-a-half years older than me. We hung out a lot in my early teens, so, by association, I got adopted by an older crew of guys. It was great because I got to do a lot of fun stuff before my time. The downside was that they all got real jobs when I was still relying on a five dollar weekly allowance. By the time they had steady girlfriends, I was just starting my first real job as a stock boy at an office supply store. I worked sixteen hours a week and made minimum wage, which at the time was $4.25 an hour. Still, the guys were always cool to me despite that I was piss-poor. Whenever I didn't have enough money to do something, they'd toss me a couple bucks for a movie ticket or chili dog. The problem, though, was that I gained a reputation with their girlfriends as a scrap-eating mooch, and they gave me hell for it. If I ate one of their boyfriend's leftover cheese sticks, they'd act like I was depleting their unborn child's college fund. As usual though, after a few of them tied the knot, that ring of friends disbanded.

A decade later, one of the guys and his wife were visiting from Washington, DC, so the old crew got together for a makeshift reunion dinner. Thankfully, my income had increased substantially since my stock boy days. So, in the interim, I tried to keep the good karma flowing by splurging on my younger brother or being generous with my pals in appreciation for how I was taken care of. Nevertheless, when I got to the restaurant with the old crew, they still had me pegged as the penniless mooch kid.

I don't mind a little good-natured ribbing, but their wives, who'd all gotten disgustingly fat, were especially brutal. They took jabs at every opportunity. They asked if I was going to eat quesadilla scraps off their plate. They calculated that I owed them thousands of dollars plus interest. When someone mentioned the Smithsonian Air and Space Museum, one of the wives pointed at me and condescendingly said, "It's right up *your* alley because it's *free.*" They were on a roll, even "warning" my girlfriend to "watch out" because I'm "so cheap." Come on bitches, I was fifteen!

The guys seemed scared of their dragon women and didn't say much, so I kept my cool despite that it sucked hanging in the stocks having cabbage hurled at my face. I honestly thought we were all good friends back then, so I was shocked to find so much pent up animosity in these women. In an attempt to reverse the flow, I said, "Hey, seriously though, I really appreciated the love you guys showed this poor bugger back in the day, so let me pick up the tab."

It was almost two hundred dollars, but it didn't matter. Instead of saying, "Wow, thanks, we accept that you've matured since we last saw you TEN YEARS AGO," they said, "That still doesn't make up for everything you mooched!" Geez-O-Pete! I should've cut each one of them a check for whatever they felt they deserved in order to avoid hearing shit at future reunions. I wanted to burn them for being fat and horrible and ruining the lives of their husbands, but I bit my tongue. I told myself I was holding it down for my expatriate homeys, pitying the fact that they married a bunch of spiteful wenches. Sorry, brozinis.

Sometimes the best way to make forward progress is to forget the past and move on. Don't judge people by how they acted as a kid, because kids go through awkward stages of being shy, weird, dorky, cocky, angry, and poor. When I see kids in a restaurant drinking half-n-half or eating butter packets, I think, "What a bunch of morons!" But then I remember how I used to pour honey on my salads and eat shrimp tails. When I'm annoyed by a bunch of loudmouthed teens in a movie theater, I think, "I'm going to destroy these little shits!" But then I remember how much of a punk I was at the same age, sneaking a water gun into the theater in the name of anarchy. Go look at your school photo from tenth grade and tell me if you'd like to be thought of like that. Seriously, look at your stupid hair.

Growing up, we spent way too much time judging others. Some of the people I avoided when I was young turned out to be good friends, while others who I thought were cool, aren't anymore. We labeled those who didn't fit our ideals, and it turned us into twat-faces. It's time to hit the social perception reset button and cut some slack for human nature, bad parenting, and pubescent failures. Of course, some douchebag teens grow up to be douchebag adults, so here's my advice: Give everyone a fighting chance to prove their worth as a grown-up. If they re-fail, go ahead and cut them out for good.

Besides, judging others makes no sense when we're all just a bunch of average Joes to begin with. We all get tongue twisted. We all get diarrhea. We all get eye boogers. We're all unsure about what we're supposed to do next. Each of us reacts to life's ups and downs like the rest of the population. The only people who those rules don't apply to are geniuses and psychopaths. They're the only ones who'll truly surprise you. If you know a genius or psychopath, I suggest avoiding the latter, unless you want a chicken bone jammed in your jugular. However, be nice to your genius friend, because when he finishes his time machine, he might let you use it to go back and warn your buddies to not marry those future fatties.

Crazy Sushi

Sometimes my mind wanders. It usually happens after I see something that bugs me. I call it *spiraling*. My thoughts are like a school bus that blows a tire, crashes through a guard rail, careens down a hill, goes over a waterfall, and then flies off the fucking earth. I feel like an OCD plagued Yeti caught in an ADD avalanche. I'll give you some examples.

Last week I stopped at Kroger to buy three things – a Monster energy drink for hockey, a pie for a dinner party, and a box of chai tea for my desk at work. I didn't bother making a list because any nincompoop can remember three measly things. Within minutes I had the energy drink in hand and was heading for the baked goods section.

While browsing a wooden table full of pies, I made the mistake of looking directly at a nearby woman's fat ass. It was repulsive. It was lumpy and grossly misshapen. It nearly made my penis fall off. She didn't quite make the cut for a carnival sideshow, but her obesity tractor beam drew me in nonetheless.

I estimated that she was in her forties. Of course, with that much fat, it's hard to tell. Enough fat can make a sixteen-year-old look forty. Nevertheless, to add to her fantastic repulsiveness, this woman had a short wet perm and was wearing a *heinous* pair of gargantuan mom jeans. Above her waistline was an enormous fat roll that made it look like she was using a waterpark inner-tube as a belt. Her ass looked like a gigantic pair of puckered lips turned sideways. It was as if she was tightly flexing her buttocks, but while the top was wide and flabby, the bottom was shaped like the butt on a skinny male rock star, yet the transition between the two was perplexingly seamless, like an M.C. Escher staircase.

During my formative years, I devised a theorem that allows me to deduce how many offspring a female has based on her ass cheeks. I didn't take this study lightly either. My calculation takes into account body type, age, ethnicity, posture, and variables like vanity, yoga pants, and whether or not the subject works in a bar. Once proven, my theorem will be up there with the one Pythagoras contributed. After a few tweaks to the formula, my guesses grew increasingly accurate.

While drinking with my younger brother at a bar called *The White Rhino*, I guessed that one of the shot girls – a young, thin Hispanic with a bare midriff – was the mother of two. *"Two?"* he said. *"No way! She's so small and tight!* One *max,* but I doubt if she has *any."*

"I'll bet you a shot she has two," I said.

"I'll take that bet for sure," he said.

She was a deceptive case. Most men in the bar were admiring her cheeky shorts, but I took note of her indented hips, disjointed strut, slight muffin top, heritage, desperate manner, hopeless expression, career choice, and shoulder tats. If she was white, I would've guessed one. If it were a strip club, I would've guessed three.

She set her tray of test tube shots on our table and engaged us in tip-fluffing small talk. Before long, she revealed that she had a son named Michael. "Wow, you look so young to have a kid!" I said. "So, does Michael have any brothers or sisters?"

"Oh, he *loves* his little sister!" she said.

"That's *so* sweet!" I said.

"So do you guys want shots?" she asked.

"Absolutely," I said, turning to my brother. "What shot do you want to buy me?"

I smiled as she began her recital, "I've got Sex on the Beach, Blow Jobs, Slippery Nipples, Redheaded Sluts, Wet Pussies..."

The point is – I'm a female ass scholar.

I stood in the grocery store bakery holding an energy drink and a pumpkin pie, dumbfounded by this fat woman's ass oddity. Obviously she had kids, but how many? Nobody gains that much weight after one, so it's *at least* two, but an ass that blown out didn't stop at two. Her last birthing session must've blew her shit *apart!* Her rear end looked like an underground nuke test site. Maybe her third pregnancy was triplets? *Five then?* No, the manner in which she was lazily perusing cupcakes in severely out-of-date jeans was a subtraction. It must be four.

I needed to find out if I was right, so I walked up beside her and pretended to check the nutritional label on a package of birthday cupcakes. Then I broke the ice. "Kids love these things, don't they?" I said.

"Pardon me?" she said.

I was already paranoid that she knew I was only talking to her because of her horrible ass. "Oh," I said, "I was just saying that kids love cupcakes, you know, more than grown-ups. So adults, like us, only buy cupcakes for kids, usually."

"Yep," she said, clearly distancing herself with her body language.

It wasn't going smoothly. She was already standoffish. I thought, "Maybe she's afraid that I'm trying to pick her up. *Wait*, shouldn't she be flattered? Maybe she thinks I'm going to rob her. Actually, she'd be easy to rob, but I bet she'd scream bloody murder if I snatched her purse. She looks like she's got a mouth on her. Everyone in the store would hear it. It'd be super embarrassing."

I thought about what it'd feel like to have everyone in the store looking and pointing at me like I was the last real human in the crowd at the end of *Invasion of the Body Snatchers*. The thought made my face go flush, which made me even less credible. I needed to get to the point. She was holding a carton of cupcakes, so I said, "Are you getting those for your kids?"

"Nope, niece's birthday party," she said.

"Ah," I said, "are *your* kids going to your niece's birthday party?"

"*No*," she replied, her tone implying that my question was strange, which it was.

"Do you *have* kids?" I asked.

"Why do you want to know?" she said.

"Because your weird-shaped ass makes it hard to guess," I said...in my head. Out loud I said, "Because, *uh*, if you *did* have kids you might know what kind of cupcakes kids like, and you could help me decide which kind to get."

"I think kids like any cupcakes," she said.

"That's true," I said, as I put down one package and picked up another. "What kind do *your* kids like?"

"Listen," she said, "I'm not sure what you're up to, if you're trying to sell me insurance or something, but I've *really* got to get going."

When she turned to walk away, I asked in desperation, "Are you going to pick up your *kids?*"

"No," she replied abruptly, clearly perturbed. "Bye."

As she huffed off, I shouted, "Tell your *four* kids I said hi!"

"Get a life!" she shouted back. Then she flipped me off without turning around and said, "I don't have any *damn* kids!"

YES!!! Victory! Sort of. The commotion caused an old lady standing by the bread stand to look over. I smiled, pointed my thumb at the fat woman, and said, "Ex-wife." The old lady gave me an "Oh, that makes sense" nod.

But wait, *no kids?* How is that mathematically possible? Then it dawned on me – her fugly ass wasn't the *result* of having children – it *prevented* her from having children. I'll have to add a genetic defect paradox to my theorem.

As the barren woman stormed off, I stared at her ass, shook my head, and said to myself, "Your jeans look *stupid.*" On my way to the register, I panned the store and thought, "*Hmm,* everyone in here is wearing blue jeans." It was true, Kroger was packed, and everywhere I looked I saw denim. Middle-aged men, old women, a group of teens, a young family, a worker unpacking bananas, a single mom *and* her toddler – all in blue jeans. "Must be giving them away at the door," I thought. Then I looked down at my jeans and said to myself, "What the *hell?* Are there *any* other types of *fucking pants?*"

I searched ferociously while waiting in the checkout line and *finally* spotted an older fellow not wearing blue jeans, his were black. I felt some relief. I thought, "If they can dye them any color, why are they always blue?" I looked at the items on the conveyor belt belonging to the woman in front of me and noticed a salmon fillet. I thought, "I should get pink jeans. Pink like salmon, pickled ginger, strawberry yogurt, and cotton candy." I was proud of myself for thinking of so many pink foods so quickly. "I freaking rule at *Scattergories!*" I thought. Then, while swiping my card, I thought, "I couldn't pull off pink jeans. I'd look queer and ridiculous. That's not fair. Who decided pink wasn't manly?"

On the drive home, I tried to imagine a world where pink didn't carry an effeminate connotation. Darth Vadar's cape was pink. The Punisher had a pink skull on his chest. The Cadillac CTS driving next to me would look better in pink. Army tanks were pink. Ninja throwing stars were pink. Black people were pink. My house was pink. My teeth were pink. I wore pink jeans. I thought of a quote from a Christian Slater movie called *Kuffs*. While sending flowers to his girlfriend, he told the florist to write on the card, "Hugs and kisses on all your *pink* parts." I thought, "*Pink parts*, that's funny. Her pink parts would be her lips, vulva, nipples, and *maybe* even her anus."

When I pulled into my driveway, I thought, "I guess the brick on my house is kind of pink. Pinkish anyway. My house doesn't have nipples though. *It definitely doesn't have an anus!*" I laughed to myself, grabbed my Kroger bag, and went inside. "*Way* too many jeans in there," I thought. "I'm going to dig out my gray cargo pants tomorrow.

I should shop for a pair of tan khakis too. That fat lady needs new jeans. Like pronto. Christian Slater wouldn't hug and kiss *her* pink parts. He wouldn't kiss them with Steven Tyler's lips!"

I put my bag on the kitchen counter and took out the energy drink. "Hockey tomorrow," I thought. "Christian Slater caught a hockey puck in the movie *Untamed Heart*. Then he checked out Marisa Tomei's pink parts!" I did a doggy-style pantomime and said, *"Aww yeah!"* in a sleazy manner. I set the pumpkin pie on my countertop and quoted the fat, black woman from *Deuce Bigalow*, "Cakes and Pies! Cakes and pies!"

"I should've picked up some Cool Whip too," I thought. "Wish I would've bought a pecan pie instead. Why is the word *piety* stuck in my head? Piety. Pie tea. Chai tea."

"Damn it!" I said out loud. I looked down at my jeans, shook my head in disgust, and said, "Fuck you, jeans." Spiraling makes me forget stuff and swear at my pants.

*   *   *

Every time I leave work, I drive a few blocks and get stopped at a traffic light in front of a place called *The Data Recovery Center*. It's a standalone brick building between two strip malls. A large red custom awning advertises their name in white capital letters. On the awning, below their name, is a blank white rectangle suited for a slogan but left empty.

The awning layout is standard for businesses. The same one is on a nearby pizza place. Below the name "Mazzola's Pizzeria" is the slogan, "Have a slice of heaven." There's one on a thrift store near my house. Under "Sylvia's Resale" is the descriptor, "Gently used upscale resale." For some reason, The Data Recovery Center didn't fill the space with a slogan, and it bothered me.

Initially, I thought, "The Data Recovery Center – We'll recover your data," would be sufficient, but it was too redundant. Something in layman's terms would be better, like, "The Data Recovery Center – Lose Data? We'll recover it." Then I thought, since the name of the business was dull, the slogan should add some personality, maybe, "The Data Recovery Center – Don't worry buddy, we'll recover your data, no biggie."

Even though *I* know The Data Recovery Center specializes in recovering *electronic* data, passersby could mistakenly think they recover *any* data, such as your family lineage or the fifth grade love notes that Kelly Pickler wrote you. To be specific, it should be, "The Data Recovery Center – We'll recover your *electronic* data."

Still, grandmas in need of their services may not understand that lingo. They might think, "Electronic data? What in tarnation is that?" So it should be, "The Data Recovery Center – We recover electronic data, like digital photos, spreadsheets, and documents, if your computer crashes." I suppose you can't accommodate everyone. Plus, grandmas having computer trouble will probably call their kids for help first, so all they really need is, "The Data Recovery Center – We'll recover your data, just not for grandmas." Actually, that sounds like age discrimination. I know how to fix it. "The Data Recovery Center – Come on in, ya old turds!" Now it just sounds mean. It should be simple and friendly. "The Data Recovery Center – We'll recover your data, pal." That sounds sarcastic. It should simply be, "The Data Recovery Center – We'll recover your data." *Crap!* I'm back to where I started, boring and redundant.

The best slogans are pointed and funny. Someone forwarded me an email with photos of some dandies. There was a furniture delivery truck that said, "Sofa King – Our prices are *sofa king* low!" It took me a second to get it, but after that I found it ingenious. There was a port-a-potty company with the slogan, "Our business is number two." On the side of a Meat Market truck was the slogan, "You can't beat our meat." There was a sign at a truck stop that read, "Eat here, get gas." Metro Transmission's slogan was, "Get your shift together." That's when I realized the trick – memorable slogans are down-to-earth, raunchy, and hilarious. I wanted a picture of The Data Recovery Center awning to be in the next email I got.

I thought, "The Data Recovery Center – We'll recover your *shit.*" That'd be pretty funny. You know what would be even funnier? "The Data Recovery Center – We'll recover the shit out of your shit." How about, "The Data Recovery Center – We'll shitlessly recover the shit out of your shitty shit?" Anyone would snap a picture of that and email it to their friends.

I tried to think like a marketing wiz *and* a comedian to come up with something that'd grab the public's attention *and* get forwarded in a joke email. I came up with, "The Data Recovery Center – No shit dude, we'll shitlessly recover the shit out of your shitty shit's shit." If I saw that sign, I'd whip out my phone to take a picture *and* take my fried hard drive there. I was finally satisfied with the slogan.

I thought I had a clear-cut winner until they screwed it up a week later by posting a sign in their window that read, "Now Offering Digitization Services." Had I placed an awning order, I'd have to go through the trouble of having it amended. It'd probably be halfway done already. I bet there'll be additional fees. I'm on a tight budget. It sucks, but I have no choice but to change it to, "The Data Recovery Center – No shit dude, we'll shitlessly recover the shit out of your shitty shit, maybe even digitize that shit while we're at it, pal. Just don't bring in your fucking grandma." Spiraling puts my bottom line in the red and makes me sound like a sarcastic bigot.

*   *   *

I used to work by a place called *Wow Sushi*. It wasn't far from a few other Japanese restaurants named *Happy Sushi*, *Ninja Sushi*, and the Irish-sounding *O' Sushi*. I found all the names peculiar, but after moving to an office on the other side of Metro Detroit, I spotted a sushi joint that topped them all – *Crazy Sushi*. Then I started spiraling.

Crazy Sushi? That's a weird name for a sushi joint. What's so crazy about it? Do you have to be crazy to eat there? Maybe they serve Puffer Fish livers. I hope the chefs aren't crazy, because they've got knives. *Sharp* knives. We're talking Hattori Hanzo *Kill Bill* shit. They'd be like samurai warriors pulling some crazy motherfucking Master Shredder shit FOR REAL! I don't want to get fucking stabbed!

Crazy Sushi sounds too cartoony. If they really wanted to convey how balls out crazy their lunatic sushi is, they should've called it *Wacky* Sushi. Or even better, *Insanity* Sushi. Or maybe *Out of Your Gourd* Sushi.

Not Fit for Trial Sushi

Paranoid Schizophrenia Sushi

Hannibal Lecter Sushi

William H. Gacy Sushi

Jack Nicholson's Portrayal of the Joker Sushi

Heath Ledger's Portrayal of the Joker Sushi

Mark Hamill Voicing the Joker Sushi

Caesar Romero Sushi

Animal the Muppet Sushi

Clockwork Orange Sushi

My Puerto Rican Ex-Wife Sushi

Duckbilled Platypus Sushi

Strange Creatures Living in the Mariana Trench Sushi.

That's actually sort of fitting.

Severe Alzheimer's Sushi

Base Jumping Sushi

Hopped Up On Angel Dust Sushi

When Danny Torrance Sees the Creepy Twin Girls in the Hallway in *The Shining* Sushi

I suppose that's an inconveniently long name for a restaurant. When my girlfriend asks, "Hey, what do you want to do for dinner tonight?"

I'd have to say, "Do you want to go to When Danny Torrance Sees the Creepy Twin Girls in the Hallway in *The Shining* Sushi?"

She'd say, "What? I'm in the bathroom, I couldn't hear you!"

Then I'd say, "I said, 'DO YOU WANT TO GO TO WHEN DANNY TORRENCE SEES THE CREEPY TWIN GIRLS IN THE HALLWAY IN *THE SHINING* SUSHI?'"

She'd say, "Oh, no, I'd rather get Mexican instead."

What a waste of time. They should just cut it down to *The Shining* Sushi. Or maybe Ghost Hunter Sushi.

Cryptozoology Sushi

Bonkers Sushi

Wigging Out Sushi

Haywire Sushi

Completely Nuts Sushi

Well, that won't work because it insinuates that the rolls are filled with peanuts and almonds instead of eel, tuna, and shit. I've seen some pretty crazy bums, how about *Bum* Sushi?

Stinky Bum Sushi

Someone once told me that bums prefer the term "homeless." Why do they even care? Anyhow, in this day and age, you've got to be all "politically correct" when naming your stupid restaurant or people will get all offended. Fucking pansies. Fine.

Stinky *Homeless Guy* Sushi

Happy now?

Stinky Homeless Guy with Bloodshot Eyes Talking to Himself Sushi

Homeless Black Guy Standing in the Snow Outside of Joe Louis Arena Wearing Hulk Hands while Chanting "Here We Go Red Wings, Here We Go!" Sushi

Honestly though, I give that guy credit. That's a pretty smart way to get spare change. I bet he makes fat cash on game nights. That tattooed Lizardman guy I saw on TV – now he was freaking crazy! That dude had scales, fangs, and a forked tongue. They should call themselves Lizardman Sushi.

Covered in Tattoos Sushi

Having a tattoo that depicts the Cast of *Gilligan's Island* Sushi

The Girl Stalking My Friend Connor Sushi

Proposing to a Woman Who Attempted to Murder You Sushi

Uncle Parker Sushi

Southern Baptist Sushi

Handling Live Snakes and Scorpions Sushi

Scientology Sushi

Tom Cruise Jumping on Oprah's Couch Sushi

Richard Gere's Gerbil Circus Sushi

A Squirrel Attacking a Great White Shark Sushi

A Walrus Attacking a Grizzly Sushi

A Man Fighting a Grizzly with his Bare Hands Sushi

Bearded Mountain Man Sushi

Wilford Brimley Sushi

Wilford Brimley Jumping Out of a Rotting Bear Carcass Sushi

Wilford Brimley Dressed as a Duck Mascot Jumping Out of a Rotting Bear Carcass Sushi

No. Wilford Brimley Dressed as a Duck Mascot *Smeared in Feces* Jumping Out of a Rotting Bear Carcass Sushi

No. Wilford Brimley *Wielding a Crossbow* Dressed as a Duck Mascot Smeared in Feces Jumping Out of a Rotting Bear Carcass Sushi

Ooh, wait. Wilford Brimley Wielding a Crossbow Dressed as a *Platypus* Jumping Out of a Rotting Bear Carcass *Punting* a Handful of Feces *while Shouting Something Vulgar in Portuguese* Sushi

No, wait, here it is. Wilford Brimley Wielding a Crossbow Dressed as a Duck Again Jumping Out of a Bear Carcass Still Punting a Handful of Feces while Shouting Portuguese Vulgarities *and Revealing a Tiny Purple Boner as he Breakdances to a Techno Remix of Aaron Neville's "Everybody Plays the Fool"* Sushi

That's *far superior* to *Crazy* Sushi! That makes Crazy Sushi sound totally normal. They'd have to rename themselves *Normal* Sushi.

They'd be like, "Come visit us, we're Perfectly Sane Sushi."

We're Reasonable Sushi

We Floss After Each Meal Sushi

Learn to Properly Utilize Your Company's Retirement Plan Sushi

Boring Life Sushi

What Do You Even Do For Fun Sushi

Your Wife Wants a Divorce Sushi

Don't Act So Surprised Sushi

You Knew She Was Cheating On You Sushi

She Thinks You Have Nothing in Common Sushi

Lackluster Sushi

Blah Sushi

Yucky Sushi

Diarrhea Sushi

Food Poisoning Sushi

Vomit Sushi

Incurable Disease Sushi

Spanish Influenza Sushi

Black Death Sushi

Mass Gravesite Sushi

Rotting Corpses Teeming with Maggots Sushi

Genocide Sushi

End of Humanity Sushi

Zombie Sushi

I've got to stop, this is so stupid.

Stupid Sushi

Retarded Sushi

Foolish Sushi

Everybody Plays the Fool Sushi

Aaron Neville Sushi

Aaron Neville Wielding a Crossbow Sushi

Aaron Neville Wielding a Crossbow Dressed as a Pirate Sushi

Aaron Neville Holding a Conan Sword Wearing a Shirt that says "Fuck If I Know" while Standing Between Satan and Chewbacca Sushi

Spiraling Sushi

Try their Rainbow Roll.

I'm Vincent Van Gogh

My age is in purgatory. I'm tied for youngest in my office, but I'm the veteran when visiting the Lansing office. I'm older than most of the guys in the Allen Park Hockey League but one of the youngest players in the Ford League. I was the oldest guy at Toys "R" Us buying the TIE fighter exclusive that came out last week, but I was the youngest one playing slots at Motor City Casino later that afternoon. On Saturday morning I went to a lapidary arts exhibit and was, by far, the youngest attendee. The average age had to be at least seventy-five. That evening, though, I was the oldest guy in the crowd at a Jason Mraz concert at EMU.

It's an odd stage of life. I can't decide whether I should knit a cardigan on Saturday night or pound liquid cocaine shots at the bar. I currently reside on opposite ends of the spectrum. Oldest, youngest. Mature, immature. Experienced, rookie. Hot, cold. Expand, contract.

Sun, moon. Day, night. Chicken, beef. Butt, mouth. Poop, pee. Penis, vagina. Cock, balls. Dick, twat.

What were we talking about again? Oh yeah. The opening act at the Jason Mraz concert was a sixteen-year-old kid named Kyle Something. When the announcer stated his age and told the audience that Kyle writes his own music, I got worried that his lyrics would be stupid and shallow, because I didn't think a sixteen-year-old would have enough experience to write anything insightful. For some reason I felt nervous before his set, fearing that he was about to embarrass himself. It made me wonder why we feel embarrassed when observing someone else screwing up.

There's an old Hungarian guy at my church named Otto. His thick accent sounds *exactly* like the Count from *Sesame Street*. "One, *ah ah ah*. Two, *ah ah ah*." You know the drill. They often give Otto the responsibility of reading a list of congregation announcements from the podium, but every time he does it, his hands tremble and his voice cracks. Watching this grown man shake in his boots makes me squirm in my seat.

Otto recently botched an onstage demonstration intended to aid the congregation with public preaching. Otto played the role of a stranger at a bus stop being offered a religious pamphlet by a woman. She recited an exemplary method of introducing herself and her purpose. All Otto needed to do was graciously accept it, but instead he got nervous and went off on a tangent about how shocked he is by homosexuality. The woman was dumbfounded. Picture an entire audience watching an old man who sounds like the Count saying, "Men are having sexual intercourse with other men, *ah ah ah*. Male sexual intercourse is on the rise, *ah ah ah*." He rambled for a while and used the phrase "sexual intercourse" five times. I was so embarrassed for him that I considered moving to Manitoba.

I felt the same way when Kyle Something started singing one of his originals. The chorus was, *"I want your es-tro-gen. Give me your es-tro-gen."* He wants estrogen? He wants a hormone produced in a woman's ovaries? I cringed. I was afraid the next line would be, *"I wanna be in your fallo-pi-ans. Let me crawl in your fallo-pi-ans."* The rest of his songs were about humping chicks at bars and trimming his pubes – things a sixteen-year-old had no business singing about. It was horrible. I looked at my date and said, "This is the most homo song I've ever heard, *ah ah ah.*"

Even though it seems illogical, we often feel embarrassed for others. We sink in our seats when someone is sucking big time, even if we don't know them. Why is it that way? It's not us making an ass of ourselves up there. Shouldn't we be pointing and laughing? I wish it were that easy, but compassion ruins the fun. If you're prone to fellow feeling, here's a doozy of a story that'll make you want to bury your head in the sand.

I used to work for a radiator manufacturer called *Kolberg Cooling Products.* They employed about two hundred and fifty people. They were having an all-hands company rally in the cafeteria that kicked off with an awards ceremony. The emcee was a stubby Italian guy from Quality Control named Tony Garacci.

Garacci did the usual microphone tap "testing, testing" thing before calling up a series of employees who'd worked for the company for fifteen, twenty, and twenty-five years. He handed them plaques and mantle clocks while everyone applauded. After that he called up

Engineers who'd won invention patents. The clapping continued as they accepted calligraphically signed certificates. A fresh batch of plaques and gift-card stuffed envelopes were set beside Garacci, and he dove into special achievement awards.

I'd been a Product Designer at Kolberg for five years and never received any form of recognition. I thought it was noteworthy that my department's output had doubled since my arrival. On a monthly basis, I completed as many Work Orders as the other three CAD jockeys combined. I went above and beyond the call of duty by lending my artistic talents to advertising campaigns and company paraphernalia. As my reputation grew, I became the go-to guy for all creative needs. I designed the company golf shirt. I sketched the layout for the company website. I drew the cover for the ISO 9000 manual *and* the company cookbook. They used my idea for the fiftieth anniversary banners. I even created the template for the certificates being handed out at the ceremony.

Additionally, when I hired in, there was a divide between blue collar and white collar personnel based on stereotypical misconceptions of class prejudice. When office personnel walked through the factory, it was like a cowboy riding through an Apache village. I, on the other hand, got along fine with the manual labor force and became a harbinger of unity. I found that they simply wanted to be treated like equals and vent to someone wearing a tie. They were comfortable around me because I took the time to talk with them. I also cussed excessively to make those lowlifes feel at home.

Garacci started with the introduction, "Next is an award for a guy we all know and love. He's contributed his talents to Kolberg Cooling in a variety of ways. His artistic abilities have impressed us all at some point. He didn't know he was getting this award for his creative excellence, so we're probably catching him a little off guard. Let's give a big round of applause for our own Vincent 'Van Gogh' Daniels! *Yo!*"

"Hey!" I thought. "That's *me*, Vincent Daniels, the 'Van Gogh' of Kolberg Cooling!" I won't lie, I was delightfully surprised. "Wow," I thought, "this is *really* fantastic, and quite frankly, it's about *fuckin'* time! *Ha ha ha.*"

There was thunderous applause as I deliberately rose from my seat. I couldn't help but exhibit a dorky ear-to-ear smile. I approached Garacci at the podium and stretched out one hand for a handshake while raising the other to accept the award.

Garacci shook my hand, but his grip was feathery. When I looked at him, he appeared distant and confused. I thought, "Is he having a stroke?" He didn't hand me a plaque. He didn't smile. He didn't say anything. Then he squinted his eyes the way you would while trying to remember whether or not you closed the garage door after driving away. That's when it hit me. He had no idea what I was doing. Two hundred and fifty employees were applauding, but not for me. I closed my eyes, dropped my head, and thought, "Oh shit."

Daniel Yotes, a janitor who'd been with the company for twenty-two years, stepped to my side and took the award. I may as well have been standing there buck naked after swimming in a chilly pool. It felt *exactly* like the nightmare where you get your books out of your high school locker and then realize that you forgot to wear clothes, only this time there was no waking up.

I shook Dan Yotes' hand, congratulated him, slunk back to my folding chair, and stared at the floor. I could hear a snakey chorus of snickering jeers. The guy sitting next to me leaned over and whispered, "I feel your pain, man."

In actuality, Garacci had said, "Let's give a big round of applause for our own Vincent Van Gogh, Daniel Yotes!" He added a famous artist's name to be clever and destroyed me in the process. If he'd have used Pablo Picasso, Monet, or Rembrandt everything would've been fine. I heard, "Vincent 'Van Gogh' Daniels! *Yo!*" and assumed "*Yo!*" was how an Italian stooge expressed excitement. It was an honest mistake. I heard my name and chopped off the rest. Daniel Yotes' "artistic" achievement was painting yellow safety lines on the factory floor. *Whoop-a-dee-doo!* I designed the fiftieth anniversary banners, goddamn it.

When the meeting ended, a receptionist turned around and said, "OH MY GOD! Did you just want to *die* up there?" A couple people sympathized with me as the cafeteria emptied. They patted my shoulder, shook their heads, and made sounds as if they were touching a scalding pot. For the most part, though, I was a leper.

When I got back to my department, my boss said, "I wish I could've shut the lights off when I realized what you were doing. It was painful, not your fault, but *painful.*"

Undoubtedly, everyone in that cafeteria felt the sour sting of embarrassment on my behalf. I'm sure their families and friends got to hear hilarious recaps about an "idiot at work who tried to steal the janitor's award." Needless to say, I learned my lesson. If I was previously prone to snickering at the unintentional idiocy of others, from then on, I felt compelled to show mercy.

So, whether it's a kid fervently singing about female hormones, a Hungarian man revealing his gay tendencies, a drunk pal trying to meaningfully karaoke *November Rain* in a crowded bar, someone's brother crashing into his mom's China cabinet while showing off breakdance moves in front of some girls, a teammate losing an edge and wiping out on a penalty shot, a friend reciting a half-English, half-Spanish rap he wrote about praising Jesus, or a cocky draftsman trying to steal an award meant for a lowly janitor – my heart goes out to them. I want to help them. I want to shield them from humiliation. I want to put my arm around them and say, "Hey, it's okay, you did your best. Keep your chin up. You'll get 'em next time!"

It won't be until *later* that I amuse myself and my friends with merciless impersonations of the aforementioned morons. Compassion, schmassion. I'm allowed, I paid my dues.

Fore!

From time to time, you'll catch me inebriated. Thanks to granny's triple-X marked jugs, I have, on occasion, puked my guts out, felt as if I'm going to die, and repeated the fib, "I'm never drinking again!" That aside, I casually drink on most weekends and weekdays. If I have a particularly boisterous drinking night, I require detox. The older I get, the longer it takes to recover. These days I can't function until three o'clock the following afternoon, and I'll shiver at the sight of booze for weeks, and by "weeks" I mean a day or two.

Last weekend my pals invited me to an Ohio party island called *Put-In-Bay*, but I couldn't go due to my cousin's wedding. The guys left Friday morning, camped, partied, chased tail, spent hundreds on alcohol, nursed hangovers, and came home Sunday evening. To my surprise, they called to hang out Sunday night. When I get back from a trip like that, I usually want to chill on my couch and not move, but somehow they were up for more. We met at a local dive bar called *Harvey's*.

When I showed up, the guys were already half-crocked because they decided to finish a case of beer and leftover bottle of Jim Beam while waiting in line to get on the island ferry. They told me a few amusing stories from their trip, something about a plastic cup full of shit, crashing rented mopeds, and two drunk, topless hags playing cornhole outside of their cabin. They said, "Let's do a round of shots! Vince, man, you want a shot?" But I stuck with draft beer.

A few standard hoochies were on the dance floor, gyrating to standard hoochie music. When the DJ mixed in the club anthem *Ass n' Titties*, a couple chicks got up from their table and screamed, "*Oh my god! This is my song!*" I recognized one of them. Her name was Stacy Murphy. I remembered her from years ago.

I used to hang around a guy named Ben in my late teens. Ben always wore a cowboy hat, cowboy boots, and an enormous belt buckle, but, despite that, we still managed to be friends. Stacy was best friends with his younger sister. They were fifteen years old the last time I saw them. Stacy and Ben's sister explored their budding sexuality as a team, simultaneously having first time make-out sessions with neighborhood boys, experiencing two-hour fingerings, and swapping blow job stories all before they turned sixteen.

They lived in the city of Taylor, Michigan – an impetuous community south of Detroit which is often referred to as "Taylor-tucky." Kid Rock is their hometown hero. The Burger King won't serve you unless you have facial hair. You're considered weird if your car doors match the fenders – nothing a couple cans of primer won't fix though. You can also regain credibility by adding a towering aftermarket spoiler to your trunk lid. The highlight of the annual city festival is when a fat, bearded guy draped in a Confederate flag lights a barrel of firecrackers in a petting farm while a band named Whiskey Creek Rattlesnake Hicks rocks the crowd. The more crooked your teeth, the more awesome it is. In Taylor, Ben's sister and Stacy were right on schedule, although the fingering was a little late. Backwoods hillbilly rules applied. If they had a father, he would've been proud.

My pal Hank pointed out Stacy's older sister, Kristy, sitting beside the dance floor. When I was eighteen she consecutively hooked up with my two closest friends. She wanted to complete the trifecta with me, but, regrettably, I remained loyal to the cheating ho-bag I was dating at the time. Back then, Kristy was pretty, perky, had a nice ass, and was a form of psycho associated with being raised by a skanky barfly mother and never-present, womanizing father. Now, at twenty-five, she looked like she was in her late thirties. She appeared worn out, used up, and trailer trashy. Too bad I didn't stuff my Luke in her tauntaun back when she was premium.

The middle Murphy sister, Bridget, wasn't present. Guys used to call her "Big Boobs McGee" because she was *exceedingly* endowed. Eventually, for medical reasons, she had her massive knockers chopped down to small B's, and nobody's noticed her since. Tough choice: Chronic back pain with popularity or painless existence with social invisibility? So maybe she was there, but I sure as hell didn't see her.

The Murphy girls are the epitome of Taylor chicks. Three sisters from two different fathers, all have illegitimate children, all have tramp stamps, all have worked in titty bars, two did military stints, one's on welfare, one served jail time as an accessory to a dope dealing boyfriend, the oldest moved in with her mother after being evicted from her father's house, two are divorced, and the one that isn't is engaged to her sister's ex-husband who is fourteen years older than her and the father of her nephew. *Yee haw!*

The two at Harvey's were wearing low-rise jeans that revealed their butt cracks, shirts that showed half-a-nipple, and the same amount of mascara Rhode Island uses in a month. They were both wearing "Taylor Wedding Gowns," a local term coined for women wearing blue jeans and a jean jacket. "Taylor tux" is the term for a guy in jeans and a denim shirt. Kristy's hair looked like straw. Her once curvy body was skinny and shapeless. The seat of her jeans sagged. As Sir Mix-A-Lot says, "The rock man got 'em, and their butts just dropped." There were constants though. Stacy still had that "dumb as a brick" look on her face, Kristy still seemed out of her gourd, and by the look of things, they're both still nymphomaniacs.

I hadn't seen Kristy in years. When she noticed me, she did a double take, followed by a happy dance, and then ran up and jumped on me for a hug. "Vincent!" she said. "OH MY *GOD!* I haven't seen you in *forever!* It's *so* good to see you! I'm *so* glad you're here! For real, I'm glad you're here because there's a guy over there that I'm not comfortable around because he raped me last week."

Huh? I looked over and saw a guy that resembled Skeletor's emaciated, goatee-wearing younger brother glaring at me with a psychotic look on his face. "Wow," I said, "that's...*fascinating?*" With Kristy's arms still around my neck, I turned to the guy, pointed at Kristy, gave a thumbs-up, and mouthed the words, "Good job."

Kristy gave me a five minute summary of her life. It basically went: Army, kid, marriage, divorce, Jesus. She pulled her shirt off her shoulder to show me a tattoo of her son in a bassinet next to Jesus' face. "Wow, you've got an excellent tattoo artist," I said.

"Thanks!" she said. "His name's Bert, but everyone calls him *Skeezer*. I can give you his number."

"That'd be great," I said. "I was thinking about getting a tat of Jesus holding a baby raptor, you know, because he loves all creatures."

"Yeah, that's an *awesome* idea!" she said.

When I congratulated her on her child, she poised herself and went into Grammy acceptance mode. Pretending we weren't in a seedy dive bar surrounded by titty-ogling men, she placed an emotional hand to her heart, slowly shook her head, gazed heavenward, and said, "*Oh...my...god*. My little Dylan just turned five (pause for dramatic sigh) and he is *the...most...beautiful...thing* in my life." One minute later Kristy was straddling Stacy in a chair, grinding her pussy into her sister's gut, while chugging a Jager Bomb. They're not lesbians, they're just having a "Taylor hug" because it draws the right kind of attention.

I imagined the music coming to an abrupt halt, cuing Kristy to pause her incestuous lap dance, look over, and say with a hand on her heart, "My baby is *the...most...beautiful...thing* in my life." Then the music restarts and she goes back to rubbing her denim crotch on her sister's beer belly. What's the second most beautiful thing in your life? Opossum road kill? A wad of boogers? A plunger from a truck-stop restroom?

Kristy showed off her sexy moves for a while and eventually came back to my table to get my number. I had a premonition that giving her my real number would lead to an unwanted pregnancy, bad credit, and a warrant for my arrest, so I gave her the number of a Chinese carry-out place that I had memorized. To her credit though, Kristy brought up a funny incident that happened back when she was dating my friend Jason, whom we called *Big Jay* because he was over six-and-a-half-feet tall and at the onset of a professional wrestling career. At 5' 10" I was affectionately referred to as Medium Vince.

When I was sixteen I had a crush on a girl named Megan Holtby. She knew I liked her, and would flirt with me a lot, but she was dating an older guy. When they broke up I thought I had a chance, but before I could make a move, Megan's family moved four hours north to Alpena. Four hours by car, that is, longer by foot of course, not quite as long by bike, much shorter by plane. A couple years later, Megan was in town visiting her aunt and showed up at a backyard barbecue at Big Jay's place. She was wearing a loose yellow top and librarian glasses, and had a long pigtail draped over her left shoulder. In other words, she looked *freaking sexy*.

During the barbecue, Megan told Kristy, "I never realized this before, but being around Vincent makes me horny." It purposefully got back to me. I was instantly like, "Shazam. I'm on it!" Armed with the scoop on Megan's horniness, I turned on the flirt boosters. The game was virtually in the bag, it was simply a matter of time.

Later that evening, six of us were hanging out, Big Jay and Kristy, Ben and some redhead, and Megan and I. We took the girls to a miniature-golf and driving range place called *The Midway*. Big Jay and I frequented the driving range's upper deck that summer to work on our swing. Megan had zero golf know-how, so I volunteered to teach her how to hit a golf ball. Doing so allowed me to get touchy-feely with her while explaining how to grip a club. I spooned her like Chubbs in *Happy Gilmore* while saying, "It's all in the hips."

After she missed the ball with a couple cute, uncoordinated girly swings, it was time to deliver the ultimate lesson. I told Megan to step aside so I could give her a play-by-play of a perfect swing executed by yours truly. I told her I had a knack for golf because I played a lot of baseball and hockey growing up, and the motions in those sports translated well into swinging a club. I placed a Titleist on a rubber tee and ran her through the basics. I adjusted my grip, bent my knees, wiggled my hips, squared up my shoulders, and lined up the club head. I turned to Megan and said, "Observe."

I took a deep breath and exploded into the ball with a full, enthusiastic swing, hoping to impress the pants off my horny friend. Ironically, though, Megan's face was in the arc of my follow through, and I clobbered her with the head of a 300cc driver. Her glasses flew into orbit, she bounced against the wooden partition, and the ball rolled up to the 200-yard marker.

Jay and Ben were in the next bays. I looked at them with shocked despair. They looked back with matching expressions – their eyes wide and their mouths open in terrified amusement. I thought, "Please tell me I didn't just do what I just did."

When I turned to Megan to assess the damage, a huge red lump was already swelling on her forehead. It looked like an apple was pushing itself through her eyebrow. My face was locked in the same grit-toothed look that little kids give their dentist when asked to show their teeth. She put her hands over her face and started crying. I apologized profusely. "Here," I said, handing her mangled glasses back to her.

I walked her to a bench and tried my best to console her, but it was no use. She put her trust in me. I told her where to stand. I told her to watch intently. Then I swung the club at her head like I was on a *Braveheart* battlefield. Megan's horniness turned into a vow of abstinence. Just like that, I created a nun – a nun with brain damage. Like many of life's pitfalls, it really sucked at the time but was pretty hilarious in retrospect. It was a good example of how tragedy + time = comedy.

Kristy and I laughed while retelling the story. Then she said, "That was *the* funniest thing I've *ever* seen in my *entire* life!"

I thought, "That's quite a feat for a Taylor queen who's seen it all."

Put up Your Bo Dukes

Fighting is totally cool. I was at Applebee's with a few friends on a Tuesday night. Connor and Mike asked to be on the same bill to take advantage of a buy-one-get-one-free appetizer deal. When two baskets of boneless wings arrived, Connor couldn't find Mike. Someone said, "He's probably outside on his phone." That wouldn't be a surprise, since Mike always has a chick or two on the backburner requiring his attention.

After fifteen minutes or so, we ate Mike's wings because we didn't want him to come back, eat cold food, and get salmonella poisoning. We care like that. After sorting out the bill, one of the guys walked back to the table and said, "Mike's in the hospital, he got jumped in the parking lot!" Well, that sucks, but good thing we ate his food, and thank god it was free!

I said, "Dude, are you serious?" because my friends are a bunch of good-for-nothing pranksters who'll say your grandmother got hit by a cement truck for a cheap laugh. However, it turned out that Mike went outside on his phone, some guy in the restaurant followed him, an argument ensued, and Mike got socked.

See, Mike recently hooked up with the guy's ex-girlfriend, an Applebee's bartender, and it somehow got back to the guy that Mike called him a "queer faggot." According to my logic, calling a man a queer faggot insinuates he's straight, but the guy still took offense. I don't know the guy who punched Mike, but in my book, hanging around the place your ex works to keep tabs on her is evidence that you're a shitty dick.

In summary, after confronting Mike in the parking lot, the guy said, "Apologize for calling me that mean name!"

Mike said, "Fuck you, bitch." Then *Pow!* The guy broke his nose. Get a load of this though, the sister of the guy who punched Mike ended up driving him to the hospital, flirted with him during the ordeal, and now Mike's boning her. Clearly, he has a knack with the ladies if he can even score a date with blood gushing from his swelling honker.

A girl at our table said, "Should we go to the hospital to see him?"

"Yeah, we should," Connor said. "We can pour this hot sauce in his IV bag!"

Fights rule! But really, do they? The answer is actually *yes.*

Last winter, I was at a crowded pub called *McCleary's* on a Friday night with some teammates after a league hockey game. The first sign of trouble came when a short, white punk wearing a skull-printed skull cap and a two-sizes-too-small *Tapout* shirt threw a greasy, wadded-up napkin on our table and said, "Throw that away for me," followed by whiny laughter.

Later, when the guys were scattered around the bar playing darts, talking to girls, and perusing the jukebox, the same punk sat down at the end of our table next to a shy girl named Emily. Emily's boyfriend was shooting pool, and she looked nervous, so I walked over and sat beside them. Obviously looking for trouble, his first words were, "You got a *fucking* problem with me talking to your girl?" He raised his hands in the universal gesture for, "You want a piece of me?"

"It depends on what you're talking about," I said.

"None of your *fucking* business," he said, putting all the emphasis on the F-word as if he was personally tutored by Steve Buscemi. Poor Emily was scared stiff.

"I like how you shout the word *fucking* each time you say it," I said. Then I quoted him, "*'Fucking* problem! *Fucking* business!' Did you just finish Rosetta Stone for swearing?"

"This guy thinks he's *fucking* funny!" he said rhetorically.

"Not bad, eh?" I replied.

"You think you're the *fucking* king of this table?" he said.

"No, I'm the *fucking* king of *fucking* dentistry," I replied mockingly, "and it looks like you've never been to my kingdom."

I was referring to his mangled yellow teeth. It was a lame insult but an evident low-blow, plus, I couldn't think of anything better at the moment. I watched his red meter rise. I said to him, "Seriously, dude, your teeth look like corn kernels."

"You wanna *fucking* step outside?" he said.

I don't know what I was thinking. I'm not tough or menacing, but without hesitation I stood up like Vin Diesel and headed for the door. I figured, since I took the reins on this fiasco, I may as well ride it out. Plus, I hate bullies, even though I don't have the moxie to put them in their place. There was a good chance that this punk got into bar scraps for a living, and I was the perfect non-intimidating victim.

The moment I stepped outside, he was in my face with a thug-life act. He said, "I'm All-State wrestling *motherfucker!*"

Lacking wrestling accolades, I countered with, "I'm All-State getting head from your mom!" Hopefully, ear chewing and eye-gouging are allowed in wrestling, because that's what I planned on doing. However, before anything could happen, the bar door swung open, and out walked Emily's boyfriend with another guy from my team followed by three guys from the punk's crew. Crap. Shit was on, and now I was worried there'd be a brawl and my friends would get stabbed. Just kidding, I was actually worried about the software training I had scheduled for Monday and the risk of damaging my mouse hand.

The guy bumped his chest against mine in classic playground fashion. In response I pulled his hat over his eyes. While struggling to get free, his hat came off in my hand, so I did what any Good Samaritan would; I rubbed it on my anus and threw it at his face. He flailed his arms as if I threw a beehive at him. When he lunged forward, his crew grabbed him and pulled him back. Then they started apologizing for him, explaining that he's a complete jackass who always acts like a fucking idiot when he's drunk. I was relieved. I had no business being out there.

Emily's boyfriend said, "Dude, *what happened?* I was about to break when I saw you walk by followed by that guy who was saying he was going to kick your ass! Then Emily came running over and said, 'Hurry, go outside and help Vincent!'"

"*Psshh.* Bub's lucky I didn't KILL HIM!" I said, as I growled, made Wolverine's Berserker Barrage face, and posed my fingers like adamantium claws. Phew, that was a close one, I can't mess up my mouse hand, bitches.

It wasn't the first time I'd been saved from a potential fight. In tenth grade, a couple jocks were bullying me at my locker, and this giant kid named Joe Ramirez, who was literally a giant, intervened despite that I'd never spoken to him before.

Joe came in like the Jolly Green Giant, grabbed the collars of their lettermen jackets, pushed them against the lockers, and said, "You mess with *Vincent*, you mess with *me!*" He dropped them like bean bags and walked away, and the jocks scurried off in embarrassment. To this day I have no idea why he helped me. Maybe Joe cheated off my Geometry tests and was showing his gratitude. It beats me. My best guess is that he just watched one of the classic '80s movies with a bully villain, maybe *The Karate Kid* or *Back to the Future*, and was moved to use his gigantism for good.

Another time, years later, I was hanging with a work pal at a popular Dearborn bar during a Friday happy hour. While exiting the men's room after a piss, I passed a Middle Eastern guy who appeared to be in his mid-twenties. I held the door for him and thought nothing of it. A minute after I got back to my seat, the guy came out of the bathroom shouting in my direction. "You fucking queer!" he said with an Arabic accent. "You want to die, *bro?*"

The place fell silent. Wondering to whom or what he was refer- ring, I pointed at myself and mouthed the word, "*Me?*" "He couldn't possibly be mad at *me*," I thought. I was confident that the guy who doinked his girlfriend or scammed him out of five grand was sitting behind me.

My friend said, "Is that guy talking to you?"

"No, I don't think so," I said.

The guy continued shouting as he got closer. I turned and looked behind me for the person he was mad at, but everyone behind me was staring at me with looks of concern. When he was a few steps away I accepted that I was his target based on his unwavering eye-contact, blatant pointing, and palpable fury. "Relax, man!" I said. "What's your *problem?*"

"No!" he shouted. "Fuck you, bro! You're fucking *dead!*"

Out of nowhere, a bouncer who looked like Ben Grimm grabbed the guy by his throat and body-slammed him. A second bouncer joined in and put his knee on the guy's chest. When he was fully restrained, I stood up and said, "What the *hell* is your problem you *lunatic?*" I said to the bouncers, "I have *no idea* who this guy is!"

"You're *dead*, bro!" he yelled from the floor.

"I think you're mistaking me for someone else!" I said.

"Fucking *dead*, bro!" he shouted.

I was *incredibly* curious as to why he wanted to strap TNT to his chest, hug me, and blow himself up, but the bouncers promptly ushered me and my friend to the door. One of them said, "Listen guys, we don't want any trouble, so please get in your cars and get the hell out of here." We gladly left, since we never paid our tab, but I still have *no fucking clue* why that guy was so mad. I'd love to say that I built an elaborate booby-trap in the restroom that caused him to fall face first into a shit-filled toilet while a spring loaded plunger sodomized him, but I'm incapable of rigging such a contraption. My best guess is that he just watched one of the classic '80s movies about going haywire, maybe *Short Circuit* or *Adventures in Babysitting*, and just lost it.

However, the *best* fight rescue I've *ever* experienced was during a skateboarding party when I was sixteen. My older brother and I, along with a few kids from church, hauled our ramps and rails to a freshly paved parking lot on a Saturday afternoon. My friend Dustin brought his grandfather's bulky VHS camcorder along to film tricks and spills.

During our session, two young gangbanger wannabes walked through, glaring at us, and jumped onto one of our plywood platforms. We stopped skating and watched them. One of them mumbled, "Bunch of faggots," and kicked a PVC rail.

"Come on, man!" Dustin said.

They kept walking, but one of them turned around and said, "You better not be talking to me!" Then they left. Twenty minutes later, a rusty van flew into the lot and screeched to a halt by our ramps. The doors flung open and seven guys wearing saggy pants, backward caps, and wife-beaters jumped out. We were outmatched in size and numbers.

One of them, presumably the ringleader, said, "Which one of you pussies called my brother a faggot?"

"Nobody called anyone a faggot," Dustin said. "They walked through here and onto our stuff. We didn't ask for any trouble."

"You did now," the guy said. "You think this is your parking lot? This is *our* lot. You ask *us* if you can use it!"

One of their guys pushed over a quarter-pipe and shouted, "*Fucking pussies!*"

It was about to go down. They started spreading out. I picked up my skateboard to use as a weapon. Just then, out of nowhere, an orange Dodge Charger with "01" painted on its doors and a Confederate flag on the roof raced into the lot squealing its tires and doing donuts. The air horn belted out the first line of *Dixie* as it drove up and skidded to a stop in a cloud of dust. Four guys climbed out of the windows. Out of the *fucking* windows! It may as well have been Bo, Luke, Uncle Jesse, and Cooter.

The driver walked to the trunk, pulled out a tire iron, and said, "Is there a problem here?" Within a minute, the punks backed down, got in their van, and sped home to watch *My Little Pony* reruns. Our saviors were the older brothers of a kid skating with us, along with their buddies. They were on their way to a sports bar and stopped to check on their kid brother because their mom told them to. Talk about good timing. During their *Dukes of Hazzard* spectacle, they didn't even realize we were about to get jumped, they were just showing off. Saved by the fucking *General Lee!* It couldn't get any better than that. Well, if they would've blown up the bad guys' van with dynamite wrapped arrows – that might've been a little better.

I play a lot of hockey. It's a competitive, emotional, full-contact sport. It's also unique in that fighting is allowed in professional games. Even at the amateur level I play, I've seen my fair share of guys lose their cool and start throwing punches. However, if I'm in a skirmish at the rink, I never go fisticuffs. I simply don't consider myself a pugilist.

When facing a player who wants to pound my face in, I usually mouth off or flash an infuriating grin. If someone hacks me, I don't go all Bob Probert on them; I wait ten minutes and check their face into the boards when they're not looking. Some guys are so stupid – they'll lose their temper during a pick-up game, drop their stick and gloves, and want to fight without considering that I'm going to leave my equipment on and swing my stick at their head. This isn't the NHL, you clown, I have the equivalent of a bo-staff in my hands, and I'm going to use it.

I used to spend summer vacations re-watching Steven Seagal and Jean Claude Van Damme movies, studying their moves, and training to be a deadly ninja. I was good at pretending to know kung fu. Remember the scene in *Bloodsport* when Frank Dux is doing the splits between two chairs in his hotel room? No lie, I could do that. I have pictures to prove it. No, I can't do it anymore. I'm barely limber enough to put my socks on now. Anyhow, I almost used my kumite skills a couple times, but not really. Thing is, when it comes to a *real* fight, forget fancy spin kicks, I'd rather smash my enemy's head with a brick or spray mace in their eyes.

People who're born to tussle can be in a fight one minute and enjoy an egg salad sandwich the next. Not me. After a hostile confrontation, I'm shaky for days and need lots of hugs. During the height of my phony ninja training, when I could kick the fastest and highest, I never wanted to actually test it. I had no desire to defend my village with hand-to-hand combat or defeat my enemies with honor. Practicing the art of Tiger Claw made me feel cool, but it didn't change the fact that my preferred method of attack was to throw sand in an opponent's eyes. Then, after confirming that they're temporarily blinded by waving my hand in front of their face, I'd hit them, but not with my fist or foot, but with a bat or pipe, Casey Jones-style. Then I'd run for it.

I don't want to be in a fair fight where I might get hurt, I want to be in an unfair fight where I have a *huge* advantage and winning is a sure bet. I rely on superior brain skills when choosing battles. I'll fight someone too drunk to stand, most pre-pubescent kids, or a blind guy, but no one that might land a blow. In a perfect world, I'd splash acid in everyone's face, but I don't know where to get that kind of acid, and even if I did, I'd be too stressed about transporting it safely in my pockets. Like I said earlier, fighting is totally cool, you just didn't let me finish – I was going to say, "Fighting is totally cool…in movies."

Eat Shit and Diet

I'm annoyed by the same stuff that annoys you. Like, remember when people used to call you at home, you'd make plans, and then you'd spend the evening conversing with one another in person? Well, those days are long gone. Nowadays, when people get together, they spend way too much time on their phones.

I met some friends for food and drinks at a place called *Bailey's Pub & Grill*. I was chatting with Connor about our inconceivable five goal comeback during Friday night's hockey game. I glanced around the table. Kate was texting Mike, who was at a different bar. Paige was texting back and forth with Rob, also absent. Brenda was on her phone searching the internet to find out how many calories were in an appletini. Hank was chatting with Becky, who was somewhere in Toledo. Trish was on her phone checking Facebook. I thought, "Are you kidding me right now, you cell phone maniacs?"

I know a girl who's renowned for doing three things at each appearance:

1. Entering fashionably late with her phone attached to her ear. Those surveyed believe she's speaking to a make-believe entity. She walks around pretending to be in a conversation until she feels comfortable, and then says, "Okay imaginary person, I have to go now, *ha ha ha*, OMG you're *sooo* funny! *Ta ta!*"

2. At the event midpoint, when most people are huddled together engaged in real conversation, she whips out her phone again and places a call to "Tyler in Portland" or "Ricky in Soho" and commences a loud exchange about how she could've been doing something way more fun that night. "Oh I know, *I know*, we *totally* could've been bulls-eyeing womprats in my T-16 backstage at the Mumford & Sons concert right now!"

3. As the event winds down, her phone reattaches to her ear, and she makes a grand exit, pretending to be overbooked and unbearably popular, on her way to an invitation-only event. "Wait, I'm on my way! Don't let Fergie unveil her time machine until I get there!"

Add the fact that she never takes off her humongous sunglasses, a style only fit for Audrey Hepburn while she's arc welding after completing her metamorphosis into *The Fly*, and it pushes her cringe-inducing aura to new heights. Mobile phone security blankets are annoying. Live in the now, people!

Smartphone pacifiers are a deplorable new low. They're systematically devolving us into antisocial primates. What's the point of hanging with friends (in real life, not the word game app) if you spend the entire time playing *Angry Birds* or online poker? I get that they're addictive as hell, but do it when you're by yourself. It's kind of pathetic that you can look around any crowded restaurant on any given weekend and find multiple tables full of people staring at their laps, hypnotized by glowing mobile devices.

Phone pacifiers are a particularly bad habit for single people who'd like to meet someone. I was at a place called *Ye Olde Saloon* on a crowded Saturday night when a group of three dolled up women walked in, squeezed into the area beside me, and ordered drinks. By eavesdropping I gathered that two of them were in relationships and were playing matchmaker for the single member of their group. One of them said, "There are a lot of cute guys in here!" and the others readily agreed. A little later I heard the single one label herself as being "on the prowl." Then she said, "I mean, I go out *a lot*, but it's hard to actually *meet* someone, ya know?"

Then, when one of her friends went to the bathroom and the other one started talking to a guy, she instantly took out her phone and buried her face in it. I looked over her shoulder and saw that she was doing nothing more than scrolling through Instagram. Not only that, but I noticed that every picture already had a red heart under it, meaning she'd already seen and liked those photos. She was sabotaging that opportune moment when a lot of guys would make their move. Guys are like Sand People (AKA, Tusken Raiders) in that they front a big game but scare off easily. We assume that a girl thumbing away at her phone is checking in with her boyfriend, husband, or one of the totally buff dudes in her contact list that already has dibs on her. It's a sure turn off to both sexes, so do yourself a favor and learn to sit quietly with your drink for a few minutes, unattached to Wi-Fi and cellular data.

Technology is advancing too rapidly for etiquette to catch up. The last time I was at Niagara Falls, I saw a family gathered at a vantage point, and the kids were playing games on their iPhones. I was thinking, "Hey, by the way, if you pause *Jewel Quest* for a second and look up, you might notice one of the wonders of the natural world in front of your dumb face." It's too bad that everyone who's glued to their phone doesn't walk into a mall fountain or black bear.

Every time I see someone veering out of their lane, turning into oncoming traffic, driving twenty miles per hour under the speed limit, or taking quadruple the allocated time to pull into a driveway – they're always on their phone. I'm not saying we shouldn't have them, I use mine all the time, but instead of designing them to be compact and stylish, they should make them look like the mustard yellow rotary wall phone in my parents' kitchen, that way people will feel dumb using them in public.

Furthermore, I'd like to remind people of all skin colors, some more than others, that wearing your Bluetooth earpiece as jewelry makes you look fuckishly dickish. If you're not on a call, please take it out. The only exceptions are if you're with Danny Ocean robbing the Bellagio or you're an agent of SHIELD. When you're sitting in Taco Bell with your family, it's not really necessary.

I was at a Caribbean resort, lounging by the pool, watching a ghetto fabulous black guy with keen interest. He was wearing three things – a baggy swimsuit, gold-rimmed sunglasses, and superfly Bluetooth technology. I'd been poolside for well over an hour, and it was in his ear the entire time, but he obviously wasn't making calls or listening to music. He was with a couple hoes who were prodding him to get in the pool. I thought, "Yeah, do it, do it, do it! Don't think, just *do it!*" Finally, he removed his sunglasses and dove in. I fist pumped as if my horse just won the Kentucky Derby. When he surfaced, his reaction proved that his earpiece wasn't waterproof. *Yesss!!!*

When you answer a call hands-free, be mindful that it's indistinguishable from starting a conversation with those around you. If you're ever a victim of this, do what I do and reverse the annoyance for self-amusement. There's a cocky Indian guy at work who parades around acting like his Jawbone makes him the office Jay-Z. We had a pleasant exchange in an elevator.

Indian Guy: "Hey, how's it going?"

Me: (Duped) "Good, thanks. How are you?"

Indian Guy: (Ignoring me) "How's everything running?"

Me: "All systems are GO!" (Gave him double thumbs up.)

Indian Guy: "Not you, I'm on a call."

Me: "Oh, my bad. We're on a 'call'."

Indian Guy: "I'm in an elevator with some guy."

Me: "I'm in an elevator with some guy too. *You!*"

Indian Guy: "Do you mind? I'm on a call."

Me: "Are you on a call with me?"

Indian Guy: "Let me call you back."

Me: "Okay, call me right back."

Indian Guy: "What's your problem, man?"

Me: "What?"

Conversing with someone while they're texting is even worse. At least you can hear someone on a call. Texting spurns paranoia that they're writing, "So bored! Help me think of an excuse to leave this jackass." If I'm talking to someone and they check their phone for a text, I usually keep talking. When they start texting back, I never know whether or not I should stop. If they say, "Oh, sorry, keep going, I just need to text my dad the name of my chiropractor," I end up talking until they hit send and say, "Sorry, so what we're you saying again?"

That aside, could someone please encourage my parents to *start* texting? They refuse to add it to their mobile plan. Currently, playing phone tag with them consists of listening to and leaving a series of long voicemails. I can't explain why, but sometimes I feel like I'd rather pour hot sauce in my eyes than listen to voicemails. To keep it perpetual, my parents end each one with, "Call us back, okay?" Not leaving a conversational message is a mortal sin to them.

Catching up on family news, confirming a visit, or reviewing health issues feels like hours of work to communicate what we could text in seconds. Morse code would be more efficient. At least they've started using speakerphone when we get in touch. I used to have to review my life status with each of them in succession. I'd spend a half-hour telling my dad every detail of a vacation, and then he'd put my mother on, who'd say, "So tell me all about your trip?" Baby steps, I guess. I should be grateful for their green-screen, mobile flip-phones.

*   *   *

Are you on the bandwagon of every new, trendy diet? If so, I've got a diet for you called *Eat Shit and Die!* Disclaimer: If you're fat, please diet, great idea. Try every proven and unproven, unethical, stupid-ass method of shedding weight. Cart around a jug of cloudy cayenne-lemon water. Buy raw almonds, acai berries, and cabbage soup. Order Tony Little contraptions. Drink spoiled milk. Join a Zumba class. Hump a dildo-shaped blow-up medicine ball. Tape magnetic beads to the back of your ears. Do lunges. Go herbal. Go meatless. Take pills. Get your stomach stapled. Get lipo. A little bulimia wouldn't hurt either.

If your ass blocks the sun, my only request is that you please stop complaining about it all the time. "I'm fat, I'm fat, I'm fat!" Yes, you're a fat ass tub of goo! We can all see that you're overweight! We're sick of hearing about it! You've been fat forever and you'll always be fat! Please quit stating the obvious! *We're not blind! Fuck!!!*

Conversely, if you're in tip-top shape with a metabolism that allows for guiltless cheesy fries at midnight, don't ever, ever, ever say, "I need to get on the South Beach Diet to get my butt in shape!" Don't reveal your self-imposed starvation habits to people whose BMI is higher than yours. Don't recite the Jenny Craig rules you live by while I'm dipping steak fries in honey mustard at Red Robin, it induces guilt. I don't want to hear about your detoxifying cleanse and how your sparkling digestive tract is now sensitive to anything deep fried. It took a lot of training to reach a level where I can eat pizza that sat out for thirty hours without getting sick. You deserve the runs.

I enjoy those articles on the Yahoo homepage that list "The Top Ten Unhealthiest Fast Food Sandwiches" or "The Highest Calorie Drinks in America" because I pick the ones that sound good and try them. Obviously, it's not smart to make a habit of eating junk food, but people who live in fear of it are annoying. When McRibs are available,

I'll grab one because they're tasty. I don't care if it's made from the same stuff in yoga mats. I could die in a car wreck, meteor shower, or terrorist attack tomorrow – let me enjoy my McRib.

I recently told a few friends that I like to pop a bag of Orville Redenbacher for myself when I rent a movie. A health nut chick chimed in and said, "You shouldn't eat that! I read that microwaved popcorn is one of the top ten worst things you can eat."

"Really?" I said. "Popcorn is one of the top ten *worst* things you can eat? You'd think that list would be reserved for things like hot lava, razor blades, and cyanide." People are idiots.

If you think your trim waistline needs Atkins, you're stupid. If you spend twice as much for organic peaches that are half the size of regular peaches, you're stupid. If you order a BLT and remove the bacon, you're stupid. If you order a hamburger and remove the bun, you're stupid. If you hang out in a bar and only order water, you're stupid. If you can fit into your high school jeans and obsess about carbs, you're stupid. If you think your beach-ready bod needs to go vegan, you're fucking stupid. Okay, I'm sorry, you're not stupid. I'm just saying there are better alternatives in each scenario than the stupid things you're doing.

People with nice bodies publicize their diets and workout plans to trick you into saying, "Are you kidding? You don't need to do that! You look great!"

They'll say, "Really? *I don't know?*"

You'll say, "What?! You're the last person who needs to worry about losing weight!"

She'll put her hand on her flat stomach, arch her tight booty, and spew out one last, "Are you sure my butt's not too big?"

She's counting on you to say, "I freaking worship your ass! Boys are jerking off to you right now!"

Don't fall for that crap! Anyone who says, "I need to lose weight," in front of people who're beefier than them is essentially saying, "I think you guys are total lards. Looking at you grosses me out."

Next time someone in decent shape says, "I need to go on a diet," just say, "I know, you totally do, everyone thinks so." Then make a fart noise and poke them in the gut. For the rest of the population who've gained a few pounds over the past decade, accept it, it's normal, buy bigger pants and be happy.

*   *   *

I was enjoying a quiet summer afternoon, flipping through a travel magazine at my kitchen table with the door to the back deck wide open, when I heard, "*EEEEEAAAAAHHHHHGGGGG!!!*" The little redneck runts who live next door ran into their backyard screaming at the top of their lungs. I looked to see what all the fuss was about but didn't notice anything out of the ordinary. They weren't on fire, surrounded by bees, or being chased by a tiger. They were simply running around their swing set screaming their heads off, literally hitting the highest measurable decibel level possible, like what Mariah Carey stunned everyone with on her first album. It's what my dad calls "screaming mimis like a wild banshee." I'm not sure what that means, but it sounds pretty loud. What if I went out on my front lawn and screamed as loud as I possibly could for thirty minutes? The cops would show up with their guns drawn. I don't understand why they don't show up and shoot these little Mariah Carey gremlins.

They cry wolf like that *all the fucking time*. They'll wade in their kiddy pool screaming as if it's full of piranhas. I peek out for particularly loud shrieks because I've always wanted to see a compound leg fracture, but they'll just be chilling with their toys. Ironically, something seems awry when they *stop* screaming. If it gets quiet, I expect to look out and see a twelve-foot-long, lumpy anaconda in the grass.

These starved-for-attention little brats constantly yell, "Daddy, look at me! Mommy, look what I can do!" I hate having to shut my windows on a warm, breezy day due to their high-pitched racket. Finally, after thirty minutes of incessant squealing, their stepfather shouted what I'd been thinking the entire time, "YOU KIDS SHUT THE FUCK UP!"

I cut my lawn regularly. I even edge it and run a weed whacker because I think those things separate good homeowners from deadbeats. However, my landscaping is nothing special, just eight square bushes that were already there when I moved in. I appreciate nice landscaping but don't plan on upgrading mine. The reason is that I consider a semi-unappealing yard a security feature. Thieves scoping out the neighborhood will take one look at my place and say, "With landscaping that lame he probably doesn't even own a TV." Inside, ten TVs. Since I never apply weed killer, my backyard is an all-you-can-eat buffet for birds, squirrels, and bunnies. I enjoy the wildlife. It makes me feel like I'm on the set of *Teletubbies*.

Last summer I caught the neighbor kids throwing rocks over the fence trying to hit grazing starlings. Before I cut the lawn that weekend, I gathered the stones and asked their stepfather to keep them from throwing them in my yard. A few minutes later, I was in my garage, and I heard him screaming at them, "If you ever touch one of them *fucking* rocks again I'M GONNA BREAK YOUR FUCKING ARMS!" The kids are six or seven years old, and I was *positive* he wasn't bluffing. I felt a little bad, but thought, "Whatever. They're bastards. Somebody's got to break their arms, may as well be their legal guardian." Nevertheless, even when they're out there screaming all day long, I can't bring myself to complain to him because I'm afraid he'll smash beer bottles over their heads as punishment.

What gets my goat, though, is that some adults have the same mentality as those kids. They're practically always screaming, "Everybody, look at me! Look what I'm doing!" An adult who can't reside in a group without coveting the most attention is annoying. We're all grown-ups here, let's share the stage. Everyone's input is welcome! But *nooo*, attention cravers always interrupt to outdo your story or disagree with your opinion, and they usually do it ten times louder than necessary. I *can't stand* those freaks. Most of their sentences start with, "No, I did/saw/had something *way* better..."

For example, I was sitting in a friend's backyard telling a story about four gray-haired old ladies who were driving beside me in a beat up Ford Taurus on the Ontario Highway 401. Out of nowhere, their rear driver-side wheel fell off. It literally detached from the axle and started weaving between lanes. Everyone was tapping their brakes, swerving around, kicking up dust, and shitting their pants trying to dodge the thing without causing a multi-car pile-up. It seemed like it was rolling between traffic forever. It finally slammed into the median and skidded to a stop. Somehow the ladies in the Taurus just kept driving along on three wheels, oblivious to all the commotion.

When I drove up beside them and looked over, I realized they had *no idea* they lost a tire. I started beeping my horn and waving to get their attention, but they must've been jamming NPR way too loud or were all deafer than shit, because they never noticed me. When they got off at the next exit, I watched their car drive up the ramp and decelerate until it finally teetered back and scraped the pavement in a flurry of sparks.

I thought it was an amusing story, but before I could finish, a loud-mouthed attention whore named Kyle butted in and said, "No, dude, it was *way* funnier the time I wrecked my Yamaha scooter!" The group did a contiguous eye roll because, A) We've all heard his scooter story a dozen times, and B) It's not that funny. As he rambled, laughing obnoxiously at himself, I imagined myself kicking the fire pit onto his lap while the group surrounded him and clubbed him with logs.

Chicks can be just as bad. I was at a housewarming party listening to the host and his wife talk about their recent whitewater rafting trip when a lumbering know-it-all named Becky chimed in with her "life-altering" Colorado River experience. She repeated the phrase "I'm a *really* strong swimmer" *six* times. She was so stuck on explaining how intimidated we should be by a Class 5 rapid that the host's wife finally got fed up and said, "*Okay!* Class five is big! *We get it already!*" The only thing I was thinking during Becky's story was, "I hope you drown in the end."

If I'm ever on a plane that goes down in the Alps and an attention whore is among the survivors, I swear I'll cannibalize them within the first hour, even if we were just served pretzels and half the plane's cargo is Lunchables.

If there's a family with an infant sitting in front of me at church, I often make the mistake of initiating a game of peek-a-boo. The amused baby wants it to go on indefinitely, whereas my attention span for such things is spent after doing it twice. The kid keeps staring, waiting for more, but I'm like, "I'm done with you, turn around." That's expected with babies, but I've also caught adults staring at me when scanning the auditorium. I don't mind if it's a cute girl, but fat, bald weirdoes give me the creeps. Psycho staring is annoying.

A measure of eye-contact is normal during conversation, but people spoil that too. There are rules. You shouldn't sustain direct eye-contact for more than five or six seconds. You shouldn't break eye-contact to look at someone's hairline, teeth, or crotch because it causes paranoia. At least it does for me. Also, try not to look like you're shooting Superman lasers out of your eyes, it's disengaging. Lastly, blinking is a good thing.

There's a woman at my church named Tammy who's in her forties and has a hilarious '80s perm. The normal expression on her face seems wild because you can always see the white of her eyes around her irises. It makes her look like the Mad Hatter's sister. Whenever I get trapped conversing with her about her fibromyalgia or her mother's gout, she maintains *unbearable* eye contact. It's as if she's whacked out on drugs and viewing me through a kaleidoscope. Tammy's gaze makes me feel like I'm going to spontaneously combust. I wish she'd relax her optic muscles or look over my shoulder instead of glaring into my soul. Save that for when you want to make out, Tammy.

Speaking of people at church, I'd also like to throat chop the baby boomers who speak in non-returnable quips. For example, if I walk in from the rain with an umbrella, they'll say, "You must've come straight from the fancy umbrella store!" If I wear a pinstriped suit, they'll say, "Look, Vincent's heading to the gangster reunion!" How am I supposed to reply to stupid shit like that? It's either, "No, I'm not," or, "Yep, I am." "No, I'm heading to your funeral," crossed my mind. Either way, they end each conversation before it starts. They mistake themselves for witty. Conversing should be like playing tennis with your girlfriend, the goal being an even, sustainable volley – not spiking the first serve, dropping your racket, and walking away like an asshole.

Truth be told, you can stare at me while on your phone yapping about your diet being better than mine and it won't annoy me as much as any act of self-righteousness. That form of hypocrisy takes the cake in the annoyance department. Sure, there are a number of things people do that annoy me despite that I do them myself, like littering empty beer cans or farting at a urinal, but I don't judge them based on it. I don't say, "That guy littered. He's an awful person. God hates him." Although I think it'd be funny to collect a barrel full of cigarette butts and dump them in the car of the next person I see flinging one out their window.

Anyhow, nothing boils my blood like people who judge others for doing the *exact same crap* they do. I don't care if you fudge your golf score, throw elbows on the B-ball court, have a filthy mouth, drink too much, are addicted to porn, cheat on your girlfriend, or smuggle drugs over the US-Mexico border, as long as you don't preach some self-righteous bullshit on the side, we're cool.

The One-Armed Pitcher

When it comes to humor, it's different strokes for different folks. Some hate Monty Python, others think its comedic Viagra. Some like repeating the material of popular stand-up comics, while it makes others flee the scene. Some laugh at the sight of a midget, some sympathize with them. An old person's walker is a hilarious prop to a fraction of the population, while a fraction of the population simply needs them to walk. Some people laugh at their own jokes but are blank-faced when trying to get yours. Some laugh at everything but rarely induce laughter. Some prefer clever wit, others are disposed to pratfalls. Regardless, a shared laugh is bonding. If a couple unacquainted dudes crack up at each other's Chewbacca impersonations, they'll each leave thinking, "He's a cool guy."

I spent the weekend at a Ludington cottage with my pals. It was intended as a fishing trip. The first fish we caught was a three-inch long perch that was punted back into Hamlin Lake. The second was a five-inch long rock bass that someone claimed was big enough for a fish McNugget, so we kept it in a bucket, but it got blown up with M-80s later. *Pardon les poisons.* It wasn't my idea. I suggested we free it back into the lake, but the guys booed and threw M-80s at me.

We brought a cooler stocked with beer, a box of cigars, a Texas Hold 'Em set, and an Xbox with some hockey and fighting games, and everyone button mashed and swore like salty sailors. A continuous mix of Big Tymers and Korn blared on the stereo, despite that everyone would've enjoyed *Chicago's Greatest Hits* and Michael Bublé a lot more. It's easy to get along with your buddies on a guy's trip because nothing serious is ever discussed. If anything pertinent is brought up, it's destroyed within seconds.

"Does anyone have a Pike lure?"
"There's a Pike lure up my ass if you want to reach in there."

"We need an RF adapter for the Xbox to work on this TV."
"You need an RF adapter to suck my dick."

"I hope we catch something worth filleting."
"I hope we catch a baby dragon with a boner."
"Why? So you can suck out some magic dragon spooge?"
"Exactly!"

Who doesn't enjoy constant, immature banter like that? The cussing was so prevalent and infectious that I couldn't shake the habit while roaming around Frankenmuth's Bavarian Festival with my family a few days later. My sister-in-law said, "Hey everyone, do you want to stop in this German bakery for some pastries?"

I replied, "Sure, if we can shove them up my ass first!"

She was like, "What?"

And I said, "Oh, sorry. Sounds good."

I'm sure my buddies' opinions on movies, literature, and relationships suck a big black dong, but as long as our conversation is confined to boobs and poop, they're without fault. Everyone dwells in perfect harmony at puddle depth. Boobs and poop are as universally acceptable as they are shallow.

One of the trip's belly laughs had misguided beginnings. We were sipping suds at a place called *James Port Brewery* when an unfortunate little boy, suffering from what appeared to be an amalgam of muscular dystrophy, cerebral palsy, and Down syndrome, was carted past our table. The poor bugger was about ten years old and in bad shape. A surge of sincere sadness flowed through my empathetic heart. The guys were in the middle of raunchy joking but fell silent as the handicapped boy passed by with his parents. Only the biggest jackass in the world would make fun of him. The moment they were out of earshot, my friend Sam turned back to the table and said in a concerned manner, "I hope that's not contagious." I sucked the beer from my throat into my sinus cavity. It deservedly stung. Each time I replayed the scene in my mind and thought about Sam's comment, I'd laugh. The timing, delivery, and taboo nature of it produced pure comedic goodness. Sometimes there's no denying it – funny is funny.

We laugh often, but not often do we laugh uncontrollably. The reasons behind untamed, heartfelt laughter are often inexplicable. I'll never forget watching my parents, along with a dinner guest, laugh hysterically after noting that the remaining saginaki cheese on the table was shaped like an oil pan. I didn't get it, but they just about needed a defibrillator. My father was keeled over the dining room table cackling down at the rug. Oil pan cheese? *That's* funny?

The hardest I ever saw my father laugh was when he and my grandfather were reading a book titled *How You Can Grow Luscious Fruits, Nuts, & Berries*. It was self-published by an old gardener at church named Henry. Due to a pesticide accident, he had a voice that wheezed like a punctured raft. He carried a vial of synthetic saliva around to wet his palette and choked down shots of it while talking. Henry forced copies of his book on church members at ten bucks a pop. Turns out the old loon had some crazy ideas about fertilizing peach trees with human feces, opening walnuts with a pickup truck, and waving a lit kerosene-soaked rag at blueberry bushes to discourage insects. Each chapter included statements like, "Consult a library or expert for information about growing strawberries." Wait, then what is this book for? My father and grandfather were in stiches as they took turns reading from it aloud.

Now that I'm older and have laughed ferociously at dumber things, I get it. Sometimes you simply "had to be there," and if you *were* there you had to be in an ideal state of mind, because things we laugh the hardest at are often difficult to recount with equal impact. For those big, hearty laughs, the joke usually starts small and grows into something large and absurd. Adding charades, accents, cursing, and sheer volume often pushes it over the edge, sending you into laughing fits. For example, I once laughed to embarrassment at a Macaroni Grill while a friend went through a routine of pretending to pour every food, oil, and liquid on the table down his pants or on his head. Go figure.

Another time I laughed my ass off was at a St. Patrick's Day cookout while trading inane comments with a friend. I said, "Nothing says St. Patty's Day like putting mustard on a hot dog," while squeezing a perfect yellow squiggle onto a beef frank.

He said, "Nothing says St. Patty's Day like wearing blue jeans in the backyard," while pointing at his pants and some shrubbery.

I said, "Nothing says St. Patty's Day like hanging out with blacks and Asians, eating tortilla chips, and listening to rap music."

He said, "Nothing says St. Patty's Day like having to take a huge dump in your buddy's basement." You get the picture. Was it idiotic? Indeed. Was it hilarious at the time? For sure.

I was keeled over laughing once while talking with a friend about Yoda's tendency to think everything is a path to the dark side. The impersonations put it over the top. "Yoda, you've got to try my wife's bean dip."

"Bean dip is the path to the dark side. Beans leads to farting. Farting leads to stink. Stink leads to *suffering*."

Another laughing fit happened at a bar while presuming the final moments of Steve Irwin's life as the Crocodile Hunter. I insisted he was barbed while sticking his feet in stingray vaginas to use them as scuba fins. It led to all sorts of made-up Crocodile Hunter animal molestation stories. It sounds stupid because it was, but we laughed our asses off nonetheless. Drunkenness may have been a factor, in our laughing that is, not Steve's demise, although you never know.

One time, a pal and I laughed to tears while discussing our assumption that females take forever in the bathroom because they're systematically shoving things up their vaginas. Pantomiming the pleasure of using a can of air freshener, a toothbrush, and a Q-Tip as a dildo had us rolling. It got worse when we started acting like we were unscrewing fluorescent bulbs, rolling up rugs, and disassembling toilet seats to jam into our imaginary twats. It was juvenile yet hilarious (to us). I guess you had to be there.

The same friend and I once laughed into oblivion while discussing a mismatched couple we knew. The wife was petite and pretty while the guy had become a sloppy fatso. We presumed that she must be as horny as he is hungry, joking that he gets home from work and walks in on her grinding her pussy into the arm on their couch, and angrily says, "You *whore!* I was going to eat that couch! Now it's all ruined!" and he's standing there with a gigantic hotdog bun under his arm. It snowballed into other stuff like him walking in on her rubbing her junk on his motorcycle seat, and him yelling, "You *bitch!* I was going to eat that motorcycle!" and he's carrying a jar of relish the size of a 55-gallon drum. It seemed really funny at the time.

I was once on a date at a restaurant called *Mexican Gardens* and noticed a guy at another table wearing a pair of shorts that revealed a beat-up prosthetic leg. The thing looked like a wizard's staff made from a gnarled piece of driftwood. "Why would a guy with an ugly fake leg wear shorts?" I asked.

My date said, "Maybe his other leg is hot."

She used the word "hot" in reference to temperature, but I interpreted it as a reference to sex appeal. I pictured the guy getting dressed at home, saying, "I shouldn't wear shorts because this prosthetic leg looks *awful*, but I've got to show off my other leg because it's *so damn hot!*" I started laughing and couldn't stop. The more I tried to explain why it was funny, the more I laughed. I sounded like a total idiot. That was our only date.

Priming, timing, and atmosphere are crucial in triggering an uncontrollable laugh. When my parents have the family over, if the weather's nice, we'll head to the garage to wail on my dad's guitars and drums. Their back door exits through a small room full of hats. Since my father throws nothing out, a lot of the hats have been there since I was a baby. Toques, ski caps, cowboy hats, ball caps, fedoras, berets, beanies, foam trucker hats, fishing hats, gardening hats, there's even a sombrero. Many of them, like his 1984 Detroit Tigers World Series hat, are stained yellow from years of sweat and body oil. If they touch your forehead, you *will* have an acne breakout. Even direct eye contact can cause a rash. Nevertheless, I customarily choose a random hat to wear during jam sessions.

One evening, while perusing the selections, I told my dad that I almost bought a Milwaukee Brewers hat earlier that day. I was at TJ Maxx and found a fitted cap for ten bucks that surprisingly fit my enormous noggin. Usually, an 8-XXL only fits comfortably after a haircut. Milwaukee's classic mitt and ball logo is my second favorite logo behind my home team's old English D. I carried the Brewers cap around until I got in line, changed my mind, and stuffed it under some jelly beans. I told Dad, "I almost bought a Milwaukee Brewers hat today."

He immediately replied, "I almost bought a *trombone.*"

The absurdity of the comment, its promptness, and the hat graveyard surroundings struck comedic gold, and we burst out laughing.

It's nice having friends who'll roll with a joke, since most legendary funnies are the result of an exchange running rampant. I was at Applebee's, sitting by a wall of flair dedicated to a local high school pitcher named Steve Avery who made it to the majors pitching for the Atlanta Braves. I confused Avery with another Michigan born pitcher named Jim Abbott who had the unique distinction of being born without a right hand. I told my pal Sam, "Avery was born in Trenton, and get this…he's a starting pitcher with only *one hand.*"

"*One hand?*" Sam said.

"For real!" I said, proceeding to explain how he switches his mitt from his nub to his hand after throwing the ball.

"No way!" Sam said.

"*Seriously!*" I said. "You can check the photos to prove it!"

We got up and inspected the wall for evidence. Oddly enough, most of the pictures made it difficult to discern whether Avery had one or two hands. However, as my identity flub became apparent, we rolled with it, saying things like, "Wait, look at his autograph on this card, it says, 'Hi, I'm Steve Avery, the two-handed pitcher.'"

"He wrote on this one, 'I definitely have two hands. Love, Steve.'"

"This one is signed, 'You know what's awesome? My two gigantic, attached hands.'"

It snowballed into charades of made-up baseball card poses of Avery holding up two hands, or using one hand to point at the other. We pointed at newspaper clippings, adding headlines like, "Avery leads team to regional championship with not one but *two* hands!"

"Here's his stat sheet," I said. "It's titled 'The famous two-handed pitcher's stats.' It has a footnote that reads, 'Steve could not have done this with only one hand.'"

We reached the stage of laughter where you can't breathe, tears are streaming, and you're afraid you'll never stop. Our beet red faces looked ridiculous. People were staring at us. Some were laughing at how hard we were laughing. Further attempts at joking resulted in wheezing and chest pain. Faced with the fact that I didn't know what I was talking about, I conceded that Avery must've lost a hand in a farming accident later in his career.

Any close circle of friends employs a number of funny catchphrases based on amusing experiences. I have a friend named Wayne who resembles Igor from *Young Frankenstein*. His bulging eyes appear to look off in different directions. His expression of surprise is well beyond anything you or I could muster.

While vacationing in Florida, he stopped at a Miami-area Denny's for breakfast. When he overturned the salt shaker to season his eggs, the lid fell off and the contents spilled out, covering his plate with a white mound. He fell for the oldest trick in the book – unscrew the salt shaker and screw the next unsuspecting patron. Wayne froze, empty salt shaker in hand, his pug eyes at the peak of hyperthyroidism. The indifferent waitress approached, saw the mess, and looked at him glumly. He threw his hands up in a Larry David pose and said, *"They got me!"* It became a catchphrase for strokes of bad luck.

My older brother and I were at a place called *Nick's Scoreboard* for lunch. A middle-aged, bikini-clad waitress approached to take our order. Her frowning face and slumped posture made it evident that she hated her job. She asked in a monotone delivery, "What do you want?"

My brother said, "I think I'll have the patty melt."

She instantly lit up and shrieked, "PATTY MELT! *YEAH!*"

It caught us both off guard. She acted like ordering a patty melt was the same as winning the lottery. We expected it to be the most mind-blowing patty melt ever served, but he said it was just so-so. Since then, yodeling "Patty melt! YEAH!" has been a phrase used for lucky bounces. It works nicely during poker games when showing the table your flush. "Read 'em and weep, boys. Patty melt! *YEAH!*"

I was at an arcade auction with my younger brother and ended up winning a vintage 1987 Double Dragon machine for fifty dollars. The game, a staple from my childhood, was in working condition, so I couldn't have been happier. The only problem was that the cabinet weighed a ton and didn't have built-in wheels. As we fussed with dragging it around, a bucktoothed, redneck kid with a mop of orange, curly hair walked up and asked if we wanted to use his appliance dolly. "Sure," I said. "That'd be a big help! Moving this thing is a pain."

The kid replied in a slow, dopey Southern accent, "Five bucks." It became our standard reply to favor requests.

"Hey, can you grab me a beer on your way back from the bathroom?"

"*Pshh…*five bucks."

When I was a teenager, my parents used to pick up an old Polish woman named Dita on their way to church. She'd already given our family one catchphrase. If she wasn't going to attend, she'd leave a message in broken English on our answering machine, saying, "Sorry *honies*, I'm going to *postpone* the meeting today." We'd repeat Dita's heavily-accented "postpone" line when running late for anything, but it wasn't her greatest contribution.

One Sunday morning, Dita got into my dad's Ford Econoline, plopped down on the middle bench, and started huffing and puffing as if she just climbed ten flights of stairs. "My *stomach*," she said, "*oh* my stomach." It sounded like she was in pain, but neither of my parents noticed. "*Oooohhh*," she moaned as she scooted down the bench, uncomfortably shifting around while panting and repeating, "My stomach...*oh my stomach!*"

It sounded like Dita was about to hatch a baby alien. I was alarmed to say the least. However, just before I could speak up to ask if she needed medical attention, she said, "*Oh my stomach...*is fat." It made for a good laugh afterward and became something we say after satisfying meals.

Another classic saying was founded by my younger brother during a family reunion dinner. My mother was having trouble opening a new jar of pickles, so she handed it to him. When he stood up and bore down on the lid, he cut the cheese. His fart sounded like it bellowed out of a tuba. Accidentally farting in front of your aunt and uncle, cousins, girlfriend, sister-in-law, and grandfather usually results in embarrassment, but not for my little bro. Here's what happened: He twisted the lid and ripped ass. *Pllbbb!* Everyone moaned in disgust. *Ewww.* Then he matter-of-factly stated, "I didn't know." Indeed. Try it next time something goes awry. "I didn't know" can nullify any malady.

F-Bombs Away!

Have a shot of tequila. Pour another. Down it. Hide your kids. Cover your ears. Put your mind on five second delay so you can bleep out the expletives – because here they come, *motherfuckers!*

I'm going to apologize in advance to all the diaper-wearing, soft-serve pansies out there, because I have a few things to say about everyone's favorite word that starts with an F. Which one you ask? Flambé? Nope. Fondle? Uh uh. Fallopian? You're getting *warmer*. I'm talking about *fuck*. Go ahead and say it a few times to get comfortable. Fuck, fucker, fug, fuuuck, fahk, fucky fuck-fuck on a fucksicle with a side order of fuck-a-bots. There, feel better? Probably not – but nobody gives a flying fuck!

Here's my disclaimer: I'm not condoning the use of the F-word, I'm just saying that it's common and prevalent, which makes it worthy of discussion. Whether or not we approve, fuck has been etched into the tree of humanity. I'm not saying it's right; I'm just saying it's here to stay. However, if you don't prefer swearing, please cover your ears as you read this chapter.

I was lounging in a cardboard playhouse in Mrs. Straight's kindergarten class when a white trash runt named Larry Ferguson, who looked exactly like a vaudeville era ventriloquist dummy, crawled in the front door and said, "This is *my* fucking house." He then wiped the snot from his nose into his hair with his palm, socked me in the nuts, and ran off. It was quite likely the first time I ever heard the F-word, and the floodgates have been open ever since.

Face it ballerinas, you've heard the fucking F-word since grade school. Fuck is basically part of the fucking alphabet. You've heard it said by all types of human beings. Schoolmates, workmates, celebrities, bums, relatives, friends, and enemies all use the F-word. Even the guy behind you at Cold Stone Creamery is mumbling to his girlfriend, "This place is *fucking* expensive." That place *is* fucking expensive! So don't cower in the corner sucking your thumb. Accept that fuck is common language. It flows through speech like gravy in mashed taters.

You've probably heard this classic joke: A black guy, a white guy, and a Mexican walk into a bar. The bartender looks up and says, "Fuck." The F-word is often heard in bars, offices, sports arenas, school cafeterias, liquor stores, grocery stores, bedrooms, bathrooms, board rooms, minivans, amusement parks, prisons, battlefields, and bowling alleys. It's all over your little brother's mixtapes (proverbial mixtapes on his iPod). There's even an Amish guy named Amos whose stringy ZZ Top beard just reverberated from an F-bomb after he stepped in a squishy cow pie. Don't tell Bishop Eli. Fuck is everywhere. In fact, in the time it took you to read this paragraph, the F-word was spoken ten thousand times within your zip code. If you live in a sparsely populated area and find that statistic hard to believe, don't worry, it's an average.

Fuck is the most versatile dirty word:

It's a proper noun: "Fucking Larry Ferguson."

A common noun: "This fucker won't budge."

An adjective: "This *fucking* lug nut won't budge."

A verb: "Ron fucked Nancy silly."

An adverb: "Debbie needs to get *fucked* up."

A pronoun: "Come here ya' fuck."

A preposition: "Come here ya' fuckin' fuck."

An interjection: "*Fuck!* This pizza is *good!*"

A conjunction: "I can't see, *fucking* hot sauce in my eye."

A real conjunction: "You want tacos, fuck, let's get burgers instead."

A word whisker: "What's that Whitney Houston song that makes you cry? Um, fuck, I can't remember."

A synonym: "We've got a flat tire? Oh no! The wedding starts in ten minutes! We're screwed, done, fucked!"

A formality: "I hate filling out these *fucking* forms."

A code name: "Operation Fuck is underway."

An animal species: "A fucking tiger killed Wally!" (Latin *fuckingus tigris* is indigenous to the Ganges Delta.)

A fruit: "This fuckberry pie is delicious!"

A figure skating move: "She pulled off the risky fuckdruple axle."

An old fashioned Spanish saying: "Querer fuck es poder fuck."

A math equation: "The square root of 4,761 is…fuck if I know."

A blasphemy: "Holy fuck!"

A song lyric: "Banana fana fo fuck."

An unfortunate name: "Hi, I'm Dr. Gregory Fuck."

Something you repeat: "Fuck, fuck, fuck, fuck."

Yeah, I ran out of good examples a while ago.

F-bombs and religion go together like Turks and Kurds, or is it Kirks and Turds? That reminds me of a sex act called *space docking* – it's when Captain Kirk inserts his turd into a Klingon orifice. Anyhow, the last place you'd ever expect to hear the F-word is in a house of worship. As previously noted, the church I go to schedules male members to read short passages of scripture in front of the congregation a couple times a year. Attending my church, though somewhat infrequently, is a hokey, under-the-radar guy named Pete. Even though he's scarce, he dragged his disheveled self in on a Tuesday evening for his reading assignment.

Pete did his best. It may not have been the most fluent reading ever, but he muddled through. Nevertheless, he was hard on himself. He finished reading a passage from the Gospel of Luke, backed a few inches away from the microphone, and muttered, "I fucked that up." It was the only time I've ever heard an F-bomb dropped over the PA system in the house of God. The audience gasped as if they simultaneously surfaced from snorkeling. It's funny how a word everyone knows, said in the wrong setting, can hit you like a King Hippo punch right in the solar plexus.

Believe it or not, there's a fair share of cursing in the Bible. It's mostly written the way Hemingway penned obscenities, by saying things like, "The Israelites cursed their existence." In other words, they were wandering the wilderness saying, "Fuck my life." Besides that, there are scenarios, such as Moses catching the Jews worshipping a golden calf, or Jesus going spazoid on the greedy merchants in the temple, where cursing is inferred. I highly doubt that Jesus was calling those shysters "dummy heads" while flipping over their tables and literally whipping their asses with a whip, or that Moses busted the Israelites bowing to a Pagan god and said, "What are you jokers up to?"

During Peter's denial of Christ, the gospels say he cursed and swore during interrogation. There he was, trying to lay low in the crowd, but people kept calling him out for being part of Jesus' posse. Finally, a servant girl said, "I totally recognize you! I'm sure you were with the Nazarene! You're busted!"

Peter said, "Fuck you, bitch! I don't know the man!" Then he heard a *cock-a-doodle-doo* and mumbled to himself, "Shit balls," or whatever the Hebrew cursing equivalent of *shit balls* was.

Besides that, the word *ass* is in the Bible numerous times, mostly in reference to donkeys, but still. Also, when Saul was pissed at Jonathan, he called him "a son of a perverse rebellious woman," AKA, "you son of a *bitch.*" The Israelites were commanded not to worship "dungy idols." Dungy is just another word for *shitty.* And when the prophet Elijah mocked Baal worshippers after their god failed to light their sacrifice during the "Whose God Will Light a Sacrifice First?" contest, he said, "LOL! Where's Baal? Is he pissing and shitting?" So more or less, yeah, swearing in the Bible.

Michael Crichton said a good writer never writes as if his mother will read it. After that he wrote the most graphic dinosaur sex scene imaginable. Ironically, his mother loved it. Crichton's rule definitely applies when using the F-word. Sorry, mom. Every time I type it, I'm as shocked as you are reading it. Strangely, the F-word has somehow maintained its taboo status despite widespread, prolonged exposure. All of us can get in trouble for saying it in the wrong setting. Even powerful, established men who run countries, armies, and corporations aren't allowed to say it in public.

Why *is* fuck a bad word? Who categorized fuck as foul language and *flub* as general purpose? Why isn't *foop* or *furb* a cuss word? Why aren't we threatening our enemies with *"Furb you, mother fooper?"* Which, admittedly, has a nice ring to it. How did funk, fork, flit, fig, fluke, and flock sneak past customs while fuck got tasered and hauled off to Guantanamo? After all fuck is just a word, right? It's just a plain old, regular word. A plain old, regular, *naughty, filthy* word...*fuck* (I whispered it).

Legend has it that the word *shit* originated as an acronym. SHIT stood for "Ship High In Transit." Supposedly it was stamped on crates of manure being transported in the hull of sea vessels, because if they sat on the floor and got wet, the doody would ferment, produce methane, and when Popeye lit his pipe, it'd blow the ship to smithereens. Shit, indeed.

Allegedly, *fuck* came from an acronym too, but there are conflicting accounts. Some say "Fornication Under Consent of the King" was a term coined during the Middle Ages when Your Highness could have any snatch he wanted. Some say it was a mandate for towns decimated by the Black Death to fuck anything that moved in order to restore the population. Another story claims the F-word is related to an old Irish law where a couple caught fornicating were thrown in the stocks with a sign above their heads that read "FUCKIN," which stood for "For Unlawful Carnal Knowledge In the Nude." There's you're history lesson. Go teach some preschoolers.

I wasn't raised in a swearing household. I'm sorry if your parents cussed each other out like bitches, but my parents were very religious, so even *slightly* off-color words had G-rated equivalents. *Fart* was considered a bad word, so we said, "Who let a stink?" We got "ticked off" instead of "pissed off." Our substitute for "What the heck?" was "What in the world?" Instead of saying, "This sucks," we'd say, "This stinks." Saying, "Oh my gosh!" was considered taking the Lord's name in vain, so we'd say, "Oh my goodness!" If I spilled Grape Faygo on the couch, I wouldn't say, "Darn it!" I'd say, "Shoot!" I habitually adhered to the fed-up idiom "Shoot!" until I started playing hockey and realized that yelling it after fanning on a shot made me sound like a total chump.

My parents classified the phrase "Taking a crap" as crude, so we said, "I'm doing my job." In my early teens I converted it to, "I'm J-O-double-B'ing." My older brother taught his kids to call it "pushing out." A lot of families call it "going number two." I'm not sure what I'll use if I have kids. Statistically, I use the phrase "I've gotta take a dump" a lot, so maybe that'll be my household terminology. I'm not particularly fond of using the word *shit* to describe a bowel movement due to the abundance of alternate colorful verbiage, e.g. poop, crap, BM, doo-doo, feces, fecal matter, dung, excrement, poppin' a squat, defecation, caca, guano, turds, droppings, dump, job.

As Christian teens, we created euphemisms to supplant swearing. As weird as it sounds, I used to say *pit* instead of *shit*. When I was thirteen, if I got spaghetti sauce on my shirt, I'd say, "Aww pit!" Pit morphed into *mitt*, as in, "You piece of mitt!" Mitt also became a substitution for the F-word in phrases like "Mitt that" or "What the mitt?" "Mitt this mitt" was, in effect, saying, "Fuck this shit."

Following standard practice, we also used the first letter of expletives in place of the word, such as, "I'll kick your A, you mother F'in piece of S." Sometimes *fuh* was used in place of the F-word. Getting to Mother Brain in *Metroid* and running out of missiles prompted a groan of, "Fuuhhh." Friggin' and freakin' were other substitutions long before *Napoleon Dynamite* sent them to stardom. Using euphemisms became so prevalent that church elders, including my father, stepped in to counsel teens on their language. They said cursing with abbreviations was reprehensible to God because the intent remained. "F that!" I thought.

After the euphemism hype died down, I was helping church volunteers replace a leaky roof on the house of an old, ornery woman. I yanked up a rotted board and a massive bumblebee flew out and circled my head. I was working beside one of my pals, and said to him, "That's the biggest bee I've ever seen!" My dad overheard me and thought I was saying it about the woman who owned the house, who was standing two stories below. "You watch your language!" he scolded, thinking I was calling her "The biggest B(itch) I've ever seen." I wasn't, even though she was.

When I was sixteen, I dropped a nuclear F-bomb in front of my mom. It was chili dog night and I was helping set the table. Mom asked me to get out the ketchup, mustard, jalapenos, pickles, peppers, nacho cheese, and relish. The table was a few feet from the fridge, but, like an idiot, I tried corralling all the items at once. While closing the door, gravity turned on me, and everything slipped from my arms. In a last ditch effort to prevent the glass jars from hitting the floor, I kicked at them, hoping for a hacky sack type of recovery. Instead, I booted the relish into the wall and it shattered. The sound of breaking glass harmonized with a saucy "Fuck!" exiting my lips.

Mom quickly denounced, "What did you say!?"

When I fearfully replied, "Nothing!" she graciously blew it off. I fucking love you, Mom.

I accidentally let one fly in front of my dad on a camping trip once. I was seventeen and in that rebellious stage where I felt forced to participate in family activities. I didn't want to be there. Instead of roasting marshmallows and horseback riding, I wanted to eat Burger King and stroll the mall with my buddies. When I complained about the cold, damp cabin, Dad told me to put more wood in the furnace. I begrudgingly did it, but while stoking the logs, my wrist touched the scalding metal door and I yelped a canary-like, "Fuck!" If I would've shouted, "Fart!" I bet he would've intervened, but he wasn't in the mood to deal with any hardcore hijinks and let me live to swear another day.

My cousin Lydia was at my house recently using my computer to download music. When she finished and walked into the living room, I noticed that the office light was still on, so I said, "Hey, you left the light on in there."

She got offended and said, "Whoa, take it easy there, psycho!"

I was puzzled. Turns out she thought I said, "Hey, you left the light on, motherfucker." That would've been shocking, because I normally refrain from weaving gratuitous profanity into everyday speech. I'm not one of those people who'll casually say, "Sorry I'm fucking late. I fuckin' stopped at the goddamn grocery store to pick up some shit. Just some fucking bread and shit." I usually keep routine speech radio friendly, saving major expletives for later.

On the other hand, if you ask me if I like tie-dyed shirts, black licorice, or Natty Ice, you'll likely get a "Hell no!" out of me. "Fuck no!" if I'm a few beers in. Sometimes I casually refer to workmates as *bitches* and *bastards*. If you're reading this and work with me, don't worry it's not you. I might call forest-green bath towels or cereal with the word *Fiber* in the title, *gay-ass*. And, when driving, I call a lot of other drivers *dicks*. But, in general, I impose cursing rules on myself so as not to come across as an ignoramus. I make exceptions in order to:

1. Be humorous
2. Accentuate excitement or pain
3. Make sexy talk
4. Intimidate bad guys
5. Express myself when inebriated
6. Reprimand myself when golfing

Nevertheless, every culture from every nook and cranny on the globe, whether it's a cannibalistic tribe, food stamp-reliant ghetto, or tea and crumpets polo club, spouts cuss words galore. You can cuss in any language because humanity requires it. If a hippo stampedes through Mbembe's Amazon Basin hut and tramples all of his stuff, is he going to say, "Frick you, bad hippo!"? No, it's a situation that requires heavier language. Mbembe is going to bust out the big guns and scream in his thick jungle accent, "Fuck you, hippo *asshole!*" During times of emotional excitement, vulgarities are the *only* language that'll get the job done. They're also key when binge drinking.

It doesn't take a rocket scientist to figure out how funny the F-word can be. I once saw Chris Rock do stand-up at the Fox Theater in Detroit, and half of his punch lines were, "What's up with *that* motherfucker?" The place was roaring. All of your favorite comedians exploit the F-word's hilarity. Robin Williams, George Carlin, Dane Cook, Louis CK, they burn through F-bombs like nobody's business. If you want a real dose of pure fuck-word merriment, watch *The Fucking Short Version* of movies like *Scarface*, *Goodfellas*, and *The Big Lebowski* on YouTube. By the fiftieth consecutive fuck, you'll be dying laughing. The *Team America: World Police* theme song is pretty good too. As a side note, I think the best use of the "One F-word per PG-13 movie" rule goes to Kevin Bacon in *Tremors*. When they jump in the ravine and the worm monster kills itself – *holy shit* that was a good "Fuck you!"

On a daily basis, though, the funniest way I hear the F-word used is at my office. On the other side of my cubicle wall is the desk of a veteran employee named Richard Glickson. Glickson is a sexist, crude, prejudiced old-school white geezer with a foul mouth and a chip on his shoulder.

When he was tasked with integrating soft-spoken engineers from India, he continuously referred to each of them as "Your drunk ass." He'd say, "Your drunk ass needs to learn how to speak English," or, "Your drunk ass needs to stop eating that stinky ass food." He couldn't pronounce their names, so he called them what he thought they sounded like. He called Yogesh "Yoda," Chinmayu "Chilly Willy," Vijaykumar "Harold and Kumar," and Anup "Pre-nup," whom he badgered for not being around during his first marriage. Glickson is as politically incorrect as they come, and as long as you're an innocent bystander, it's pretty funny.

When someone approaches my desk, I usually greet them by saying, "How's it going?" or, "Hey, what's up?" Glickson's version is, "So, what the *fuck?*" I hear him say it every day. When his manager walks up and says hello, he replies, "So, what the *fuck*, Dale?" When his phone rings, he answers in his gruff cigar-smoker's voice, "This is Richard." There's a brief pause while the caller states their name. Then he says, "So, what the *fuck?*" The best part is that he draws out the word *fuck* in a little song. "*Fuuuck.*" It's truly amazing. He's the Tony Bennet of saying fuck. Whether it's his doctor, wife, kids, HR, or the Shanghai plant, he always starts with, "So, what the *fuuuck?*"

Glickson is one of those people you *have* to swear around just to keep up. He could influence a kindergarten teacher to swear in front of her class. This guy would say fuck in front of your grandma, four-year-old, and priest. He truly doesn't give a fuck. I've only worked with him on one brief project, but it was a real treat. He'd stop by my desk, coffee in hand, and say, "Vincent, good morning, sir. So...what the *fuuuck?*"

Assuming that means, "What's new?" I'd answer, "Fuck if I know."

Joan Fett: Office Bounty Hunter

Work has been busy lately. It sucks because I don't get as much time to sit here and write about life's minutia. See, I have the delusion that my 401K, dental benefits, and direct deposit are linked to a full-time writing job instead of an automotive electronics job, or whatever bullshit I'm really supposed to be doing. Admittedly, though, being busy here is an anomaly.

Last week, IT set me up with a new PC, and unlike my last one, the DVD player on this one worked. Their bad. Yesterday I clocked overtime watching the *Star Wars Trilogy* re-release bonus material. Man, George Lucas was a pimp in the '80s, and now he's a pulsating bag of farts. The prequels suck Nien Nunb's dick, assuming he has one. Anyhow, my new PC is ten times faster than my old one, which was cool at first, but actually kind of blows now. My old one took thirty minutes to open a headlight assembly, which necessitated lengthy breaks. All that stuff opens in seconds now, and I can't blame my laziness on anything but, well, laziness.

White collar America has *massive* amounts of spare time, trust me, I know. I'm pushing management to give me a laptop so I can work from home because I'd finish my weekly workload in an hour and bake chocolate chip muffins the rest of the day. We've got "fake work" down to a science. Some fly under the radar as their guise. Some bug others as a diversion tactic. Some suck up to the boss. I generally try to do what post-hypnosis Peter did in *Office Space*, because for some reason, not giving a shit actually endears you to management.

It's an unspoken rule, if you haven't done a lick of work all month, and someone says, "Keeping busy?" you're bound by honor to respond with an exasperated sigh and then bitch about system crashes, cutback rumors, faulty databases, the room temp, and the deadline of a made-up acronym. "I'm going gray thanks to the fucking VP4F project!" When your visitor leaves, you can get back to your online crossword puzzle. What kind of employee have you become? What's a four-letter word for "phallus" that ends with K? After writing that clue, I realized there're at least four, doesn't matter, *you're all of them.*

Office Survival Tip #33 – Suffering from an incurable yet easily faked ailment is a fine diversion from having to work. The professional scoundrel contracts a disability because nobody's comfortable giving a pink slip to someone with sciatica, fibromyalgia, migraines, or a gimpy left arm. Submerge your hand in a deep fryer and you'll secure your job for at least three years.

Have you ever pointed out a window and said, *"What the!?"* in order to steal a fry off someone's fast food tray? That sort of trickery is invaluable at the office because diverting attention is the best way to keep the focus off your deficiencies. Some who exhibit no usable skills become what we call "Talk Radio." They float around the department making snide remarks to others. For example, by calling a tardy employee "Part-timer" you draw attention away from *your* early exits. If you see someone glued to their monitor, stressing over a project, and say, "Saving the company, Design Guru?" the sheer sarcasm will cover your two hour lunch. Ray Malton, a non-contributor here since 1988, is my group's talk radio host. If he sees an industry magazine on your desk, he'll say, "Wow, wish I had time to read magazines!" Truth be told, Ray has time to read every magazine on the Walgreens rack, including the teen girl ones.

There's a worthless guy in my group named Bob who prides himself on showing up at 6AM every morning. When I get in around nine and walk past his cubicle, he always hollers, "Good afternoon!" It's super funny and never gets old. From what I've seen, his only job is snooping everything that comes off the department printer. Every time you print something and walk over there, he's standing there handing you your stuff. If it's more than two pages, he'll say, "Are you printing a novel?" or, "Someone felt like chopping down a forest today!" You can also rely on him to sarcastically shout, "Wake up!" every time he walks by your desk. I laugh a little more every time I hear that funny joke.

About once a week I see a guy with a Rollie Fingers mustache roaming the aisles in a white lab coat. He looks like Tom Selleck's mad scientist uncle. I have no idea who he is or what he does here. He attends the Holiday luncheon every year and always says, "Drink up! Vincent's buying!" followed by a hearty laugh. I've been to five luncheons and he said it at each one. Who are you, weird lab coat guy? How come you know my name and I don't know yours? I want to know because I look up to you. You're a comic genius.

Worthless workers have to be creative when refuting their worthlessness. Let's say the company announces that they're phasing out the ASX Supplier Database. When Larry Riggs realizes that the only thing he ever learned to use in the whole universe is the ASX Supplier Database, what can he do to avoid being fired? No worries, Riggs! Find a spare cabinet and turn it into a pay-as-you-go snack drawer! This job requires buying Ritz Bits and Reese Cups in bulk, which can be done on company time. Overnight, Riggs transforms from "The Guy Who Knows Absolutely Nothing" to "Snack Drawer Guy." When it's time for cutbacks, who would you fire, the guy who knows how to use the new database or the guy who provides Doritos? *Cool Ranch* Doritos? *Delicious* Cool Ranch Doritos? What does that so-called "database" even do?

Alan Dutton, one of our skill-depleted veterans, does nothing but run the coffee club. He charges twenty-five cents per cup and pulls in roughly two grand a week. I heard he paid for his new Mustang convertible with quarters. The last valid project he worked on was designing a bumper for the Model-T. It's been so long since Alan's done any actual work that he forgot how to read and write. In his defense though, he has other duties. He's the self-nominated weather whistleblower. If there's a storm brewing on the Doppler radar, he makes the rounds. He's also on traffic duty. Accident on Southfield Freeway? Alan comes a knockin'. He tapes Dilbert comics to the lunchroom fridge. Even when he doesn't get the humor, he still enjoys the drawings. He collects for the lottery pool. He's got menus from every restaurant within twenty clicks. He gets five weeks of paid vacation but doesn't work fifty-two weeks out of the year.

There's a woman here named Joan Rivers, while she's not *the* Joan Rivers, they do share the same cancerous voice. This Joan Rivers' "skill" is with a CAD program that went belly up in the mid-nineties. How has Joan lasted so long? She became the Holiday Luncheon Planner. That's her job 365 days a year, and yes, she works overtime from October onward. Once in a while she'll choose a spot for someone's retirement luncheon too. Talk about unwanted stress! Her official title is "Research Analyst," which translates to, "Someone Googling Restaurants." She also tacks on an auxiliary title of "Human Factors Logistics Engineer" since she makes a seating chart for the event.

Joan's responsibility is not to be taken lightly. Tough decisions are involved. Mexican, Chinese, or American cuisine? Will carpooling be encouraged? When should the pre-invite email be sent? When should the actual invite be sent? What about that tricky reminder email? Who's wearing the Santa costume? How do we avoid offending the Hindus in the test lab? Does anybody know if Larry Riggs is Jewish? How do you sneak the company's alcohol policy into one of the emails without causing an uproar? Those emails have to be spellchecked too. The date and location have to be approved by management. Joan might need a PowerPoint refresher course to make the flyer. For her sake, the holiday luncheon should be once every three years.

When mid-December hits, Joan turns into Boba Fett. Statistically, 37% of the staff won't reply to emails, so they have to be hunted down and interrogated for a proper head count. Jetpack, check. Grappling hook, check. Flamethrower, check. Spiral notepad, check. The supervisor unleashes Joan with one request, "No disintegrations." Employees hide out in conference rooms, bathroom stalls, and the cafeteria. Some are smoking in the alley. Some are faking sick at home. Some are at the strip club down the street. Riggs is at Costco. Ray is at Walgreens. Han is in Cloud City. Joan *will* find you.

Others might gripe, "That's not my job," but not Joan. The holiday luncheon is her life's purpose, and she'll do whatever it takes to pack the room with hungry ingrates. She's immune to layoffs based solely on her lunch planning superpowers. We're lucky she crash-landed on Earth after her planet of restaurant-choosers was destroyed. Last year she held the holiday luncheon at Panda Buffet and received the maximum profit sharing bonus for thinking outside the box. Clearly, Joan is a risk taker.

Office Survival Tip #108 – Hide the fact that you're a burden on the budget by displaying any of the following in your cubicle: Bowling trophy, snapshot of you in waders holding a trout, 1/18 scale 1967 Shelby Cobra GT 350, Gary Larson calendar, certificates from non-required training (e.g. Safety Committee, ISO Awareness, CPR Certification, Completing an Expense Report, Proper Record Retention). If anyone seems interested in your stuff be sure to engage them in conversation. Who knows, they might be above your boss on the corporate ladder and can save your ass during cutbacks.

I work in a high-end tech center where vehicles of the future are conceived, R&D for a multi-million dollar corporation takes place, and well-paid, pressed-shirt wearing degreed adults work. You'd assume this type of place would be a professional environment, but it's not. Every day there are new boogers smeared on the bathroom mirrors. Dry-erase markers are used for board meetings, brainstorming new ideas, and writing above the urinal, "Harriet in HR sucks dick." Everyone whines about the cafeteria menu and lack of parking space. Anyone who's fat, skinny, tall, short, old, bald, or resembles an amphibian, sitcom character, or Muppet gets a nickname (e.g. Mudpuppy, Fonzie, Dr. Bunsen). People steal lunches out of the fridge and swipe shit off of other people's desks. There are flasks in drawers, pictures of naked ladies coming off the printer, and women crying after their presentations were criticized. It's worse than junior high.

I'm part of a young alliance that handles 90% of the actual workload, and by 90% I mean all of it. We're the group that would be laid off first during cutbacks. We sit in the back corner of the room where its ninety degrees in July and we click our mouse wearing mittens in the winter. The old-timers call our area "The Nursery." Someday, we hope to be the lazy bastards whose job duties include nothing more than sucking down infinite pots of coffee and harassing newbies.

I can't imagine what the supervisor says during their performance reviews. "Well, Ray, I honestly have no idea what you do here, but I've never heard any complaints either *so*...keep it up, I guess."

During review season they hang around the boss' cubicle, brown-nosing. If Alan shows up to work wearing a tie, you know that's the day he'll be knocking on the boss' partition, saying, "Excuse me, Dale, I wanted to talk to you about the paper jams in the HP LaserJet. I took the initiative to switch to a thinner stock to improve morale. Oh, and I turned the thermostat down because it seemed stuffy in here." A week later, what else can Dale do but write in his review, "Alan streamlined office procedures. He was proactive in resolving climate issues, assisting workflow, and improving morale." Alan receives the full merit increase.

The workstation of a typical Mechanical Engineer has a Xeon 3.5 GHz processor with 8 gigs of RAM, but it's mainly used for playing solitaire. *But OMG can those computers run solitaire!* You can open ten thousand sessions of solitaire without bogging that fucker down. Go ahead and open Minesweeper, WeatherBug, Google Earth, Pandora Radio, a CNN stock ticker, and a YouTube video simply because you can. You're the Bobby Fischer of desktop gaffing.

I keep my desk neat and orderly. Ironically, it's a demerit in my field. Project milkers leave their desks littered with graphs, memos, manila folders, old work orders, and defunct prototype parts. One of the wire harness guys has a dismantled 8-track player from a '66 Thunderbird spread out on his desk as a decoy. A cluttered desk is the perfect alibi for refusing new assignments. All you have to do is gesture to the surrounding landfill, raise your hands apologetically, and say, "I'm totally swamped."

Office Survival Tip #17 – Keep two dozen empty Coke, Mt. Dew, or Red Bull cans lying around to give the illusion that you've been working late.

If you work in a large office, try playing a fun game called *Hide All Day*. By charting an effective path past key personnel, you can cut at-your-desk time by a whopping 82%. The key is to have your presence confirmed by your boss once in the morning and once in the afternoon. Stand up for a stretch if you hear his voice, or browse the supply cabinet by his office for a black rollerball pen, which is never stocked. After that, go see a movie or sleep in your car. An all-weather jacket is your accomplice, preferably a windbreaker or cardigan, that way no one can tell whether you're coming, going, or just a bit nippy.

When your supervisor wants to assign a project to you, he'll try contacting you by email, phone, and eventually, in person. If he can't find you, he'll give it to the next sucker he *can* find. Your stress levels will plummet. If confronted with, "I stopped by your desk three times. Where've you been?" don't fret. There are endless alibis for the old disappearing act. You were having a smoke, getting some fresh air, making a pot of coffee, taking a dump, forced to take a late lunch, bumped into an old colleague in the lobby, had a family emergency, forgot something in your car, had a dentist appointment, had a follow-up dentist appointment, had to "give your eyes a break," or were over at Steve's desk helping him again. Steve can never remember how to process files correctly. Steve is such a pain in the ass. Read the online documentation for once, *Steve!* By the way, Steve is imaginary. It doesn't matter. You're the office ninja.

These antics may sound pathetic, but they're all true. So next time you read about an auto manufacturer reporting third-quarter losses, understand that it's not because sales are down – it's because they pay lazy, worthless employees to do nothing but plan luncheons and buy Doritos.

Jumper Cable Guy

Diners and cafés have counters lined with stools for folks who want a meal but don't have a dining partner. Otherwise, watching someone eat alone can be a little heartbreaking. Culturally, we categorize it with other awkward solo activities like going to a movie, vacationing, or dancing alone – all of which seem way more pathetic after 5PM. But that laminate counter, that's what it's for – it makes eating alone acceptable.

I was attending a training seminar in Auburn Hills, Michigan and stopped at a place called *National Coney Island* for lunch. I was rolling solo, but instead of sitting at the counter like I should've, I seated myself in a narrow two-person booth. After ordering a Greek salad and fries, I was approached by an old man who looked like a sickly hobo version of the Gorton's Fisherman. He stared at me for a second, pointed to the seat opposite me, and said, "Is anybody sitting here?"

"*Uh*, no?" I replied.

"You mind if I?" he mumbled.

I did a quick scan of the restaurant. The counter was wide open and half of the tables were empty. I hesitantly replied, "*Uh*…sure, feel free."

The old man sat down and commenced one of the dullest exchanges in lunch history. After he ordered a cup of soup and a Chicago-style hot dog, I tried to spark up a conversation. "So, do you prefer natural casing hot dogs?" I asked. He shrugged. This geezer wasn't outgoing or friendly, he just didn't want to eat by himself.

He coughed violently and hocked up a chunk of lung butter into his napkin. Trying to eat in front of a surly old stranger who's coughing as if he's in the opening scene of an epidemic movie is just fucking gross. "You all right there, buddy?" I asked.

He ardently waved off the question as if he was shooing a fly. The only other "communication" that took place was an incessant "*mmm*" noise he made after each spoonful of beef barley. It wasn't a "This is delicious" *mmm*, it was a "This shit stings my ulcer" *mmm*. The whole scene was so awkward that I started peeking around the restaurant looking for hidden cameras. Nevertheless, for reasons unknown, Old Man Jenkins zeroed in on me as an ideal table mate, and it totally ruined my lunch.

A woman named Janice sat behind me at work for two years. Unbeknownst to her, her nickname was *Eighties*. It didn't have anything to do with her age. I called her that because her hair and fashion were stuck in the 1980s. I'll be the first to admit that I had an '80s childhood full of *Alf*, Huey Lewis, and Members Only jackets, but unlike Janice, I didn't perpetuate feathered hair and pleated acid-wash Jordache jeans into the next millennium. Sure, a little retro is cool, but not the way she did it.

Bruce, our department's mullet sporting, Z-Cavaricci wearing '80s guy, once said to me, "Dude, you are *so* lucky you sit next to Janice!"

"Why?" I asked.

"Cause she's so fucking hot!" he said.

"Really?" I said. "Maybe you two should hook up. Get a little *Wang Chung* action going."

"*Totally!*" Bruce replied.

Janice and I rarely spoke. We occasionally greeted each other when passing in the aisle. I'd say, "Hi." She'd reply, "Hi." And that was about it. One time she asked about the weather when I came back from lunch. "How's the weather?" she said.

"It's nice," I said. Then we nodded, spun around in our chairs, and went back to ignoring one another.

One time, instead of just saying "Hi," I added, "How's it going?" and she started complaining about her achy knees, forcing me to pretend I had diarrhea to get away from her. "Oooh, sorry," I said while rubbing my belly, "the Thai food I had for lunch is already on its way out. I've gotta go."

Janice and I had nothing in common. We didn't work on related projects, I didn't share Bruce's attraction to her, and attempts at conversation were painful. Thus, we rarely spoke.

I have a regular lunch crew at work. They're comparable to Kramer, George, and Elaine, which, by default, makes me Jerry. They're a cool bunch, and we never seem run out of amusing conversation topics. When Janice announced that she was relocating, we decided to be nice and take her out for a farewell luncheon at Mexican Fiesta. None of us really gave two shits about her departure, it was simply an excuse to take an extended lunch break and drink margaritas. We were joined by Bruce and an old lady named Marge who is the spitting image of a mother hen complete with waddles. At the restaurant, Janice bored us with company conspiracy theories, the monotonies of data-entry, and more details on her achy joints. After splitting the bill, we sighed and thought, "Thank God that's over."

Janice moved to an office a few miles away. Did I mention that we pretty much never spoke during the two years we sat by one another? Since that damn luncheon, she's been constantly emailing me corporate rumors and requests for more "team building lunches" as she calls them. I don't understand why she emails me and nobody else. Chimichanga consumption is hardly bonding. Marge does data-entry; the two of them have *way* more in common, especially if you include genitalia. Mullet-man has a Debbie Gibson crush on you, email that dude! He'll think it's totally rad! We never talked when you were here, Janice, let's not talk now. Not to be mean, but leave me the fuck alone.

I stopped at Meijer recently to buy a space heater. While browsing the small appliance aisle, a nerdy, middle-aged, bald weenie – a guy who wouldn't have the balls to talk to a puppy – started making small talk with me for no reason. I tried to field his inane questions to be nice, but when they started getting personal, like where I live and what I do for fun, I couldn't take it anymore, so I pointed over his shoulder, shouted "Pterodactyl!" and fucking ran for it. It was more of a power-walk, but, whatever.

Similarly, I was minding my own business in the movie section at Best Buy a few weeks ago when a random couple asked me if I had any recommendations, because they said, and I quote, "You look like someone with good taste in movies."

How the hell do you project that? I wasn't wearing a turtleneck and blazer, smoking a pipe, and petting a Siamese cat. I wasn't wearing 3D-glasses and holding a tub of popcorn either. I was just standing there staring at the clearance section. I told them *Romy & Michelle's High School Reunion* should've won a Grammy and bee-lined the hell out of there. I don't know why people bother me. It's not flattering. I just want to be left alone.

I'm worried that my look is too approachable. I try to project the opposite but still end up being accosted by panhandlers, rose peddlers, out-of-gas scammers, and garbage pickers who want to recap their life story. I wish I could just pump gas in peace. I consider that "me time," not "bug me time." Strangers in restaurants approach me when they need ketchup. Bums show me their bullet wounds. Goths show me their tats. Tourists ask me for directions. Chubby girls who're normally shy have no trouble complimenting me on my wristwatch. Strangers ask to borrow my phone at concerts. Lost, crying children cling to me in hotel lobbies. I swear I have "Jumper Cable Guy" written across my forehead. I'm afraid to leave my house, because someone might need an emergency kidney transplant and shout, "Hey, that guy will give us his!"

I don't understand. Why not the guy at the next table? Why not the happy couple over there? Why not the smiling mother in the corner booth? Why approach *me?* I wish I was scarier. I try to wear a scowl but it only makes people curious about my ethnicity. Is there nothing dissuading about me? Seriously, I wish I had anaconda eyes or my left arm was an octopus tentacle. Sometimes I even wish I was black. I just don't want to jumpstart stalled cars anymore. I seriously considered taking the jumper cables out of my trunk for good, but then I thought, "What if *my* battery dies? *Shit!* I can't win!"

There's a conveniently located Walgreens in my neighborhood that I can never set foot in again. I put a discomfort ban on the place thanks to my fucked up approachableness. I went there to pick up a few essentials. I put toothpaste, batteries, and butt-wiping paper on the counter. The girl behind the register was a short, chunky brunette wearing glasses. "How come you're all dressed up?" she said.

I looked down at my faded navy T-shirt and loose jeans. I glanced behind me expecting to see someone in a tuxedo, but I was the only one in line. "*Uh*, I'm not really that dressed up," I said while unsheathing my wallet.

I paid, took my bag, and was two steps from the door when she shouted, "Hey, wait!" She walked around the counter and trotted at me with an outstretched hand as if she was going to plunge it through my ribcage. After we shook hands, she said, "I'm Rebecca. Do you live around here?" We engaged in deflective chatter until she insisted we hang out on Saturday.

"Well," I said, "I'll be back in here soon, so we'll figure it out then, okay?"

I left knowing I could never go back. Now I have to drive to the Walgreens on the other side of town when I need a goddamn tube of chapstick. Thanks Rebecca, you friendly-ass bitch, thanks for ruining my *fucking LIFE!* You owe me like $6,000 in gas money!

Here's another one. I own an air hockey table. I was searching for one on Craigslist and found a good deal. When I went to check it out, a mother of two showed it to me in her attached garage. A few minutes later she said, "You know, my father runs a landscaping company. You should come work for us!" It was completely out of the blue. We weren't talking about her family, and I never said anything about needing a job. After we settled on a price for the game, I loaded it, drove away, and assumed our relationship was over.

Three days later she called and left a voicemail, saying, "Hey, hope you don't mind, I still had your number on my caller ID. My husband and I are having a barbecue this Saturday, and, well, you were just a really personable guy, *sooo* I was wondering if you'd like to come!" I didn't think haggling was a shoe-in to making friends. And I wasn't interested in meeting any of the desperate women she wanted to hook me up with either.

I also own a bubble hockey table. Again, I saw an ad for it online. When I went to check it out, a mom and her teenage daughter showed it to me in their detached garage. I told them I'd take it, backed my truck in, and started disassembling the legs. I was working up a fresh sheen of sweat when the daughter came out and asked if I wanted to stay for dinner. *Stay for dinner?* Let's ask this random guy, who could be a psycho rapist, to come inside with two females for pork chops. If I was picking up your bubble hockey in a horse drawn wagon after a three day journey, maybe I would, but nowadays, that's abnormal. In fact, I found it so odd that I got suspicious that *they* were psycho rapists. I started sizing them up, wondering if I could fend off their strangulations. When I told her I already ate dinner, she invited me in for a movie. "A movie?" I said. "Are you going to watch *Romy & Michelle's High School Reunion?*"

"I think we have that!" she said. A few seconds later, I peeled out of their driveway.

I want to know who's putting these people up to this. Seriously, did they lose a bet and were forced to befriend the next person they saw? I'd love to say it's because they want to make out with my puffy bottom lip, but I'm pretty sure they're simply picking me to be their new, non-sexual friend. If not, I wish they'd be more direct. There's nothing wrong with telling a stranger, "Hey, I'm being nice to you because I want to do you." Well, most guys don't mind anyway.

I won't be a complete chump though. Some of the instances I encounter seem flirtatious and shouldn't be confused with the convergence phenomenon. Like the time I was test driving used cars at a Chevy dealership and the saleswoman who drove around with me said, "We should get some chow mein for lunch." I'm pretty sure that's code for, "You should chow my bush." My test drive skills are like funky cold medina. Or maybe she was a psycho rapist. Or maybe she was just hungry.

The cafeteria in my office building is run by an all-female, all-Hispanic staff. After weeks of putting up with a half-dozen Latinas giggling every time I ordered food, the thick-accented girl working the cash register finally asked, "You wants to know why we always laughs when we sees you?"

"Actually, yes, very much," I said.

"It's because you look like Selena's husband," she said. "If you had long hair, I'd be like *mmm hmm* (as in, I'd cream my pants)."

Aye mommee! She gave me a complimentary oatmeal raisin cookie for putting up with what I long assumed was belittling mockery. I wish I would've known sooner because they were giving me a complex. Every time one of them would look at me, snicker, and turn away, I'd nervously check my zipper, brush my nose for dangling boogers, and head for the men's room to see if my hair was messed up. Turns out they just wanted to gangbang me while I wailed on an electric guitar. Who knew. I went back to my desk and Googled "Selena's husband." I don't know what those mamacitas were talking about, I'm not Mexican. Regardless, I started growing my hair out.

I've been hit on by gay men a couple times. One time was at Suncoast Pictures as I was checking out the back cover of a Jean Claude Van Damme DVD, which is pretty much the rainbow bumper sticker of movie perusal. A skinny guy with curly hair and one hand on the back of his neck said in an effeminate tone, "Oh, that is a *must see!* Are you *into* Jean Claude?" I could tell by his accentuation that he meant, "Is your *penis* into Jean Claude?"

Conversely, I hit on a gay guy once because he was the final obstacle between me and a flight to Vegas. I missed my original flight, and he was the agent at the Delta Airlines counter. He said, "I'm sorry, but the next flight is overbooked. There's nothing I can do for you, sir."

I said, "What a drag…*hey*…that's a nice watch you've got there," while putting a bi-curious finger to my chin. I got to Vegas. I don't want to talk about it.

I attempt civility with the cleaning crew in my office because I'd feel like a jerk if I ignored the person who's reaching at my feet to empty the rotting banana peels out of my wastebasket. For a long time it was an old man who barely spoke English, but one day he was replaced by a girl of indiscernible age, maybe seventeen, maybe thirty-seven, but definitely Frankenstein's sister. I stuck to my routine. Around five o'clock she'd grab my trash can and I'd acknowledge it by saying, "Thank you."

Courtesy backfired the morning I found a folded-up love note sitting on my chair. Now, before I relay the contents, I want to assure you that I'm not writing this to stroke my ego. It's way too late for that. Anyhow, the note started, "I've been dreaming about being in your strong arms. I want to stare into your beautiful eyes and talk until the sun comes up."

I thought, "Sorry *sistah*, but I've gotta work in the morning!"

And for the record, my arms aren't that strong, so if she was hoping to be carried anywhere, it better be within four or five steps max. Everything she wrote was spelled phonetically instead of grammatically. For example, the front of the note read, "Your hott!!!" The back read, "Hope too here from you!" You get the idea. In conclusion she asked me to check one of two boxes, "Yes" or "No."

I was like, "Fuck..." and begrudgingly got out my pen and notepad to write back a polite explanation that started with, "I'm flattered but..." I wrote a couple lines but eventually gave up and used the out she made available. Admittedly, checking the "No" box felt horrible. It felt like telling your five-year-old daughter you don't like the picture she drew for you. But I got over it because I don't have kids.

Being subjected to unwelcome advances left me feeling somewhat violated. It gave me a rare glimpse into how attractive women must feel when a guy like me hits on them. And let me tell ya, it's icky. These poor women are just trying to go about their business when another unwelcome, schmoozing creep pops up to bug them. I think I finally understand how irritating that is. So ladies, I'm sorry for all the times it was me. Really, I feel terrible. I'll tell you what, let me get your number so I can call to apologize...*and find out what kind of panties you're wearing.* Yeah, that's right. We should totally hook up later!

Nevertheless, most of the accosting I'm subject to has nothing to do with flirting. I'm not bombarded due to Hollywood looks. I'm an ordinary-looking motherfucker. Instead, it's as if my soul exudes an aura of friendliness, like I was a used car salesman or Walmart greeter in a past life. It's as if strangers already know that I'm completely harmless despite that I want them to think I'm a psycho rapist. It's as if they recognize me from a reoccurring dream or something. Wasps and dogs hone in on me too, so maybe I'm emanating enticement pheromones. Who knows.

Don't get me wrong though, I get it. Last summer I stopped at a red light in front of a coin car wash. Coincidentally, when I looked over, I saw my dad hosing down his Buick in one of the bays. When I beeped my horn and waved, my dad, along with the people in the other bays, looked up, smiled, and waved back. They couldn't see one another and each assumed they were the recipient. I'm sure they wondered who I was after I drove off, but it probably brightened their day nonetheless. The point is that we're all eager for a friendly face to say hi. We all want to connect with another human being. It's a lonely planet, and we're all desperate for a friend, but, seriously, the next person who approaches me is getting kicked in the crotch – man, woman, or child. I'll even kick a fucking dog in the nuts, I don't care.

Tweety from Compton

My mind has an egg timer that flips when I'm listening to someone blabber about something boring. Maybe it's their job, car troubles, medication, or new carpet. When the timer runs out, no matter what they're saying, I interrupt and say, "Is that when you beat your meat?" Then I make sexually explicit hand gestures and sounds. Try it. Adapt if necessary. For example, if someone is droning on, "So, yeah, this clunking noise is coming from my driver-side wheel well. It's most noticeable when the car hasn't warmed up yet. My mechanic checked it out and said it was the ball bearing, but I said, 'I'm pretty sure I had those replaced last year.' So he said, 'Well, it could be your strut mount...''

I'll interrupt, "Oh yeah? And is that when he whipped out his wang and started stroking his sausage right in front of you?" Then I pantomime an enthusiastic jackoff motion.

See how it shocks some entertainment value into the exchange? Did you notice how I customized the interruption to fit that particular situation? Feel free to use it on anyone, except maybe your parents, because that'd be weird.

There seems to be a run-of-the-mill, factory-produced, generic personality going around these days called, "Hi, I'm boring. Let me bore the living shit out of you." Reruns of city council meetings broadcast on community access channels are more exciting than these motherfuckers. So, in an effort to remedy this issue, let's do a little self-analysis on your bore factor.

First of all, if you have no form of expression, technically, you're boring. You'd be more exciting if your hobby was gluing rocks to paper, which is useful in creating wildlife dioramas. With the dull breed of humans being churned out in today's society, I'm happy to find someone who played the clarinet in eighth grade. Granted, accusations of boredom don't apply to everyone. I base that statement on the fact that when I peruse my friends in any online community, I see photography, art, music, and swashbuckling listed as their hobbies. They might suck at their hobbies, but that's beside the point. Whether it's out of procrastination or narrow-mindedness, it seems like most people are only interested in money, celebrities, partying, and getting laid – all fine pursuits, mind you, but better when combined with activities that have some depth, history, or intrigue.

The average person spends each morning in rush hour traffic, goes to Subway for lunch, watches something on TNT when they get home, and goes to bed after a handful of Pringles. On Saturday, they sleep in, do laundry, eat at Chili's, drink a bunch of booze, and pass out. They don't play an instrument. They don't read books. They don't draw.

They don't bake. They don't create anything, study anything, or practice anything useful. Their lives are devoid of uniquity, culture, and learning.

To boring people, cellulite can be the most important thing in the fucking universe. I'm starting to believe conspiracy theories about the government putting fluoride in our water as a mind-numbing agent to prevent uprisings, because it seems like everyone's main hobby these days is gossip, whether it's about Kim Kardashian's cellulite or the cottage cheese on "Paul's ex-girlfriend, Tracy." Boring people are always more interested in the lives of others, and I don't blame them. Fundamentally, I have nothing against gossip. I'm like everyone in the nail salon. I want to know who's getting a divorce and who's cheating, but boring people rely so heavily on gossip to communicate that they lose all social aptitude. It's like the country's filled with homeschoolers whose mom's didn't bother getting their GEDs.

America is brimming with boring humanoids because pop media lambastes us into thinking that listening to music without words, growing beans and artichokes, collecting butterflies, or having a model railroad is for losers. Such thinking turns interesting people into outcasts, which in turn causes eccentricity. Eccentricity is a tightrope. Some eccentric people want everyone to experience Django Reinhardt, while others want to join a militia and bomb city hall. Pop media saturation dulls the masses and is a forbearer of rebellion. Celebrity cellulite will systematically end civilization. You've been warned.

On the flipside, dispelling popular people who're considered cool or hot isn't necessarily the answer either. You have to cut through the fat to equalize your disdain for boring, eccentric, *and* popular people based on how much heart they lack. Finding a virtuous balance has been a battle ever since we were teens. Everyone relates to this character challenge because, while most of us openly appreciate good-natured people, the rest are like Darth Vader in that they're jerks with a glimmer of good buried inside of them. In other words, even jerks recognize other jerks as undesirable. It's like the fact that fat, ugly people still find fit, beautiful people attractive. It's like that Dave Chappelle skit where he played a blind, black Klansman. Being a target doesn't necessarily deter anyone from targeting people like themselves. The biggest douchebag I know refers to guys he doesn't like as douchebags. Boring people are boring to boring people too.

After I escaped the awkwardness of high school, it turned out the "cool" life was a farce, and it was the geeks who were genuinely enjoying themselves. Join the geek revolution! I have. I attended the epitome of Geekdom last weekend – the *Motor City Comic Con*. Cooler people were eating in the mall food court, perusing their recent purchase of *Total Club Hits vol. 19*. Later, they primped for hours, waited in line, and paid twenty bucks to get into (cue obnoxious DJ hype voice) CLUB DOMINATE-NATE-NATE-NATE-NATE. When inside, they complained about the lack of vodka flavors, ripped on people's outfits, and turned their nose up to anyone who walked by.

At comic con I hung out with scout troopers, ring wraiths, DC villains, and centerfolds. The guys from *Boondock Saints* were there. My celeb look-a-like Dean Cain was there. Even the Soup Nazi from *Seinfeld* was there. "NO SOUP FOR YOU!" I saw Kenny Baker, the midget inside R2-D2, waddling down one of the vendor aisles. "Hey, Kenny Baker!" I said.

"Oy!" he replied.

"You and Artoo are *one!*" I said, as I raised my fist for Shake-spearean emphasis.

"Well, we both have achy joints!" he joked as he darted off. I'd been drinking. Hopefully he was too.

My post-show fanboy tradition is reviewing convention finds over a Denny's Dagwood. I was there with the crew of guys I regularly talk sci-fi and comic books with. Coincidentally, they resemble Emperor Palpatine, the Rancor Keeper, Sparkplug Witwicky, and Clark Kent. My geek crew and I laughed the entire time. How could you *not* laugh while wearing an Admiral Ackbar mask with matching Mon Calamari hands and replying to everything with, "It's a *trap!*"

"Vince, could you pass the ketchup?"

"It's a *trap!*"

In addition to the Ackbar getup, I also got a vintage Stormtrooper blaster from 1980 with working sound effects. I used it to shoot our waitress' big butt every time she walked away. I picked up a *Megaman* shirt bragging, "I Beat the 8 Master Robots." I got bootleg *Sealab 2021* DVDs, a Punisher statue, a Bo Duke carded action figure, Frank Miller's collected work on *Daredevil*, and a Lando Calrissian disguise which consisted of nothing more than a black, stick-on Billy Dee Williams mustache.

I waited in line to get Peter Mayhew's autograph on a Chewbacca crossbow toy. Mayhew, the actor who played Chewbacca, looks like a Wookie in person and seemed pretty brain dead. He illegibly scribbled his name in gold marker on the box. When I requested that he write *Chewbacca* beside it, he turned to his agent who muttered, "Okay, but write *small.*" Overall, the signature looks like Chewbacca pissed on it from twenty paces. Regardless, the convention was awesome. Yes, it has its share of pale, overweight, smelly, zit-faced attendees, but that's part of its charm.

Don't get me wrong, I love mindless leisure activities too. Hanging out in bars is plain old-fashioned *great*. I love sitting around with my chach-bag pals, sharing pitchers, doing shots, watching sports, throwing darts, and messing with waitresses. I'm certainly not anti-TV either. I have a 57" LCD screen in my living room that gets ample use. I also love fast food. Half of the items on Wendy's value menu are surrounding me right now. I love chain restaurants too. I've been eating the Triple Play at Chili's since it was called the Mombo Combo. I even like shopping. I can spend hours in a TJ Maxx sifting through discounted designer gear. And when the weekend hits, I listen to radio stations that repeat the same top twenty songs over and over.

Scolding the populous for being boring is not to bash common activities by any stretch. My point is, if the *only* data you're retaining is the current cast of *Dancing with the Stars*, *Survivor*, or *American Idol*, maybe it's time to buy a cookbook, scrapbook, sketchbook, guidebook, telescope, metal detector, aquarium, piccolo, or *something* to add depth to your trite existence. Seriously, anything is better than nothing. Get a goddamn potted plant for Pete's sake! Here's an example:

I was at a cocktail party thrown by a friend of a friend and got into a pleasant conversation with the host's wife about art. Her name was Sophie. She was in her early twenties, petite, and had an olive complexion. She had long, raven hair and was sporting a generous amount of cleavage in a lacey, black top. She got married young, and, in my opinion, her husband was a dweeby, arrogant little Smurf.

I was admiring a Renoir print in their hallway when Sophie walked up and introduced herself. I told her I had a Renoir print above my kitchen sink, and that I recently viewed some of his work at the Art Institute of Chicago. "Me too!" Sophie exclaimed. "I was just there two months ago! It was one of the greatest experiences of my life!"

We discussed the museum's remarkable Impressionist collection. She laughed at my jokes about Manet being pissed at Monet for copycatting everything from his brushstrokes to his beard. We even swooned over the delicious parfaits served in the museum cafe. Then she said, "I've heard that *you're* quite the artist!" One of my friend's wives had mentioned it to her. I told Sophie I was currently into Japanese styles and that I preferred working with a standard Pentel pencil, Prismacolor markers, and Alvin Penstix. She seemed genuinely interested in hearing about my illustrations and the methods I used to store or display them.

Sophie effortlessly laughed at my quips and continuously touched my arm. A Madeleine Peyroux CD was playing in the background. She sipped on a glass of Chardonnay, I had a Manhattan. Our exchange felt like a scene from a Woody Allen movie, and I was thoroughly enjoying it. "I don't tell many people this," she said, "but painting is kind of my *secret* passion."

"No kidding?" I said. "Well, I'd love to see your work!"

"I'm not very good," she said. "I've never had formal training or anything. It's just a hobby."

"That's awesome," I said, "and you don't have to be shy about it. I enjoy *any* artistic endeavor no matter how humble."

"Okay, but there's no way I'm bringing it out for everyone to see," she said. "You'll have to come with me into the other room."

I followed Sophie down the hallway into an unused but furnished bedroom. She reached into a drawer and pulled out a large wire-bound pad and handed it to me. "I'm so nervous!" she said. "I hope you don't hate it!"

Her meek manner was inviting. She made me feel as if she looked up to me and respected my artistic opinions despite that we'd just met. We sat on the edge of the bed. She sat close enough to maintain body contact. There was good energy between us, a fresh and flirty vibe. I was excited to see her work and eagerly flipped open the cover of the pad.

The first painting was of an animal, specifically, a coyote. To be more specific, it was a cartoon coyote. To be even more specific, it was Wile E. Coyote. In addition, Wile E. Coyote was portrayed wearing gangster rap getup while striking a Kris Kross pose. Furthermore, the quality of the art was on par with that of an average fifth-grader. I held my expression and turned to Sophie, waiting for her to burst into laughter to confirm my suspicion that she was pulling my leg. I thought she might say, "Just kidding, that pad belongs to my nephew! *Hahaha.* This one is mine." Instead, she stared back, doe-eyed, anxiously awaiting my reaction. I slowly started nodding and said, "Wow. *Yes.*"

"Really?" she said.

"Yeah, really, *wow,*" I said, still expecting her to shove me, laugh, and say, "Look at your face! I got you good!" but she continued sitting there sheepishly.

The next page was the Tasmanian Devil wearing a thick gold chain and unlaced Timberland boots, flashing a Westside gang sign. Next was Marvin the Martian impersonating Vanilla Ice. The next page was Bugs Bunny if he were part of 2Pac's entourage, then Sylvester and Tweety from Compton, then Foghorn Leghorn with a non-Acme gun shoved in his baggy Fubu jeans. When I got to thug life Daffy, she said, "You can probably tell that urban, hip-hop *Looney Tunes* is sort of my thing."

"No shit!" I said with poignant sarcasm. She giggled.

When I got to bust-a-cap-in-yo-ass Elmer Fudd, she said, "I just use cheap poster paint from Target."

"No shit?" I said with subdued sarcasm.

She needed a lot of affirmation, and rightly so, but I blamed myself for insisting to see her stuff, so I laid the compliments on thick. "You're *really* good at this!" I said. "This Elmer Fudd should be in a frame next to that Renoir in your hallway!"

"Thank you *so much!*" she said. Then she clammed up a little and said, "My husband thinks they're kind of...*stupid.*"

"Well, your husband wouldn't know good art if it walked up and kicked him in the dong!" I said. Sophie laughed.

Even though I wished her paintings were of pine tree landscapes and still-life pottery, I said, "At least your paintings aren't of pine tree landscapes and still-life pottery!"

I don't know why Sophie was hell bent on superimposing Warner Bros. characters and G-Unit, but, to be honest, it thoroughly bewildered and delighted me. One thing was certain, Sophie embraced something peculiar, profound, and far from boring. I wouldn't display one of her pieces in my living room, or attic for that matter, but I give Sophie mad props for doing it. One thing's for certain, I'll never forget what I saw that day.

If you suspect yourself of being a bore, try collecting something. Collecting is good for the soul. It gives you purpose and a renewed sense of awareness. It doesn't matter what you collect – comic books, die cast toys, farming tools, postage stamps, Coke stuff, Civil War relics, heads in formaldehyde, dolls that come to life at night – again, anything is better than nothing.

If you don't know what to collect, revert to your childhood. You had to like something as a kid. Hunt down your favorite records and frame them. Collect posters from your favorite movies. If you enjoyed the beach, start a seashell collection. If you lived by the railroad tracks, build a model railroad. If your dad took you to baseball games, collect MLB memorabilia. If he was drunk when he took you, collect shot glasses. If you were chubby, collect Hostess merchandise. It's that easy. And trust me, no matter what you choose, there's already an entire subculture of people madly collecting it. Thimbles, scratch 'n sniff stickers, and burlap sacks have their own associations and newsletters.

People with hobbies are more passionate about life and therefore less boring. It's the difference between a guy who works to pay his cable bill, and a guy who works so he can afford a mint condition 1979 Ricky Raccoon Scooter to complete his Fabuland Lego collection. At the end of the day, who's more prone to feel like life is pointless? It ain't Lego guy. Lego guy could crash land in the middle of the Sahara with no supplies and make it out alive just to get his hands on that Raccoon Scooter. Non-Lego guy would die on impact.

Another reason to take up a hobby is to prevent yourself from becoming your career. Are you only capable of talking about your job? If you answered *yes* you should immediately enter the Kumite and yell,

"Frank Dux sucks Chong Li's dick!" which I've heard will get you killed. I'm sure there's a ton of drama to be told about your dental hygienist or retail job, but I'd rather hear about your uncle's miniature castle collection. Sorry, but your office politics blow. What are they going to say at your funeral? "The only thing I remember about Jim was that he couldn't stand his regional manager because he dogged on his TPS reports." Your eulogy would sound better with the line, "Jim was an avid salsa dancer."

Sadly, our generation is severely lacking people with hobbies and personal endeavors. As hip-hop Elmer Fudd once said, *"Niggas be boring as shit!"* Keep in mind that get-rich-quick schemes and anything hateful doesn't count as a hobby, you're just an ass. If all of this "boring talk" reminds you of yourself, then do yourself a favor and dust off your old clarinet, buy a deep fryer, or order a goddamn Chia Pet. At the very least go borrow a few books from the library. If not that, then please borrow Chewbacca's crossbow from him so you can shoot me in the temple the next time you're rambling on about your car troubles.

Bradley's Going Pro

If you know what's good for you, steer clear of Ecorse, Michigan. It's a dilapidated, low-income city just south of Detroit that's only good for getting drugs, prostitutes, and speeding tickets. A meth-head hooker cop gave me a speeding ticket there last month. I was on my way to my parents' place for dinner and was forced to take a construction detour through the heart of Ecorse, and by "heart" I mean *anus*. A jerk-off cop trying to meet his quota pulled me over for going 34 in a 30 mph zone. He wrote me up for going five over. I'm not surprised. The city's entire budget comes from non-resident traffic fines. The detour is a sham to get people who can afford fines to drive through.

Today I spent the morning in Ecorse court. Ecorse court is funny, but you aren't allowed to laugh, at least not out loud. You can laugh, but only on the inside. Laughing is disrespectful to the judge. The judge likes to be called "Your Honor." "Your Honor" just wants "your money." There were over thirty people in the courtroom. I was the only one wearing a tie. I was the only one *not* wearing something advertising an NBA team or Fat Albert. Next time I will not wear a tie. A guy with cornrows wearing an Iverson jersey that hung to his knees had his case dismissed. The chump wearing a tie got a $165 dollar fine. Wearing a tie in Ecorse court is for suckers. Also, the judge is a 76ers fan.

Before my speeding ticket was addressed, the court held a case between two of Ecorse's finest. They were a couple of big, black broads who were neighbors disputing an altercation that occurred after one accused the other of stealing a bag of corndogs from her freezer. The argument escalated and resulted in one of the women being pushed through a window where she "sustained lacerations." The transcript would read as follows:

Judge: Were any words exchanged before the incident?

Woman 1: Um yeah, she said to me (whispering) "You, um, you a bit…" (She proceeded to cover her mouth as if she almost said something naughty.)

Judge: Go ahead and tell me the *exact* words that were exchanged if you remember them.

Woman 1: (Bellowing into microphone) She said to me, "You a bitches, you a bitches, *YOU A BITCHES!*"

Judge: (Speaking to the other woman) And did she say anything to you at that point?

Woman 2: She said, "You a bitches!" She called me *a bitches!* She said "You a bitches, you a bitches, *YOU A BITCHES!*"

Apparently, after being called "A bitches," Woman 2 pushed Woman 1 through a pane of glass, proving that she was indeed "A bitches." Corndogs will do that to you. They're so fucking delicious, they'll drive you bonkers! I'm pretty sure the Civil War started because of stolen corndogs. A lot of people don't know this, but the forbidden fruit in the Garden of Eden was a corndog. Eve was like, "Hey Adam, which way is that mustard tree?"

"It's right next to the napkin tree," he replied.

Later on, I retold an adjective-laden, colorful version of the Ecorse court incident to some friends and was granted a few laughs. It made me think about the ability to spin an amusing tale and how much it's appreciated. If it has several peaks and doesn't drag on, a real life story beats a sitcom recap, sporting event review, or retold joke any day. Stories about taking a drunken crap on someone's front lawn, breaking your collarbone, vomiting in public, hooking up with a drunk fatty, and other forms of ripened embarrassment are utterly amusing. A good storyteller can even entertain with lesser events, like having a one-armed waiter or killing a huge-ass spider. However, some subject matter makes for storytelling disaster. Topping the list are stories about the cute thing your infant, niece, or pet did.

Here's the disclaimer: If your dog bit off your uncle's nutsack, please tell us. If your dog relentlessly sniffed your mother-in-law's cooch during a dinner party, that's not bad either. If your six-year-old niece blurted out the F-word when she saw Minnie Mouse at Disneyworld, give us the quick version. If your four-year-old blinded a dog with hairspray while trying to give it a mohawk, that'd be a good story. If your baby sprayed pee directly into your mouth, go ahead and run us through it. That's the disclaimer.

It's all about prudence, people – knowing which occurrences are story worthy and which should be locked in a secret treasure trove in your heart forever, because no one else gives a hoot. I used to have a white Persian cat that would chase a flashlight beam so frantically that it'd slide across the wood floors knocking over potted plants. It amused me, but I never told anyone because nobody would give a shit. I did, however, once relay a story involving that cat.

I bought an Ikea media shelf, laid out the parts in my living room, and committed to spending the entire evening assembling it. My cat, being a curious little fucker, wanted to stand on every plank and paw at every screw I set down. "Will you please get out of here?" I said. "It's already going to take forever to finish this without you getting in the way." Its feelings now hurt, it wandered off.

In the meantime, to be a better follower of instructions, I poured myself a stiff Crown & Coke. I took a sip, set it on the coffee table, and got my build on. Fifteen minutes later I thought, "Oh crap, I forgot about my drink!" I looked over and saw my cat standing on the table with its head crammed in the glass, lapping up daddy's nectar. "Aw, you little *shit!*" I said, while lifting her off the table.

When I set her on the floor, she walked face first into a heating vent. She pawed at the ground and got into a poop stance, so I grabbed her and put her in the litter box, but she stood there motionless. Eventually she stepped out, stumbled into the kitchen, convulsed a few times, and projectile vomited everywhere. It's okay to tell your friends a story about your blitzed cat yacking its guts out if you keep it brief.

A single mother from my congregation told me an appreciable story about her five-year-old boy. One Sunday morning, while leaving for church, he said, "Mommy, do you have your purse?"

"Yes I do!" she answered.

"Do you have your Bible?" he asked.

"Yes, sir," she said.

"Do you have your songbook?" he asked.

"Uh-huh."

Then he said, "Do you have your *vagina?*"

See, that's funny, *vagina*.

The congregation used to divide members up into smaller groups to meet for weeknight book-studies in people's homes. It was the lowest attended Jehovah's Witness meeting, so they finally cancelled it after realizing that between Sunday services, Tuesday night meetings, Thursday evening book study, Saturday morning field ministry, mandated family study hours, and preparation for all that religious fervor, members didn't have time to do laundry. And with all the fancy duds Witnesses wear, they need time for laundry.

I used to attend the book-study in the basement of a guy named Brent. Brent had a preschooler named Max who had a penchant for saying funny things. On one occasion, the conductor was reviewing the Genesis account and asked an easy question aimed at the children in attendance. He asked, "Who did God have guarding the entrance to the Garden of Eden?"

Brent whispered the answer into Max's ear. He said, "Raise your hand and say, 'Two cherubs'."

Max raised his hand up high, the conductor called on him, and Max enthusiastically said, "Two Japs!"

Everyone burst out laughing. I felt bad when Max got pouty and buried his head in his Noah's Ark coloring book, but his answer provided an amusing visual – God sitting up there racking his brain over who should guard the entrance to Eden, and then it dawns on him, the answer is obvious, "Two Japs!" I pictured two samurai warriors.

Max went through a rhyming phase too. It was mostly basic stuff, like if someone said, "That's funny," Max would follow with, "That's funny *bunny!*" But when someone in the group used the expression, "You rock!" Max hollered out, "You rock *with your cock!*" His parents were embarrassed, but I got a cool new saying. Nevertheless, such instances are few and far between. More often than not – infant, niece, and pet stories are mucho lame-o.

You've heard it before. "The other day, it was *sooo* cute, I came home and Bumpkins was *sooo* excited to see me. She was running with her little paws on the tile and slipped on the rug (cue annoying whiny voice) and her cute *wittle* nose slid into my shoes, and she made the funniest little noise, *arf arf.* It was *sooo* funny!" Not really. Can I please punch you now? Can I punch your dog too? Can I at least punch myself? Don't put your friends through that crap.

If your niece hugged you and told you she doesn't want you to leave, keep it to yourself. If your kid put a bucket on his head and said, "I'm Buzz White-year," be internally amused and move on. If your nephew gets excited about Pokémon cards, nobody fucking cares. If your seven-year-old knows all the words to a bunch of Lady Gaga songs, don't tell me about it as if I'll be tickled. I like kids and all, but when I hear something like that, I just want to uppercut your kid in the stomach and tell him to drop dead. Before you consider telling a story about how cute your sister's kid looked in a snowsuit, or how your beagle gives you pouty eyes when resting in your lap, do this calculation – think about how excited you are and reduce it by 99.9%, because that's the level of interest your listeners will have.

This message is especially important for new dads. While watching the game or playing poker, they'll blindside longtime drinking buddies with, "Dude, my little Brittany is adorable, man." Stop it. Just...please...stop. Go somewhere else if you want to reassure yourself that having a kid was the right choice, because we don't give a flying squirrelly fuck. If you finish that sentence, I'm crossing you off my list of guys to invite over. Check yourself, old friend, recover and end it properly, "My little Brittany is adorable...but I wonder how much I could get for her in Mexico."

Here's the thing, if you're complaining one week about your baby keeping you up all night, spitting-up on your favorite shirt, tearing apart your movie collection, and being so fussy at a restaurant that you had to take your prime rib and baked potato to go, which we all know does not reheat well, don't bother telling me a couple weeks later that having a kid is awesome and rewarding, it sounds flakey. Sorry, but not sleeping, being hosed with vomit, losing my kung fu movies, and not being able to eat at my favorite restaurants doesn't sound "awesome and rewarding." In my self-centered world, sleeping in, looking spiffy, having a meticulous movie collection, and dining out are pretty much the best things ever. A couple hugs combined with an "I wuv you, da-da," isn't going to make up for all of that torment.

I have several friends who are new parents, and I appreciate when they're candid about it. I don't need it sugarcoated, I can handle it when they say, "Every day, I'm *this close* to throwing my kid off a cliff." When I run into an old pal who had children, I usually ask, "How's the kid thing going?" Here are some of the honest answers I've heard:

"*Ehh.* It's more for the chick."

"Well, my little guy and I aren't really friends yet. In fact, he's kind of my mortal enemy."

"Not bad, but my advice to anyone who's considering having kids is to wait until you're *completely* done using your time for things you enjoy."

"Dude, my life's over. I'm just a dad now. I've got the dad bod and everything."

Another daddy torture method I've been hearing lately goes like this, "I got Bradley one of those little toy hockey sets, and let me tell ya, that kid can *really* shoot a puck!"

Listen, I'll gladly have a discussion with you about how Alex Ovechkin or Al MacInnis "can really shoot a puck," but not your five-year-old. Bradley doesn't have natural talent, and he's not going pro. Bradley's going to grow up to be a beer-bellied loser like daddy and daddy's friends. While we're on the topic, quit giving me wallet-sized studio portraits of your funky looking kid. He's not cute. He looks like the Creature from the Black Lagoon. I feel guilty throwing them out, but the only way I'm putting his ugly mug up on my fridge is if I'm trying to suppress my appetite.

There are subtle ways to even the scales though. One of my old drinking buddies has three kids now, so I hooked them up with the game *Hungry Hungry Hippos*. I did it as sort of a gag gift, knowing that the racket, mayhem, fighting, and lost marbles that game produces is legendary. Giving them a junior drum set would've just made me an asshole. I had *Hungry Hungry Hippos* when I was a kid. My brothers and I loved that game up until the day my dad, who was working midnights at the time, came downstairs and stomped the shit out of it. Here's an insider tip: If you buy one for your friend's kids, spend a few extra bucks and grab a vintage one off eBay. The real marbles that came with the old version are *way* louder than the new plastic ones.

Tambini Tone

The greatest impersonation I've ever done took place at a radiator manufacturer I used to work for. The Quality Control Manager was a towering, bald, deaf man named Greg Tambini. Tambini wasn't 100% deaf, only 95%. He could "hear" with the assistance of two earmuff-sized hearing aids that made him look like Lobot from Cloud City. He was difficult to understand because he could barely hear his own voice. The result was that he sounded like he was speaking from the bottom of a pool over an airport PA system.

For reasons unknown, the gods gifted me with the ability to do a spot-on impersonation of Tambini's muffled voice. Sure, it was bad for ethical reasons, but it made me and my work pals chuckle, which in essence was bringing happiness to others, so that kind of made it okay. Someday, karma will probably pay me back by giving me a deaf child with huge, furry, mutant ears. Still, even when the tabloids nickname him *Bat Boy*, you won't hear me complaining, "Life's not fair!" Well, *you* might, but Greg Tambini won't. I'll be like, "Man, this sucks!" but I'll say it in Tambini's aquatic voice and perpetuate the cycle. Then I'll take my son spelunking. He finds comfort in the caves.

Anyhow, you know how people in movies access their secret lab with a voice recognition system? A female computer voice says, "Please state your name."

Patrick Stewart says, "Charles...Xavier."

The computer replies, "Access granted. Welcome Professor." Well, I'm confident I could get into Greg Tambini's secret lab via mimicry. Unfortunately, though, Tambini didn't have a kick-ass secret lab – not that I knew of anyway – so the most thorough use I ever made of my talent was in a company shitter.

One afternoon, I entered the men's room and saw my boss' beat-up, brown leather boat shoes under the stall divider. He was obviously going number two. My boss, John Culver, had known Tambini since they hired in twenty years ago. I stepped up to the urinal, unsheathed my potty maker, and, since no one else was in there, figured pretending to be Tambini was worth a try. I got in Tambini mode, adjusting my voice box to sound like a Speak & Spell with a sinus infection, and said, "Is that you in there, John?"

"*Heeyyyy* Greg," he replied, "how the hell are ya?"

"*Aww*," I moaned, "Marino (the CEO) is really pushing to get the Caterpillar tractor job out ahead of schedule, but I told him, 'Hell no! There's no way! It'll never happen! Not in a jillion years!' He *pisses* me off!"

I paused to calm my laugh reflex. I never realized how funny it was to say, "He *pisses* me off!" in Tambini tone. While John replied, I stared at the ceiling with my mouth wide open, laughing without sound, or, in other words, doing what Tambini sees when people laugh.

John said in a sympathetic tone, "I know, I know, he's always pushing us to the limit, 'Get it out, get it out!' We can't keep up. He wants the impossible. He just doesn't get it."

"I think he's a *bastard!*" I said. "A real son of a *bitch!*" I tried to raise my voice but nearly gagged because the impression requires pushing my tongue against my tonsils. "I don't care," I continued, "I'll say it to his face. 'You son of a *bitch*, we can't finish the Caterpillar job!'" I faltered from character and said the last line in a hearing-impaired Louis Armstrong voice. I repeated, "Son of a *bitch!*" and accidentally snorted, but recovered by pretending to clear my throat and cough.

"I'm with ya, Greg," John said. "He's going to run this company into the ground." He ranted for a minute while I made deaf agreement grunts. Since it was going so well, I figured I may as well squeeze in a little self-serving plug, so I said, "Hey, how's that Vincent kid working out? I like him. He seems pretty sharp."

"Vincent?" John said. "Yeah, he's a pretty good kid. I like him too." *Word.*

I was shaking with silent laughter as John began unrolling toilet paper, so I tried to compose myself for a grand finale. I wanted to top it off with something incredibly inappropriate but was on the verge of completely losing it and had to abort the mission. I wanted to tell John that his deuce smelled rancid, or say something about motor-boating the owner's daughter, but could only pull it together enough to say, "Okay, bye, John."

I exited the bathroom, walked straight into the parking lot, hid behind a dumpster, and laughed my ass off. It was the whole "watery eyes, forehead vein bulging, out of breath" deal. John had no suspicion of being had. All I could hope for was that he'd reference our exchange with the real Tambini and it'd result in confusion. I hoped John would walk by Tambini the next day and say, "Fuck that Caterpillar job, eh Greg?" and Tambini would say, "What the hell are you talking about?" I high-fived myself.

I can do a pretty good Gilbert Gottfried. I can nail Clive Owen, Frodo, and Yoda. I can do Heath Ledger's Joker and Michael Caine's Alfred. I could get into Jerry Seinfeld's secret lair. You'll do a double-take if I karaoke James Taylor, Garth Brooks, or anything by the Counting Crows. I'm decent at singing *Hakuna Matata* as Timon, Pumbaa, *and* Simba. My Sean Connery is so good that I use it on my voicemail greeting. I do a convincing Seth Rogen, Officer Slater, and Fogell from *Superbad*. Oddly enough, I can also do a spot on impression of a newborn baby. However, ultimate impersonation amusement doesn't come from celebrities – it comes from nailing the phrases, tics, and mannerisms of nutty people in your daily life. Your glam rock neighbor, your nerdy cousin, the dopey chick working at Arby's, a persnickety bank teller, your friend's valley-girl wife, your offbeat father-in-law – they're a gold mine of material.

On the other hand, while everyone loves a good impersonation, few truly enjoy being impersonated, since most impressions accentuate a person's unflattering quirks. I know a black guy named Davis who reminds me a lot of Carlton from *The Fresh Prince of Bel-Air*. I can nail Davis' key phrases, such as referring to everything as *dope*, *fly*, or, his personal favorite – *off the hook!* His laugh is the phonetic pronunciation of "*Ha ha ha.*" When you ask him, "How's it going?" he always replies, "Chillin', chillin'." He says all the aforementioned things while doing a hand gesture that appears to repeatedly stuff a vote in a ballot box. Whenever Davis isn't around, my friends badger me to impersonate him because they think it's hilarious. Before you get the wrong idea, you should know that Davis and I get along just fine. I do impersonations of him out of admiration – but, yeah, mostly to make people laugh.

One evening I was sitting across from him at Chili's and a girl named Paige said, "Davis, Vincent does a great impression of you! It's so funny! Show him Vince!" I just about shit myself. Davis' expression was easy to read. He looked slightly perturbed, a bit puzzled, and moderately betrayed.

"No, I don't," I said.

"Yeah, you do," Paige said.

"What're you talking about?" I said.

"It's so funny. Do it!" she said.

I sighed. Davis was waiting, his curiosity piqued. "You're retarded!" I told Paige, blowing off the entire notion. "I'm not good at impersonating anyone!" After that I stared at my chicken crispers and refused to look up.

Later, I scolded her. "What the *hell* is wrong with you?" I said. "Impersonating someone to their face is not *off the hook, ha ha ha.*"

I wish I could say the shame fizzled, but I get a sinking, sleazy feeling around Davis ever since that incident. The last time I saw him, I got worried because when I said, "Davis, how's it going, man?" instead of saying, "Chillin', chillin'," he just said, "Fine."

The same thing happened with my friend Gabe. I'm good at imitating a few of his odd mannerisms. For example, when explaining anything, he makes a gesture where he puts his palm in the air as if he's a tuxedoed waiter carrying a tray. He also shakes his head sporadically when talking and says, "Swear to god," way too much. He also has a hint of a lisp. My classic impersonation of Gabe is to hold the invisible tray, shake my head, and effeminately repeat something I once heard him say to his wife, "I swear to god, Ashley, go make me a burger."

I did the impersonation for everyone in our circle of friends with the exception of Gabe. It was funny until the time we were at a bar and my pal Dave, after a few cold ones, blurted out, "Gabe, have you ever seen Vincent's impression of you? It's hilarious!"

"Oh crap, not again," I thought. For the record, I like Gabe. I think he's a cool guy with a good sense of humor, but that doesn't mean he'd find a faggy impersonation of himself amusing. I panicked for a moment, and then I said, "No, I can't do Gabe, but I've been working on my Davis – *off the hook, chillin' chillin', ha ha ha!*"

As before, I think Gabe grew leery of me after getting wind of the fact that I may or may not have done demeaning impersonations of him to mutual friends without his knowledge. The moral of the story is that impersonating someone behind their back is nearly as bad as talking crap about them behind their back – so make sure they don't find out.

In my defense, Gabe pranked me pretty darn good one time and arguably deserved the mockery. Years ago, when I was eighteen, he tricked me into watching a low-budget, campy horror movie, and it cost me a set of perky boobies. I was at Blockbuster with Gabe, a couple other pals, and some girls. Our plan was to rent a scary movie to assist in under-the-blanket hook-ups in the basement of a friend whose parents were out of town. Gabe had somewhere else to be, but before leaving, he recommended a horror flick that would aid us in getting touchy-feely with the chicks. His argument was straightforward and convincing. He said, "Dude, I promise," followed by a humping motion. Then he handed us the movie *Basket Case.*

Back at the house, we popped in the movie, turned off the lights, and got cozy with the girls, but it didn't take long to realize we'd been royally scammed. The movie was about a polite young man taking care of his evil, cowpie-shaped "brother" – a tumor that grew on his ribcage until being surgically removed. The little freak looked like a deformed potato with arms where his ears should've been. He basically flung himself around, raping and murdering in B-movie fashion. Coincidentally, the monster loved cock-blocking his brother.

For the previous three weeks, I'd been trying to get to second base with a doe-eyed, rusty blonde named Lindsey. After suffering through half of *Basket Case,* she closed up like a clam. That retarded, disgusting movie removed every drop of libido from the basement. I could only shake my head, admit defeat, and respect the fact that Gabe got us good. So if you're ever leaving people who are trying to decide on a rental, suggest *Basket Case,* the ultimate pootang-getting horror flick. Pump it up beyond belief, because it totally sucks. Gabe, you're an invisible tray holding bastard, but that prank was *off the hook, ha ha ha!*

The Cheese was Heavenly

My father had three favorite snacks that were off-limits to me and my brothers when I was a kid. Unattainable snack number one was *Laughing Cow Cheese*.

Like all American men, Dad loved cheese. He enjoyed bricks and mounds of cascading cheesy wonderment without paying mind to the one-way ticket to Constipation City. When he turned fifty, a physical exam revealed that all thirty feet of his intestines were clogged with cheese. He shrugged it off and went out for enchiladas. To him, cheese made every dish better, but *Laughing Cow Cheese* made *life* better.

Laughing Cow is a malleable swiss spread that comes in a round cardboard tub. The tub contains eight individually wrapped wedges. It's intended as a spread for gourmet crackers, but Dad ate the wedges like chicken nuggets. The packaging depicted the image of a beet red cow with horns and hoop earrings as if it was some sort of netherworld bovine demon. Dad called the cow Elsie, despite that Elsie the Cow was the mascot of another dairy brand. After his cheesy snack, my father would imitate the laugh of a red-faced, hysterical devil cow while chasing me around the house. It was terrifying. Because of this, I assumed Laughing Cow Cheese was laced with LSD. Since I was well-versed in Bible stories as a kid, I associated the red cow with the calf idol the Israelites worshipped while Moses was away getting the Ten Commandments. That cow caused anger, diarrhea, and mass murder. From what I saw, Elsie was capable of the same.

Why was Elsie laughing? It's hard to say. Maybe she was sadistically laughing at my unfulfilled yearning for a taste. Maybe she was watching the rhino birth scene from *Ace Ventura 2*, the mirror scene from *Duck Soup*, or the viral video *David after Dentist*. Either way, only a top echelon comedic moment could make a cow laugh hard enough to poop out a treat so creamy and delicious.

After Dad finished a wedge, I'd ask permission to lick the foil wrapping. One time, in acknowledgment of my fervor, he gave me half of a wedge, which calculated to roughly five percent of his serving. I savored the chunk in twenty tiny nibbles. My lips tingled with pleasure. It melted on my tongue. I thought, "This is better than cake frosting!" The cheese was heavenly. Remember that creative writing exercise from high school English where the teacher had you write a one-page story based on an awkward, pre-determined sentence? If I'm ever a teacher, that'll be the sentence I use, "The cheese was heavenly." Work a story around it kids, preferably one with elves and wizards.

The second snack on maximum lockdown was Dad's *Pimento Spread*. Pimento spread is a pink, tangy, creamy delight best consumed on crackers, ideally, Wheat Thins. Kraft's packaging showed the spread tucked into a piece of celery, but that's utter crap, as such use would be blasphemy. It'd be like a can of gravy picturing its contents poured over a salad, or bacon bits advertised as fish food – just an obscene waste. This stuff wasn't made for vegetables; it was made for crunchy gluten products! *Stuff yo' face, fool!*

The easiest way to open a jar was with a hammer and chisel. If that wasn't available, a pair of pliers might work. It's the kind of container that makes you wonder if old people ever die of starvation because they can't open the jars in their pantry. Every time Dad pried open a jar of pimento spread, the lid catapulted behind the stove. I'd like to see the injury statistics related to pimento spread lid removal. It's probably the leading cause of blindness in New Jersey. You could rob a liquor store using the jar as a weapon. *"Empty the register now! Don't make me pop open this lid at you!"*

They really missed the mark on the jar design. Much like Pringles, you simply can't reach the bottom product because the diameter of the container is too narrow for a normal human hand. In this case, a person with a deformed, shriveled hand would be considered fortunate. Dipping crackers into a half-empty jar of pimento spread requires using your fingers like tweezers. Doing so leaves your knuckles coated with salmon-colored slime. After Dad finished a jar, he'd sit on the couch licking his hands like a cat. Sure, you could use a butter knife to spread the stuff, as long as you don't mind slowing your pace of consumption to a crawl, but people like my father tend to be in a lifelong eating contest, so that wasn't an option. He often cursed the little jar and went on lengthy diatribes about how they should switch to a wide, plastic tub. Are you reading this Kraft? If so, please put your pimento spread in a wide, plastic tub. Do it for my dad. You're driving him insane.

Mom peeled the labels off empty jars, washed them, and used them as a kid-sized juice glasses. They'd be perfect triple-shot glasses if you needed that sort of thing. Dad would watch a Tigers game and finish an entire jar by the third inning. He'd watch thirty to forty games a year. So we had *scads* of juice glasses. When stacked incorrectly they'd tumble in the cupboard like a Jenga tower. The next unlucky soul who opened the door took a wave of fifty pimento jars to the face.

Dad's final and most-coveted snack were his *Chocolate Éclair Ice Cream Bars*. My brothers and I could break from the summer heat and help ourselves to a variety of frozen goodies. We ate sherbet push-ups, grape twin-pops, and fudgsicles up the wazoo, but we had to keep our dirty nubs off Dad's éclairs.

Behind my parents' house is a gravel alley. I spent a lot of time back there with my bros and friends shooting hoops and pitching into chalk strikeout boxes on the adjacent cinderblock warehouse. At the end of the alley was a muffler shop full of grease monkeys. One afternoon, a mechanic who looked like Charles Manson interrupted us during a game of PIG to give us a carton of Fla-Vor-Ice. To clarify, he wasn't giving us a *box* or *family pack* – he gave us a *carton*, as in what they deliver to Kroger on a wooden palette to stock the coolers. After the shock of being offered sweets by a bearded guy in an oily jumpsuit subsided, he explained that the guys in their shop watch us playing ball every day and it reminds them of when they were kids, so they wanted to surprise us with something cool. Then, without much fanfare, he handed over the frozen juice treats. We didn't have to show him our dingies or anything.

That summer we thought of 101 different ways to eat Fla-Vor-Ice. We smashed them into slushies, emptied the juice into ice trays, drank them warm, and crushed them over cereal. One time, as an experiment, I bathed in Fla-Vor-Ice. Eventually we got sick of them and started using them as ant bait, doorstops, whips, watercolor paint, and currency in neighborhood transactions. A kid named Jimmy Bickerstaff traded me an Autobot hovercraft named *Seaspray* for ten Fla-Vor-Ices on the condition that he could choose the flavors. He took seven purples and three greens. Motherfucker did his research. I tried to trick him into taking a couple orange ones by telling him that they have the most sugar, but he didn't fall for it.

While a gazillion Fla-Vor-Ices circulated through our freezer that year, only six éclairs chilled beside them, and my father ate them *all*. I had a better chance of scoring a passenger pigeon kabob from the World Wildlife Federation. On the rare occurrence that I was allowed a taste, I quickly discerned why he hoarded them. Fla-Vor-Ice was piss compared to an éclair. Straight up goat pee. Éclairs were opium den, happy-ending massage parlors for your mouth. I assumed the ingredients of an éclair were:

1. Vanilla ice cream crystallized in a cumulus cloud over the Bermuda Triangle.
2. Chocolate coating harvested from a lush valley on Halley's Comet.
3. Nuts grown under a rainbow by leprechauns.
4. Fudge cake stolen from Betty Crocker's window ledge by the Good Humor Ninjas and recovered by Indiana Jones after traversing a

bobby-trapped cave, outwitting an immortal Knight Templar, and fighting a bunch of Nazis.

When Dad finished one, I'd lick the residual ice cream off the stick. I often fantasized about stealing one, but the fear of getting in trouble and displeasing God dissuaded me. In retrospect, I could've easily gotten away with it. God wouldn't have even noticed, since he was undoubtedly distracted while eating éclairs on his couch in heaven.

My father was generous with his Cordial Cherries, Ruffles, Fudge Stripes, and Vienna Sausage, so popular demand for those snacks remained low. Laughing Cow Cheese, Pimento Spread, and Chocolate Éclairs were the Sasquatch, Mokèlé-mbèmbé, and Loch Ness Monster of our kitchen. Rare glimpses of the untouchable trio led me to believe that Laughing Cow Cheese came from extinct cows. I estimated that a jar of pimento spread went for fifty gold bars on the black market. I assumed that the reward for saving the planet from an apocalyptic asteroid was a year's supply of éclairs.

Years later, when I moved out of my parents' place and embarked on my first grocery store run, I did the predictable. "Screw milk and bread," I told myself, "I'm buying a dozen jars of pimento spread, a case of éclairs, and fifty tubs of Elsie's cheese." I did. It was beyond awesome. I gained twenty pounds during checkout. Opening my fridge and seeing a wall of formerly elusive snacks brought oodles of contentment. It gave me warm, bubbly feelings. I felt in touch with myself. I also felt like touching myself. I felt domination over tyrannical forces. I had a revelation.

I'd taken an unresolved childhood desire and fulfilled it as an adult, or "pseudo-adult" if my girlfriend's reading this. I realized that aging forces us into adulthood before we're ready to stop being kids. And since aspects of our childhood stint influence the type of person we become, including our insecurities, perspectives, and goals, I may have just stumbled upon a formula for making peace with our inner child, thereby enlightening our adult existence. Or maybe it was just an excuse to buy a Millennium Falcon toy since I never got one in the '80s.

Either way, I've completed this exercise and can proudly say that I've fulfilled, by purchase and consumption, all of my childhood desires. I now have more toys, games, comic books, and tasty snacks than I could've ever dreamed of owning when I was little. Thanks to individually wrapped cheese wedges, I've found that playing catch-up with your childhood can be very healthy, symbolically speaking of course, because in a literal sense, the sugar, sodium, and saturated fat are pretty bad for you.

Face It, You're a Four

(On a Scale of 1 to 10)

A woman places her items on the conveyor at a grocery store checkout. Toothpaste, bread, milk, and dish soap. The guy behind her says, "*Hmm*, you must be single."

She replies, astonished, "Yes, actually I am! But how could you tell from these basic items?"

"Oh, it's not your items," he says. "It's that you're super ugly."

It makes calm folks jittery. It turns tough guys into whimpering babies. It turns pacifists into pugilists. It transforms trusting people into jealous freaks. Cheapskates drop major dough. Articulate people stutter. Graceful people bang their leg on a table, spilling drinks everywhere. It's the leading cause of spontaneous mental retardation. Yep, *beauty* can really fuck things up.

Generally, it's not their fault they were born with perfect symmetry, softly sloping cheekbones, and every line of their face was drawn on the Etch-A-Sketch of God. Don't be mad at them because your family has been cursed with ugliness ever since your great, great grandfather refused to sell eggs to the town witch. Don't be pissed off because they got the Schwarzenegger genes and you're the Danny DeVito of the litter. Beautiful people – we love *'em*, and we hate their *friggin'* guts!

Beauty is in the eye of the beholder, unless of course you're undeniably hot. What are the odds of being a gorgeous human specimen? One out of fifty? One out of *five hundred?* I guess it depends on what city you're in, but a good spot to survey is the gas station. The corner Mobil is a place everyone visits, good looking or not. Next time you're filling up, take a glance at your fellow filler-uppers – chances are they're a bunch of ugly mo-fos. If they're all attractive then you better sit down because I've got some bad news for you...but let me know where you fill up so I can check out all those fueling hotties!

Over years of careful observation, I've noticed that, besides crying, people look ugliest when overheated. Picture the hideous face everyone's making at mid-July street fairs or baseball games when its ninety degrees out and they're sitting directly in the sun. If you're from Northern Canada, it's the face everyone makes when it's in the upper-sixties. When suffering from heat, a person's face looks like a theater tragedy mask. Look at the droopy face on the next jogger you see. It's disgusting. Step in front of a mirror and make your best "It's hotter than shit out here" face, and you'll see what I mean. Stay cool, stay attractive.

I work in an office with thirty ugly men, six ugly women, a transgender person, and one decent-looking girl. I said *decent*, not *beautiful*. I honestly wouldn't even put her in the *cute* category. She looks like a chubby Princess Diana. The other department females are not only ugly, they're also fatter than shit, so by default this girl is the "hot chick" because she's blonde, wears skirts, and her BMI falls on the low end of obese. Dudes flirt with her every day. They stare at her ass and stand in line to walk her to the cafeteria. They're called "work husbands," and in the automotive engineering field, a halfway decent chick can score at least *five*.

I was waiting behind Chubby Di at a vending machine in the break room once and felt compelled to give her the old, "How you doin'?" I then realized I was pulling a Joey Tribbiani on a second rate skeeze and snapped out of it. The lack of office options makes her *seem* attractive, but if you dropped her in any other setting, whether it's a nightclub, gym, or Starbucks, you wouldn't give her a second look. So ladies, if you want a daily ego boost, become a Mechanical Engineer and you'll feel like Helen of Troy Monday through Friday. To keep it up on the weekend just wear a push-up bra to a dive bar.

Women often take advantage of the basic rules of comparison when assembling their gaggle of girlfriends. If you go out with three girls who're fatter and homelier than you, *bam*, you're instantly the "hot one." I need to start doing that. Next time I head out, I'm calling Kool-Aid Man, Chewbacca, and Cher's son from *Mask*, that way I'll appear to be fit, groomed, and handsome. Girls will be like, "That guy next to Chewbacca has great hair." Her friend will say, "Are you talking about the guy standing next to Kool-Aid Man? Yeah, I was just thinking he has a nice body." As I'm leaving with the girls, some Joe

Schmo who just walked in with Joseph Merrick will give me an approving head nod. Cheating? Perhaps. But there's nothing wrong with playing your angles. Sometimes you've gotta concoct a plan like a mother-flippin' concocter!

Beautiful people are often stereotyped as being understocked in the personality department. That's only as true as the assumption that ugly people are pleasant by necessity. Both are fairly accurate. Regardless, beauty is an intangible element we constantly focus on, and it's hard to put a finger on why it's so important. In this day and age, you don't need character or personality if you're good looking, because society puts far too much emphasis on physical appearance alone.

We all spend immeasurable amounts of time, money, and effort trying to look attractive. We'll fall for any ad that triggers our voyeuristic or exhibitionist instincts. We'd wear a stick-on Hitler mustache if someone told us it would make us look like a model or score one. Even the packaging for a pair of XL tighty-whiteys portrays an athletic dude slightly lifting his shirt to reveal a tan six-pack. The actual guys buying cheap Walmart underwear have bald spots and slightly lift their shirt to reveal a hairy gut.

Nobody would buy a *Maxim* with my Aunt Linda on the cover, that's why we all know who Scarlett Johansson is. Victoria's Secret didn't meet success by modeling realistic women. Even when the service at Hooters sucks, we still tip over twenty percent. We're all the same. We ogle and admire beauty as if it's virtuous and meaningful. So if *Dateline* reports that they sent ordinary-looking qualified candidates and sexy under-qualified candidates to the same job interview, and the sexy ones were hired, don't moan and groan about discrimination because you'd do the same thing. You'd say, "This girl may not know her ABCs, but *damn* she's got nice stems!" Nobody wants a fugly secretary. The hiring staff at *Dateline* would fall for it too.

There's a twenty-seven-year-old single woman at my church who's soft-spoken, fit, and fashionable. She makes kick-ass lasagna, keeps her apartment spotless, and gets her oil changed regularly. She's a successful physical therapist, watches sports, and has a good sense of humor. She's top notch wife material. Most females her age have already been snatched up by prowling Christian bachelors. What gives? Oh yeah, did I mention that she's *butt-freaking ugly?* I mean, the monsters chasing you in your nightmares are simply running from her. They use her face as a mold for Halloween witch masks. She looks like Andy Kaufman after sticking his face in a beehive. Throw a hood on her and she's Emperor Palpatine. Unless a blind guy moves into town, she'll be single forever. It's a bloody shame.

A gorgeous girl who's incapable of microwaving a Hot Pocket, has dirty clothes strewn all over her bedroom, and acts like a self-entitled diva, will *still* have guys lined up around the block to be with her. Of course it's not fair! *Duh!* The problem is that pretty girls are *constantly* told they're pretty. A nice looking woman can't buy tampons without getting hit on. When you spit your game and tell her how beautiful she is, you're nothing more than creep number two-hundred and thirty-three. Get in line buddy, we were here first!

However, if you settle down with an ugly chick and muster up the gumption to say, "I think you're so…*beautiful*," she'll cry, blow you, and cook you a steak dinner. Now *that's* the sort of reaction you want when dishing compliments. It truly means something to her. You made her genuinely happy. You touched her heart. Sucks you're lying though.

You've probably played "Attractiveness Trivia" before on a scale of 1 to 10. While I can judge how hot a girl is in a millisecond, I often refer to that scale when inquiring about other dudes, since I suck at judging male attractiveness, mostly because I'm not gay, although I can appreciate a nice man can. Girls have a much better grasp on judging their same-sex counterparts, probably because they've all got a little dyke in them.

I'm not claiming complete ignorance. If a guy looks like one of Maurice Sendak's Wild Things, I can tell that he's ugly. I know that fat, bald guys with splotchy, bad skin are unattractive, and I'm in touch with my masculinity enough to appreciate the appeal of dudes with chiseled abs who look like GQ models. But all the guys in between, the level three through eight guys, they all look the same to me. If I date a girl for a while, I'll get a few drinks in her and ask her to rate my close pals so I can know whether she thinks I'm in a team of superheroes or ogres.

Recently, one of my longtime, platonic gal pals started dating a new guy, so I asked one of her girlfriends, "On a scale of one to ten, ten being Brad Pitt, one being Brad Pitt's steaming turd, how does this new guy rate?"

She answered, "A four," meaning he's a standard, run-of-the-mill goober. That works because she's a six, even though she thinks she's an eight. Most of us fall somewhere between four and seven. Typical relationships pair people no more than two levels apart. Bars and clubs should post their clientele average to expedite the mating game for patrons. The Birmingham Martini Lounge is hovering around eight-and-a-half, so turn your hatchback around and head straight to Denny's Gin Mill. They're at an even four.

Can a level four dude score a level nine chick? He can, based on the premise that beautiful women are often discriminated against. *Huh?* Sure, hotties get more attention, cushier jobs, free drinks, voluntary tire repair, friendlier service, extra latte flavoring, better medical care, smarter FBI agents when they're kidnapped, and everything else you could ever want, but seriously, it can suck too. I know that's a tough sell, but try this on for size:

A gorgeous woman sits alone in her apartment on a Saturday evening with a Lean Cuisine and *Forget Paris* DVD because she can't get a date. She gets catcalls galore, but decent guys are either too intimidated to approach her, assume she's spoken for, or peg her as a snob. She's an object of admiration but not a magnet for engaging conversation. Most men who approach her are schmucks who break the ice with sappy pick-up lines and cheesy compliments. So if *you*, a regular looking homeslice who couldn't land a modeling contract even if you and the Morlocks were the only beings left on the planet, can get the balls to treat her like a normal human being – *voila!* – you just scored your fantasy girl.

Now wake up…you were dreaming. Truth be told, that girl will think you're *nice*, but she's waiting for *at least* a seven, and that's only if he has money. Sorry to burst your bubble. While we're at it, the farmer's daughter you're hoping to find while passing through Idaho, the one with the cute face and huge boobs who's never dated because the men in her town were wiped out by a flash flood, sorry, she's imaginary too (sad trombone).

Most relationships start with physical attraction. Are there compatible people out there with common interests who could share a lifetime of happiness together that won't hook up based solely on frumpy faces? You bet your begonias there is. That's what internet dating is for. Rest assured though, beauty fades, and the hot guy who got the hot girl you always wanted will, in roughly twenty years, not have a super-hot girl anymore. What a sucker! But hey, like it says on my friend Sam's keychain over a picture of a sexy, big-breasted babe, "No matter how good she looks, someone, somewhere is tired of her shit!"

There was an episode of *The Twilight Zone* where a beautiful but vain woman woke up in a world where beauty and ugliness did the old switch-a-roo. Everyone who saw her was repulsed and she had a total meltdown. You probably know a vain person who needs to wake up in that world. I have a friend who married a prima donna chick who loves bragging about her looks. I heard her tell a story at a dinner party about her Chiropractor, whom she described as "really handsome and rich," telling her that she is "literally, God's gift to men." Gag me. She once wore a tube top to a church picnic and told everyone at her table, "I must be driving all the men here crazy!" If Shallow Hal looked at her, he'd see Salacious Crumb.

Hopefully you've learned to separate beauty in the simple eye from beauty in the mind's eye. When you're young and immature it can be difficult to differentiate between the two. Maybe you pined for a shallow, self-absorbed slut, or maybe an arrogant, punk-ass player was your Adonis. When I was twenty-one, I had it bad for a girl named Hannah. Being around her gave me all the side effects of attraction – butterflies, stuttering, acute lack of cool, paranoia of dangling boogers. I thought she was *exactly* what I wanted based on her looks, so I worked up the nerve to ask her out.

Since she only listened to country music, we ended up going to a Western-themed bar called the *Rattlesnake Saloon*. I'd never had an actual conversation with Hannah before that evening. I wanted her despite knowing nothing about her. Unfortunately, she turned out to be a total letdown. After seeing a black couple in the bar, she sounded off like a pre-Civil War plantation owner. She said, "What are *they* doing in here?" And that shit spewed out after only two beers! You're supposed to keep racist tirades to yourself until *at least* your fourth beer. It didn't take long for her to reveal her dull and ignorant ways. By the third John Michael Montgomery song, her appeal had vanished, and I started thinking of ways to ditch her. JM² would've been so disappointed.

All in all, the pursuit of beauty is futile. If you're beautiful, we're only going to rip on your outfit, point out your moles, and assume you've had plastic surgery. Do yourself a favor and quit pursuing something so fleeting. Learn to accept and embrace yourself no matter where you fall on the scale of attractiveness. That is, of course, unless you're below a four, because there's no sense in trying to fool yourself.

Doppelganger

I wrote the majority of this book while sitting in a cubicle posing as an auto industry stooge. My company provides just about everything a writer needs – a word processor, plenty of spare time, and internet access, although the internet here is limited. They restrict it with software called *Websense*. Links from friends to check out a video of a fat kid emulating Darth Maul, Tay Zonday's latest hit, or an episode of *Tourette's Guy* are inaccessible. The web-filter categorizes blocked content with tags like Tasteless, Personals & Dating, Alcohol Related, Illegal, or the one I got while searching for a picture of Alessandra Ambrosio to put in my wallet – Lingerie & Swimsuit. It can be a real stickler. Brazilian models and just about anything worthwhile is off-limits.

Writing takes research. Sometimes I need to look up a specific MacGyver episode, a superhero's secret identity, or the name of a bar where I got plastered. When I Google that stuff at work, nine times out of ten, it leads to blocked sites. It's frustrating, but I understand why they restrict it. The folks in my office waste most of their time surfing the web. They scour it for accessible crossword puzzles, funny video sites, and casino emulators. If they find one, the link gets forwarded to the entire department, minus supervisors and suck-ups.

I was in the habit of scribbling new ideas and queries on index cards and waiting until I got home to research them, but I'd often get sidetracked with after work stuff, and by the time I'd dig into my notes, sometimes several days later, I wouldn't be able to remember why I wrote "Aragorn's ass," or figure out what "Tacos and tatas" was supposed to mean. It was a pain. Then, one afternoon, while lamenting the slow progress of this book, by sheer coincidence *everything* became accessible on my work computer. I knew it was a sign from the spirit realm to get crackin'.

Some coincidences can burn you. If you take your secretary to Red Lobster to commemorate a successful business year, and your wife's loudmouthed cousin strolls in, the one who's always been skeptical of you, that's coincidence punching you in the face. That happened to a friend of mine and he still hasn't lived it down. His wife's drama-loving cousin took her time to observe every aspect of his behavior, reporting every smile and nuance of body language, and even recorded video of them on her iPhone. He wasn't having an affair, but he took so much shit for it that he wished he was. While I haven't experienced anything that drastic, I have gotten the short end of the stick with coincidence before.

One Friday afternoon, I saw my boss pack his briefcase, shut off his cubicle lights, and leave at two o'clock. I had a hockey game that night and needed to get my skates sharpened, so, assuming the coast was clear, I snuck out early and drove to a sporting goods store. After my skates were finished, I paid, walked to my car, and got inside, but just as I shut the door, my boss pulled into the spot next to me. Coincidentally, his computer repair shop was in the same plaza. He left early to drop off a virus-infected PC. He looked over at me. I was busted. I rolled down my window and we spoke briefly, stating our errands, but felt too awkward to address the obvious issue – why I was there and not at my desk. I sped back to the office and adjusted my timecard to show that I left early. While that coincidence sucked, others can be astounding.

When I was seventeen I got a summer job as an electrician's assistant running wires above the ceiling tiles in a large grocery store. The job required a hardhat. I didn't own one, so on my first day they let me borrow the one that belonged to a guy named Miguel who was electrocuted a couple days earlier and recuperating at home. My boss collected it at the end of the day and told me to go to the hardware store to buy myself a hardhat for tomorrow. It was a conundrum because I took the job to make extra cash and didn't want to spend money on something as dumb, stupid, and retarded as a hardhat before I got my first paycheck.

I went to Home Depot, but the cheapest hardhat they had was fifteen bucks. I was so piss poor that I didn't buy it, justifying to myself that Miguel was still on the mend, so I'd just borrow his again. I was uneasy as I left for work the next morning without one, worried that my new boss would be upset with me, mostly because he was definitely going to be upset with me.

Around 7AM, on my way to the jobsite, while merging onto the freeway, I spotted a yellow orb on the shoulder. "It couldn't be," I thought. Regardless, I quickly pulled over, flipped on my hazard lights, and backed up to the spot. I hopped out, and sure enough, there was a yellow hardhat just sitting there in the rubble. "You've got to be kidding me!" I said.

I shook it out and got back into my car to inspect it. It wasn't too shabby, definitely used, but in one piece. I put it on and it fit perfectly. I took it off in complete disbelief, thinking, "What're the odds of that? It must be my lucky day!" I tried to think of a logical explanation as to how it ended up there but had no idea. I assumed it was a sign from my astral guides that I'd have a long and prosperous career as an electrician, but they let me go a week later when Miguel returned to work.

To be fair, getting full web access on my work PC may not have been as coincidental as initially conveyed. One afternoon, I befriended an IT guy named Albert during a software upgrade. While watching over his shoulder as installation progress bars crawled across my screen, I asked him, "Have you guys been busy lately?"

"Yeah, Mathilda's got us working sixty hours a week," he said, referring to the tech support manager Mathilda Reinhardt. That led me to reference the character Mathilda from *Leon: The Professional*, which led to a buoyant conversation about it being one of the sweetest movies of all time, and even though you shouldn't think Natalie Portman is sexy as a preteen, for dang sure she is. It turned into a discussion on female assassin movies, which led to a *La Femme Nikita* query, which led to a Google search, which resulted in a blocked website, which led to me bitching about my limited access.

Albert stopped by several times over the next couple months to update my computer and discuss movies. We had similar tastes. We both thought *Empire Strikes Back* was the best of the Trilogy. We both thought Tim Burton's first *Batman* was better than Christopher Nolan's. We both thought *Kung Pow* was hysterical. Each visit resulted in a query. Which themes were composed by Danny Elfman? Who voiced Remy in *Ratatouille*? Which actress played the female lead in *Mission: Impossible II*? We'd search Google and get blocked every time. "You can't even get to *IMDb*?" he said, exasperated. "*Man*, I'm on there *every day!*"

I told Albert, "Dude, you've got to get me access!"

He never really said if he would or wouldn't, but a week later my web blocker disappeared. So perhaps it wasn't a *total* coincidence in the full definition of the term, but I was still pleasantly surprised. When it comes to coincidences though, I've experienced greater.

I can karaoke the Fresh Prince song *Summertime* without looking at the onscreen lyrics. If you karaoke that song at a bar at the end of spring when the weather's been in the seventies for a solid week, people love it. I know it by heart thanks to tons of practice. WNIC is a Detroit radio station that used to have a nighttime program called *Pillow Talk*. The DJ, Alan Almond, whose voice was one part Barry White, one part Harley Davidson, and two parts Satan, ended each show with the song *Summer Madness* by Kool & the Gang. That song doubles as the background music in *Summertime*. So every time I caught the end of *Pillow Talk*, I'd rap the Fresh Prince's lyrics, and I got pretty good at it.

One hot August night, while rapping *Summertime* on my drive home, I got to the line, *"The temperature's about eighty-eight,"* and pointed at the thermometer in the dashboard of my Toyota Camry. Coincidentally, it read "88." *"Hop in the water plug just for old time's sake."* It was sheer, albeit meager, coincidence. However, the Fresh Prince left DJ Jazzy Jeff and became Will Smith, thereafter filming the blockbuster movie *Independence Day*, which is based on another highly coincidental event in my life.

I was watching hockey and drinking beer with a few buddies in a friend's basement on a Saturday evening when a guy named Jake said he saw me driving up Southfield Road earlier that day. "Today?" I asked.

"Yeah, today around two o'clock," he said.

"That wasn't me," I said. "I was home all day."

"It was *definitely* you!" he said. "Red Isuzu, Tigers ball cap, two hockey sticks in the backseat, Mardi Gras beads hanging from your mirror."

"Well, that's definitely a detailed description of me in my ride," I said, "but if it was today, it wasn't me. I woke up at noon, made a Stouffer's French bread pizza, and watched *Office Space* twice. I never left my house."

"Whatever, dude," Jake said, "I know I saw you!"

"Are you sure it wasn't a couple days ago or something?"

Jake swore it was that afternoon. He was so sure it was me that he got irritated at my denial and tried to make me feel like a filthy liar. I blew it off thinking, "Time to lay off the cheeba, you idiot."

A few days later, I was waiting at a red light, about to jump on the freeway, when I spotted a red Isuzu Rodeo a couple lanes over. I had the same thought anyone has when they see their exact make and model on the road, "Is that how my ride looks? Damn, I'm a *pimp!*"

The light turned green and traffic crept forward. As I veered away from the road and drove up the onramp, I noticed that the driver of the other Isuzu was wearing a ball cap, had beads hanging from his mirror, and there were two hockey sticks protruding above his back seat. The handle of each shaft was wrapped in orange tape. I turned around and looked at the two hockey sticks in my backseat – they were also wrapped in orange tape. Normally, I use black, but I recalled the reason I used orange last time. When I went to the hockey shop, they were out of black. They had every other color imaginable, so I chose orange to match my Philadelphia Flyers-colored league jersey.

So here's a guy driving the same SUV, wearing the same ball cap, with the same beads hanging from his mirror, and he has two hockey sticks in his backseat, each of them wrapped in the *same orange fucking tape?* If the other likenesses weren't enough, that put it over the edge. I slammed on my brakes and shouted, *"What in the shitty hell is going on!?"* It was too late to go back. I was too far up the on-ramp and the cars behind me started honking. I had no choice but to continue onto the freeway and let my doppelganger get away.

What sort of parallel universe, glitch-in-the-matrix weirdness was happening? Was an alien shape-shifter cloning me in order to collect data on our civilization's weaknesses? Probably. Therefore, I highly encourage everyone to eat their favorite meal and get laid tonight, because an interstellar war is about to begin, and we all know that alien weaponry is *way* sweeter than ours.

As I drove off, contemplating the demise of our world from imminent alien invasion, and completely bewildered by the magnitude of the coincidence I just witnessed, I had a grand epiphany: Noteworthy coincidences only happen to me while driving.

A Career in Origami

I've tried my hand at many-a-talent since childhood. You probably tried some of the same stuff. I got into juggling, gymnastics, magic tricks, origami, skateboarding, karate, playing saxophone, playing piano, drawing comics, singing, and performing choreographed hip-hop dance moves. The results, though, were consistent proof that I was not the reincarnation of a world class entertainer.

My Casio keyboard skills peaked with a hunt n' peck rendition of Phil Collins' *Another Day in Paradise*. My mom thought it was pretty dope, but I got more satisfaction from pressing the DEMO button and pretending to play Rick Astley's *Never Gonna Give You Up*. I gave keyboarding one last shot when I bought a beginner's book of sheet music from *The Little Mermaid*, but I ended up spending more time looking at the pictures than practicing.

When my elementary school took part in a relief campaign to send a thousand paper cranes to Japan, I got pumped for origami. I can't remember the purpose of the relief effort, except that it probably relieved Japan of a forest or two, but I'm sure Japanese officials got our crate full of cranes and said, "What the fuck are we supposed to do with these?"

Then a secretary explained, "American schoolchildren made them to support our country."

"Gee thanks, this *totally* makes up for Hiroshima (eye roll). Send cash, *assholes!*"

Within a month I'd forgotten the steps to make a crane. I borrowed an origami book from the library, but the paper frog, squirrel, and dragon I folded looked more like their corresponding feces. Plus, I used a lot of scotch tape, which removes all credibility. Even my paper planes crashed and burned. The only thing I could consistently fold were "fortune tellers," the things where you'd pick a color, then a number, and lift a flap to reveal, "You're queer."

I tirelessly practiced dance moves in my bedroom, but the only glory it got me was twenty seconds of applause while doing the Hammer Dance and Running Man in a circle at my cousin Laura's wedding reception. When it came to card tricks, I'd forget how to do them halfway through, exasperating family members in the process. My superhero creation the *Hornet* was a shameless Batman rip-off. His costume was identical with the exception of a little flame tattoo I added over his right eye. And my original superhero team, the Ninja Dinos, was a little *too* inspired by the Ninja Turtles.

My success as a gymnast was hindered by the fact that I couldn't do a cartwheel without bending my knees, and every handspring attempt ended with me on my back. I was scared to drop in on a full size half-pipe, thus my skateboarding career never flourished. I didn't have the lungs to play the sax I bought. I could barely string together two notes on it, so I sold it at a pawn shop. The owner took it out of the case, wailed out a Kenny G solo, and said, "This thing sounds pretty good." I was like, "Fuck you."

I drove my mom crazy when I'd juggle anything from her fruit bowl, because she hates bruised peaches. I wasn't allowed to hone my inborn karate skills because violent sports were against our religion. For a while, I could hit Sarah Brightman's high notes from *The Phantom of the Opera* soundtrack but totally lost it after my bush grew in.

I was consistently awesome at two things – mashing a Nintendo controller and napping, but, to my chagrin, neither was considered a marketable talent. I used to think, "If the Cold War culminates in a Nintendo tournament, pitting the US versus the Soviets for world supremacy, I'll be a national hero!" After much deliberation, I concluded that the games we'd square off in to prevent nuclear war were *Track & Field II*, *Excitebike*, *Ice Hockey*, and *Marble Madness*. I served my country by practicing a lot but was never called to duty. It was just another thing that I spent a lot of time daydreaming about that would literally never happen in a billion years.

As each hobby fell to the wayside, the corresponding How-To book would collect dust on my bookshelf. The only hobby I didn't ditch was playing guitar. I had a knack for strumming melodies and writing lyrics. Obviously, I'd trade in all of my musical talents to be sweet at karate, who wouldn't? You can't save your village with mushy love songs. But in lieu of that, I'm happy songwriting stuck around. It definitely helped me get some snatch a couple times.

After recording an album of ten original songs with the cheapest equipment available, I got on MySpace because it was touted as the best promotional tool for musicians at the time. Everything I read about web-promotion said *content is king*. In other words, if you wanted success, you'd have to post status updates, photos, blogs, bios, lyrics, critic reviews, descriptions, song meanings, events, and your wiener size at a constant refresh rate to keep fans interested. So I sat down in front of a blank HTML page with the intention of capturing a wide audience with my winsome words.

I thought it'd be nice to post this review: "With his debut album, Daniels delivers a homegrown acoustic masterpiece full of provocative subtleties, delectable melodies, and heartfelt lyrics." But nobody had written that yet, so I was kind of screwed. I tried writing words of praise in the third person, but it came across as self-serving. I tried the opposite and switched to self-depreciating put-downs but hurt my own feelings. I tried to apologize but ended up holding a grudge until I promised I'd cook myself dinner, rub my shoulders, and do all my chores for me. After that I felt a little better.

In order to have nice words to quote about myself, I employed a bit of trickery by including a line in my voicemail greeting asking callers to "leave a message and say something *nice*." The best I got was, "You have meaty calves," "You're not bald," and several instances of my mom telling me I was a good boy. I tried to twist them into an out-of-context quote to describe my music, but it was like trying to make dessert with cauliflower. "Critics say renowned good boy Vincent Daniels delivers meaty songwriting to compliment his meaty calves, and the best part...the guy's not bald." That notion ended up in file thirteen.

I found self-promotion awkward in a "Come give your Aunt Linda a big kiss!" sort of way. Yet, at some point, we're all forced to promote ourselves first-date style in the pursuit of progress. Describing yourself sucks because we're afraid of coming across as shallow and mean-ingless, ignoring the fact that those things will surface no matter what. Besides, self-praise only sounds sincere in a British accent, which adds nobility, which is why Jude Law scores on first dates. A Michigan accent adds spite and indolence, which is why I'm glad I'm not reading this to you aloud.

The clumsiness of self-praise is why we procrastinate updating our résumé. Job hunting is a part of life where self-promo is required. A job interview is an act of utterly uncomfortable self-promotion where anything less than gloating is detrimental. When asked why you're a good fit for the position, you may as well say, "Because *I'm the best in the biz!* The only entity that could rival my awesomeness would be a clone of me with metal teeth, a dorsal fin, and BBQ grills for hands, but until evolution creates that marvel, I remain your top candidate!" Top it off by jumping on the interviewer's desk while singing Carly Simon's *Nobody Does It Better* and you'll get the job for sure.

I should try that "Go for the gusto" approach on my next date. When she says, "So, tell me a few things about yourself." I'll say, "Well, for starters, I'm so attractive that I use Victoria's Secret catalogs as toilet paper. I'm also funnier than every episode of *Whose Line Is It Anyway?* combined. Oh, and the counterfeit money I make is accepted by banks, casinos, and vending machines." For some reason though, while trying to hype a few songs on a website, I felt totally inept.

Getting on MySpace taught me a painful truth – there are fifty thousand other weenies with guitars out there who are writing, recording, and promoting their music just like me. I quickly reached 5,000 friends, but most of them were dudes who wrote in their add request, "I released a CD, come check out my music!" It seemed like we were all the same guy trying to bring the same talent out of the doldrums. We all wanted to score a few female college fans in hopes that album sales would grow enough to supplant our Taco Bell fund. Realizing you're a musical speck ruins the dream the way *Attack of the Clones* ruined Boba Fett. I hope John Mayer appreciates his career.

Nevertheless, I was *pumped* when my first song reached 10,000 plays. 10,000 felt substantial. I blew away Nolan Ryan's strikeout record. I surpassed the total amount of head punches Jet Li has delivered. 10,000 is the amount of maniacs it takes for Natalie Merchant to trouble me. I bumped Salmon P. Chase off his dollar bill. 10,000 is the number of light years to my home planet in the Crab Nebula. My song plays exceeded the number of bird species inhabiting the earth. It was equivalent to the gallons of chili I'd consumed in my life (circa 2006, likely quadruple that by now).

Sure, I realize that total could've been the same 294 people listening to the song 34 times each. Cut me some slack Captain Bubble Burster. Don't crap on my fantasy that 10,000 unique, screaming fans would show up if I hosted Vincestock. 10K is a feat in my book. I posted a note for the 10,000th listener to notify me because they'd won a half-coke, half-cherry Slurpee mixed perfectly by yours truly, as long as they were willing to meet me at the 7-Eleven by my house.

Web promotion also taught me that zealous ideas need filtering. I was so green and excited at the onset that I ended up posting a lot of corny shit. I wish I would've thought it out more. The same thing happened when GM promoted the Buick Lacrosse to young buyers in Quebec and found out afterward that "lacrosse" was regional slang for masturbating. It also happened to Hyundai when they unveiled the all-wheel drive Spanker at the Detroit Auto Show. Same story with the Fiat Beanroller. I'd love to keep rolling with this joke but feel like three is pushing it. Subaru Meatbeater. It's a minivan. Okay, I'm done.

Sometimes you need unbiased, third-party perspective to iron out the kinks in fresh endeavors. For example, there's an ice cream parlor in my town called *We Scream Ice Cream*. I understand the nostalgic innuendo but never go there because I'm afraid I'll be chopped up and added to the Moose Tracks. There's also a deck-building company that advertises on freeway billboards around here called *Killer Decks*. Again, I get the intent, and I can hear Otto the Bus Driver saying, "Killer deck, dude!" But the name seems misguided when considering the safety of your family during a barbecue.

Another local business called *Tittle Roofing* is proof that using your family name for your company isn't always the savvy choice. The worst part is that the "L" in their logo is shaped like a chimney that looks more like an "I." Nobody wants to hire a contractor called *Tittie Roofing*. It's embarrassing. I wonder if they offer areola-shaped roof vents. Similarly, there's a business in my neighborhood called *Tait's Barber Shop*. Someone, perhaps a vindictive customer, insists on spray-painting an "N" in the sign to keep the place called *Taint's Barber Shop*. Come to think of it, mine could use a trim.

Just because a business purchases a custom sign and prints business cards doesn't mean reevaluation isn't necessary. *Dick Blick Art* was around for decades before they renamed themselves *Blick Art*

Supply. The edit was long overdue. Their presumed reputation as a framing shop for porn was instantly updated to a respectable place to buy an easel and brush set. If Google stuck with its original name, we'd be "Back-Rub'ing" for answers on the web. Good thing Nintendo ditched its original name, Marafuku, because it had "Fuck You" in it. If Pepsi didn't reconsider its original name, you'd be ordering a "Brad's Drink" with your Arby's combo, which sounds totally gay.

Similarly, I cringe a little when looking back on early promotional blurbs I wrote. Don't worry; it's not a "Watch a grown man get socked in the nads" cringe, just a "This Kool-Aid could use a little more sugar" cringe. Regardless, it was a learning experience, and thankfully I made a few bucks selling CDs and MP3s along the way. I used half of what I earned to buy a bag of Gardetto's and donated the other half to a foundation bringing awareness to musicians who find promoting themselves viciously awkward. In retrospect, I wish I would've stuck with origami.

The Dive Bar Language Barrier

It takes balls to walk into a dingy dive bar for the first time. I'm talking about the ones with gravel parking lots full of broken glass, weeds, puddles, and rusted out hoopties. I'm talking about bars where the dumpster, grease bin, and a shitload of cigarette butts crowd the entrance. I'm talking about seedy places with uninviting windowless exteriors to keep you guessing whether or not Greedo is inside waiting for you. The building used to have windows, but they've been covered by a mason who wasn't paid to match the existing block. The joint would be completely nondescript if not for the burned-out bulbs surrounding the rusted *Denny's Gin Mill* sign. If you're brave enough to enter, don't expect happy hour to live up to its name.

After your eyes adjust to the darkness, you'll see a row of guys bellied up to the bar welcoming you with their welcome stare, which translates to, "Who the *fuck* are you supposed to be? I'll stab you if you sit by me." Your first thought is, "Isn't smoking banned in public places?" In places that give a shit, yes. Here, not so much. When customers have smoked crack, snorted coke, and dropped acid in the bathrooms, cigarettes hardly factor in.

Your Old Navy hoodie may as well be a golden jacket. It stands out like a sore thumb despite that you bought it at a thrift store for three bucks. The 350-pound guy with the Grizzly Adams beard whose ass is plastered across three bar stools is wearing what he mines coal in. The skinny guy next to him with two black eyes and boils on his neck looks like he spent the day digging graves without a shovel. Put it this way: If you ran a marathon in a ratty T-shirt, wore it while doing underbody work on your car, sopped up a pot of spilled pasta sauce with it, then held onto a whip while dragging behind a Nazi caravan on a dirt road, you might chuck that shirt in the trash at the end of the day. Well, guess what – these dive bars guys would dig it out, put it on, and say, "Look at the nice shirt I found!" The fact is, you didn't stand a chance. The clothes you reserve for yard work and painting would've been too dressy.

When the barmaid says, "What'cha drinkin'?" you notice that her cleavage looks like a wrung paper bag, and her bottom teeth look like Indian corn. Choose wisely, my friend, because they don't drink liquor here, they drink *booze*. If you usually drink single malt scotch whiskey, order Wild Turkey. If you usually drink martinis, order Wild Turkey. If you prefer a mixed cocktail, order Wild Turkey. You like wine? How about a nice, warm glass of Wild Turkey instead? If you don't like Wild Turkey, quit being a pussy and order Wild Turkey. If you usually drink Miller Lite, replace the "Lite" with "High Life," or, of course, Wild Turkey is an acceptable alternative. If you want water, order Wild

Turkey, down it, then sneak the empty glass into the bathroom and fill it from the faucet. Don't mind that green gunk on the rusty spout. Minerals are good for you!

To be clear, when I say "dive bar," I'm not talking about the place your Brita-filter using friends refer to as a "dive" that has a hipster bartender and a great selection of craft beers to go with their *amazing* fish tacos. Food at a real dive bar is a bag of chips. Or on the high end, dollar hot dogs or things made edible by submerging them in a deep fryer that would make the *Bar Rescue* guy throw up. Even after that, it's only going down with a shitload of ketchup. Mini tacos might *sound* good, but don't picture a crunchy taco from Taco Bell hit with a shrink ray; picture Shaquille O'Neal's toenail. Trust me; you'd rather eat a chunk of bark. Get them with a side of sour cream if you enjoy being up all night with food poisoning.

Still, these lowly joints manage to exude a medieval charm; a kid-fort clubhouse coolness, if you will. So if for some reason you wish you were one of the regulars, don't fret, it's within reach. Just be there five hours a day, every day, for the next three years, and they'll accept you. That includes Christmas Eve and Christmas Day. They'll still think of you as the highfalutin, snooty guy who wears fancy hoodies, but hey, every bar group needs a Frasier Crane.

There are several dive bars in my neighborhood. Denny's Gin Mill is the diviest of them. Shotmakers is the white-trash, thug-life dive. Biergarten is the bearded hippie dive. The Dugout is the fat, old lady dive. Breaktime Bar is the factory worker dive. Boom Booms is the karaoke dive. My favorite, though, is Perry's Pub, because they've got five dollar pitchers, free shuffleboard, and ice-filled urinals, which makes pissing a game. I pretend I'm a superhero freeing buried survivors from an avalanche, or melting a glacier that I transported to a drought-stricken third-world country to provide them with clean drinking water.

I haven't attained "Regular" status at Perry's, but at least the initial fear of entering has subsided. The next step is to get the barmaid to refer to me by a nickname like she does the other customers. There's Boner, Dooley, Pounder, Big Mike, and a guy who calls himself "The Dude" because *The Big Lebowski* is "his movie." Obviously, it's not just silly girls who say things like, "*Something About Mary* is *my* movie!" Apparently, old bearded drunks do too.

When I was growing up, my dad would watch *Cheers* after dinner. That show led me to believe that neighborhood bars were filled with rich, sturdy woodwork and bubbly, witty people. *Cheers* made me think that bars were a place "*where everybody knows your name – dun dun dun – and they're always glad you came – dun dun dun.*" I looked forward to the day when I'd be old enough to hang with the likes of Sam, Cliff, Woody, Carla, and Norm.

I grew up in a small town just south of Detroit. My hometown used to be in *The Guinness Book of World Records* for having the most bars per capita in the United States. As a kid I thought it was normal for a residential block to have a bar on each corner and one in the middle. It was carryover from the Prohibition days when the city became a blind pig haven due to its close proximity to Canada, bootlegging residents, and booming population of auto workers. My grandfather was an old Sicilian who told stories about mafia turf wars, working in secret distilleries, and his father's ties to the Purple Gang.

When he was a teen, his dad put him to work with an Italian construction company. They were building a longstanding local speakeasy called *Charlie's* during a period of heated Mob competition. One afternoon, Grampa said he climbed up the scaffolding and found a row of guns lying on top of the cinderblocks. Fascinated, he picked up a shotgun and accidentally bumped a pistol into the hollow wall. He told me, "If they ever tear Charlie's down, I want you to find the forty-five in the east wall and give it to Leo 'Lips' Moceri's kid."

Leo's son is named Stuart, and he's an orthodontist in the area, which, technically, makes him Stuart "Gums" Morceri. I'm looking forward to the day he's adjusting a thirteen-year-old girl's braces and I walk in, slap a gun on the instrument tray, and say, *"Fuhgeddaboudit."*

I was curious about Charlie's for other reasons too. I passed it on my paper route and wondered how they got away with a door sign that read "No Colors Allowed!" Dad said it referred to gang colors, but Grampa said it was for "spicks and negroes." Charlie's had artwork on the side of the building depicting people (white people) dancing and laughing, so I assumed that's exactly what was going on inside. However, when I was finally old enough to go to bars, including Charlie's, I was disappointed to find that they're nothing like *Cheers*. Real neighborhood bars were dirty and intimidating with scary, zombie-like clientele. My dreams of slamming my mug with other patrons in a spontaneous rendition of *We Will Rock You* were dashed to pieces.

I recently bought tickets to a rock concert at a small venue in downtown Detroit. Before the show, I moseyed next door into a bar named *Sebastian's*. The place was a testament to the fact that most real-life watering holes are the diametric opposite of *Cheers*. It was dank and lonely, appeared to be illuminated by candlelight, and smelled like urinal cakes. Besides me, the bartender, and a blind black guy sitting in the corner playing an out-of-tune five-stringed guitar, the place was empty. "Which way is the men's room?" I asked.

The old bartender raised a wobbly finger and whispered, "Down those stairs."

After traversing a labyrinth of dark hallways, creaky stairwells, and musty indoor alleys, I got to the men's room and literally had to limbo under a clothesline of drying socks and rags to get in the door. The remainder of the laundry that had yet to be washed was in a bucket underneath the sink beside an antique wash board and yuck-green colored bar of Lava soap. Afraid that I was about to be attacked by a vampire, I quickly pissed and ran back upstairs.

The bartender and owner, Sebastian, was an old, thick-accented man with the posture of Treebeard and the face of Yoda (puppet, not CGI). Obviously, he lived in the dungeon beneath the bar. I ordered Jameson and sipped it while he recalled his participation in the Civil War...the *Greek* Civil War that is, still a long time ago though. I used the opportunity to flex my broad periphery of knowledge on Greek culture, which depleted after asking where I could get good *avgolemeno* (lemon-rice soup). I was hoping for the name of a local restaurant, but the answer ended up being his dead mother-in-law. It's going to be tough securing a bowl of that.

During the time I was there, three separate groups of people, presumably other concert goers, walked in the front door, took one look at the place, and left. "You don't have to keep it so dark in here," I told Sebastian. "You heard they repealed Prohibition, right? And there was this guy named Thomas Edison who invented these cool bulbs that produce light. You should check into it."

The more comfortable Sebastian got, the more he elaborated on his life. The more he elaborated, the less I understood, phonetically speaking. I was catching no more than thirty percent of what he was throwing at me. I kept repeating, "Really?" to ease my confusion. Maybe I was distracted by the fact that he was holding my hand on the bar, and his hand looked like it was covered with leeches. Maybe it was because he was staring down, whispering in a shaky voice as if he was about to cry. Maybe the whiskey he served had fermented into moonshine, evidenced by the fact that I was so drunk at the concert, I spent the entire time waving two middle fingers at the bands while shouting "Fuck you guys!" I swear I meant it as a compliment. Either way, our language barrier perplexed me. I dearly wanted to understand Sebastian, but the harder I tried, the worse it got.

I used to date a girl who had Hispanic grandparents that lived in Michigan for over twenty years but never learned to speak English. Her grandfather seemed like a jovial fellow, but he only knew a few words regarding baseball and women. When visiting with them, we'd communicate with exaggerated facial expressions and wild hand waving. It got the job done, but I still had a hard time grasping how anyone could live in a country for that long without learning the native tongue. I later learned that it's fairly common.

An old Slovakian guy who doesn't speak a lick of English works as a janitor in my office building. The first time he grabbed my trash bin, I said, "Thank you," and he replied with something that sounded like, "You're welcome." When I asked him if he was new, he looked at me with a blank stare of terror followed by awkward smiling and double-hand waving. Realizing there was a language barrier; I pointed at myself and told him my name. "I'm Vincent," I said, gesturing as if I was repeatedly pressing an elevator button on my chest.

In return, he patted himself like a Comanche chief introducing himself to a frontiersman and said, "Helk."

For the record, it's highly unlikely that his name is actually Helk, but that's what I heard. Harry the Elk. Van Helking. The Incredible Helk. Good ol' Helk the Janitor.

Every day after that, Helk would grab my trash, I'd thank him, and he'd reply with a garbled, "You're welcome." I soon realized that he wasn't really saying the words "You're welcome" as much as he was simply grunting a few syllables that sounded like them – similar to how my girlfriend and I communicate when brushing our teeth. Somebody taught him to reply, "You're welcome," but either his thick accent jumbled it, he mumbled too shyly, or he simply gave up on getting it right because cordiality wasn't a priority while on a work visa trying to make enough money to buy a goat for his nana in the old country. Our daily exchange sounded like this:

I'd say, "Thanks."

He'd reply, "Urine welgum."

As time went on, his "You're welcome" got weaker.

I'd say, "Thanks."

He'd reply, "Ew velga."

Pretty soon it sounded like this:

I'd say, "Thanks."

He'd reply, "Velveeta."

To follow suit I started slurring my thanks.

I'd say, "Thuns."

He'd reply, "Vel vun."

I think he caught on and started messing with me.

I'd say, "Thun."

He'd say, "Vulva."

Our current exchange is:

I say, "Buh."

He says, "Neh."

I have a similar struggle when I get my hair cut at a local place called *Super Cuts*. The barber is a short, fat woman of dark complexion and indiscernible ethnicity. She could be Portuguese, Aleutian, or Hmong, I have no idea. We converse the entire time, but I gather very little. I try to pinpoint key words and hone in on sentences that end in the tone of a question. For example, if she says, "Hue gong show ciabatta *wort?*" I'll run a mental algorithm and extrapolate that she asked me if I have to go back to work.

I'll answer, "No, I'm off work for the day."

"*Oyyyeee!*" she'll reply, followed by laughter.

After a dozen haircuts, I've collected this much – I remind her of her son who's in the army. I've gathered that he's enlisted with either the United States or a country fighting the United States. Evidently, he was either killed in combat, is still in active duty, is retired with a family, or was never in the army to begin with. It's also possible that she doesn't have a son.

"Yip yip eva longoria tits raining odd pair?" *Beep boop beep bop* – translation options – "Hey, aren't Eva Longoria's tits a really nice pair?" or "Is it ever going to stop raining out there?"

I was tempted to reply, "Yeah, I'd love to bury my face in those fun bags," but ultimately chose, "I know, it's been such a wet summer."

"Wheeeee!" she replied, laughing.

She could be telling me about the dead bodies stuffed in her crawlspace, but I've found that the easiest response is to express agreement followed by bouts of self-conscious giggling. She does a decent job with my hair, but sometimes, after asking her to *not* trim my sideburns, she lops them off. Why don't I go somewhere else? Because Super Cuts haircuts are $7.99 on Tuesdays. Buy more books and I'll go somewhere better.

Language isn't always the barrier though. Sometimes a person's English is fine; it's their delivery that's puzzling. We usually refer to such people as "weirdos."

I was on my way to a swanky bar one night to attend a going away party when I got a text from one of my buddies. He wrote, "Heads up. My wife's bringing a friend who just moved back here. She's divorced and hot. Her name's Fiona." I was single at the time, and as any bachelor will attest, that sort of news is *super fucking rad!*

Being attracted to Fiona was easy. She had an athletic build, long, dark hair, and resembled Keira Knightley with a softer jawline. She gave a nice first impression when we met, offering a soft handshake, and politely introducing herself while maintaining a pretty smile. Even though I didn't know a single thing about her at that point, my first thought was, "Wow, the jackass that lost this girl *really* fucked up!"

I bought us a couple beers, and we started conversing. The first few minutes of our conversation consisted of silly back-and-forth banter, which I initially found amusing. "So, Fiona, I heard you recently moved back here. Where were you living before?" I asked.

"I was doing my thing in Vermont," she said.

"Vermont, huh? That's where Bob Newhart does his innkeeper thing," I said.

"Bob like bobbing for apples?" she said.

"No," I replied, "more like Bob in the Bobula Galaxy."

She giggled and said, "You may not know this, but Bob is short for Robert, as in *Robert* Pattinson."

"Yeah, the *Twilight* guy," I said, and kept the joke rolling with, "I heard he's a fan of *Robert* Redford."

"Who has a crush on *Robert* De Niro," she countered.

"Who's scared to death of the Dread Pirate Roberts," I said.

"And *really* scared of Julia Roberts," she said.

"Robert Muldoon," I continued, "the game warden in *Jurassic Park*, now *there's* a Robert who isn't scared of anything, except maybe raptors. But I think it's more of a respect thing than actual fear."

Fiona laughed and rattled off a movie quote in a corny pseudo-man voice, "Grant's like me. He's a digger."

"Dodgson!" I said. "We've got Dodgson here!"

As Fiona laughed, I thought, "This girl is pleasantly offbeat, and she really knows her JP!"

She took a sip of her beer and quoted Ian Malcomb in the T-Rex chase scene, "Must go faster!"

"Think they'll have that on the tour?" I said with a smile. "That movie is classic, isn't it? One of the best! I was *completely* obsessed with dinosaurs as a kid, and that movie blew my mind. So tell me though, what we're you doing in Vermont?"

Fiona stared at me for a moment, and I thought she was searching for an appropriate answer, but it turned out she was trying to think of another *Jurassic Park* quote. "That is one big pile of *shit!*" she said.

I chuckled and replied, "And I thought they smelled bad…on the outside. Oh wait, that's from a different movie. So, anyways, I'm curious, Fiona, why does one move from Michigan to Vermont and back?"

She took another swig from her glass, and with an odd look on her face, she said, "Hold on to your butts!"

Ohh-kay. Did this girl just watch Jurassic Park five times this afternoon or something?

"Good one," I said. "So, really, did you move there for work or something?"

"Dinosaurs eat man," she said. "Woman inherits the earth."

Oh shit, is she a malfunctioning android?

"Is it safe to assume that you *don't* like talking about Vermont?" I said.

She grabbed my arm, leaned into me, and started laughing. It seemed like she finally snapped out of it. I was relieved because the *Jurassic Park* quote machine had gone on a little too long. "Must've been tough times in Vermont, eh?"

"Oh, no, not at all!" she said, except she said it in an uppity British accent. "I'll tell you *all* about it, but I can only say it while talking like *this*."

"*Hmm*," I replied, "I'm guessing you were a Colonial museum tour guide in Vermont."

"I'm sorry," she said in the ridiculous accent, "but I can only understand you if you talk like *this*."

It was obnoxious, but I gave in because she had boobs. I replied in a scallywag accent, more Australian than English, "Right-O. So do tell, why'd ya bugger off to New England in the first place?"

Fiona looked at me and said in her best Mrs. Doubtfire voice, "What do you call a blind dinosaur?" I pressed my lips together and awkwardly raised my eyebrows. "Do-you-think-he-*saurus*," she said.

This girl is a space cadet.

"Shoot her!" she yelled. "*Shoot her!*"

Indeed.

"Welcome to Jurassic Park," she said, followed by what I assumed was her impression of a shrieking velociraptor.

"I can do felines too," she said, followed my meowing.

This chick belongs in a loony bin.

After that, Fiona started barking, growling, and whining like a dog for no apparent reason, "*Arf arf grrrrr arf arf nnn nnn nnn arf!*"

Somebody actually married this freak? I'd rather be gutted by a pack of raptors!

Fiona continued acting bonkers until I thought of an appropriate excuse to ditch her. "I'll be right back," I said. "I need to take a shit."

"That is one big pile of *shit!*" she said in her British accent as I turned and walked away. I didn't even bother making a fake trip to the men's room. I just walked straight to the bar and ordered a shot of Johnny Walker Black. "Spared no expense," I thought.

Later that night, my buddy pulled me aside and asked with a gleam in his eye, "So, what do you think of Fiona?"

"I think she forgot her meds," I said. "Pretty girl, but *completely cuckoo.*"

Reading is another area that can give you that queasy, "I thought I was smarter than this," language barrier feeling. I remember seeing the category "Reading Comprehension" on my elementary school report cards and thinking, "What's that mean?" If you remember flipping through your first algebra textbook, or trying to understand Shakespeare in seventh grade, then you know what I'm talking about.

What I told Fiona was true; I *loved* dinosaurs as a kid, so when renowned paleontologist Robert Bakker released his game-changing book *The Dinosaur Heresies* in 1986, causing waves in the dino community, I was beyond excited to borrow it as soon as the library got a copy. However, at age ten, I didn't understand a damn thing about his endothermic theories; I just thought the cover art was cool. Additionally, since I was raised in a religious household where Bible reading was mandatory, I was no stranger to reading things beyond my grasp. Hebrew law, First and Second Chronicles, and John's Revelation were all head scratchers as a preteen.

Recently, while recording a second album of songs, tentatively titled "Way Better than the First One," or maybe "Teeny-Bopper Chart Toppers" – I haven't decided yet – I undertook an endeavor to learn more about sound engineering. Generally touted as excessively technical and scathingly boring, it's the part of the recording process that musicians usually flash a garlic crucifix at. I did some research on Amazon and settled on a highly recommended book titled *Mastering Audio: The Art and the Science.*

A week later, when the book showed up on my doorstep, I eagerly unwrapped it and did what any pretentious, up-and-coming sound engineer would, I drove to Starbucks to read it. I ordered a chai tea latte and felt cool for about ten minutes while trying to cozy up to the book in an oversized chair. It didn't take long to realize I'd bitten off more than I could chew. I grew paranoid that the baristas knew I wasn't grasping the concept of "low-level dither" and "soft knee clipping." I could feel them eyeing me up from behind the counter, condescendingly thinking, "You're never going to get it!" So I packed up and left.

On my way home I got stopped at a red light in front of Denny's Gin Mill. I noticed that they replaced the burned out bulbs in their sign and resurfaced the lot with a fresh layer of gravel. "Maybe they're trying to drum up business," I thought. "Well, I should probably just head home and try to read this book."

I looked up at the red light and then down at the thick, intimidating guide resting on the passenger seat. "On second thought, I should go in and check it out. How bad can it be? It can't be any worse than those barista assholes."

I parked my car, worked up the nerve, and headed in. I figured, *"Sometimes you want to go...where nobody knows your name – dun dun dun – and they're not particularly glad you came – dun dun dun"* – but at least I get to feel like Dr. Frasier Crane compared to the other drunken lowlifes in there. "Fuck reading," I thought, "it's time for some Wild Turkey!"

About the Author

Detroit native Vincent Daniels is a writer of fine writing. Believe it or not, he's written some of the finest writing he's ever written! I shit you not. His style is refined and *extremely* sexy in a perverted yet huggable way. His essays are about social inadequacy, taut bowel pressure, being a golden phoenix of love, and personal matters that are so personal, he refuses to write about them.

Daniels was following in the footsteps of Steinbeck, Hemingway, and Salinger to pen the next great American novel but got sidetracked with doing shots, eating chili dogs, and having what seemed like perpetual diarrhea, so he decided to write about that stuff instead.

In comparison, he's a lot like the Ewoks from *Return of the Jedi*, you know – cute, cuddly, rabid, hilarious, skilled with rudimentary weapons, suckers for chicken nuggets, skittish, but down to party. He didn't want to be stingy, so he wrote the greatest book ever written (by him, until he finishes the next one) so you could finally attain ultimate happiness while enjoying a long, sustained reading orgasm.

In *Meaty Balls*, Daniels' debut collection of essays, expositions, and insightfully elegant potty humor (which we heard you're into) he has authored a touching work of epic scale, proving that he is one of the greatest authors of our time and every other time including the Mesozoic Era and whatever time the movie *The Fifth Element* took place in.

Email: vincentdanielsbooks@gmail.com
Facebook: www.facebook.com/authorvincentdaniels
Twitter handle: @quite_meaty

Made in the USA
San Bernardino, CA
08 December 2016